MCSE IIS 4

The Cram Sheet

This Cram Sheet contains the distilled, key facts about MCSE IIS 4. Review this information last thing before you enter the test room, paying special attention to those areas where you feel you need the most review. You can transfer any of these facts onto a blank sheet of paper before beginning the exam.

PLANNING

1. The IIS 4 components are: WWW service, FTP service, Transaction Server, SMTP service, NNTP service, Index Server, and Certificate Server.

2. HTTP 1.1 provides support for pipelining, persistent connections, chunked transfers, and proxy.

INSTALLATION AND CONFIGURATION

3. IIS requires:
   - NT Server 4
   - Service Pack 3
   - IE 4.01

4. Default IIS ports: Web is 80; FTP is 21; SSL is 443.

5. HTTP keep-alives sustain communication links between the client and server and are enabled by default.

6. HTTP headers are used to host multiple Web sites over a single IP address.

7. Allocated free disk space for Index Server should be at least 40 percent of the corpus.

8. MMC snap-in configurations saved in .MSC can be used during later sessions.

9. IIS configurations are stored in the metabase.

CONFIGURATION AND MANAGING RESOURCE ACCESS

10. Directory authentication methods are: Allow Anonymous access; Basic (clear text); and Windows NT Challenge/Response (automatically uses NT login).

11. Secure Web Communications: SSL digital certificates, 40-bit/128-bit, required/enabled, https://, client certificates.

12. IP Address And Domain Name Restrictions: grant or deny all, fine-tune with exceptions (single IP, IP and subnet mask, or domain name).

13. Content for a resource URL can be hosted on IIS, over a network share, or redirected to an alternate URL.

INTEGRATION AND INTEROPERABILITY

14. Index Server files:
    - **.HTM** Query form
    - **.IDQ** Query parameters
    - **.HTX** Results formatting

15. IIS communicates with ODBC via IDC (Internet Database Connector).

RUNNING APPLICATIONS

16. ASP is used to enable server-side scripting.

17. Users need IIS Script access and NTFS Execute permissions to run an ISAPI application.

18. Perl scripts require a Perl interpreter on the server.

19. The SMTP service (default port is 25) is used to send out email messages from a site and accept all mail sent to a hosted domain.

20. The SMTP service can hide source domains by using a masquerade domain on all outbound messages.

21. The NNTP service (default port is 119) is used to host threaded discussion groups.

22. NNTP service discussion groups can be indexed and searched via Index Server.

MONITORING AND OPTIMIZATION

23. Bandwidth throttling can be turned on by server and by site; a site setting overrides the server setting.

24. Tune performance based on the number of hits to optimize memory allocation.

25. HTTP keep-alives sustain communications across multiple requests. Turn it off to improve the performance of IIS without limiting corrections.

26. To maximize performance with SSL, increase processor speed and encrypt only the necessary directories.

27. Avoid unwanted hits by taking advantage of the noise word list and by having separate catalogs.

28. Site Server Express Content Analyzer is used to generate statistics and verify links.

29. Usage Import and Report Writer uses IIS log files to generate site reports.

30. The installation of IIS adds the Internet Information Services Global, Web service, FTP service, and Active Server Pages to Performance Monitor.

TROUBLESHOOTING

31. After a virtual site is created, the site must be started manually.

32. 400-series HTTP error messages are related to the client; 500-series HTTP error messages are related to the server.

Pertinent HTTP error messages:

400 Bad Request	Request could not be understood by the server.
401 Unauthorized: Logon Failed	The credentials passed to the server do not match the credentials required to log on to the server.
403 Forbidden: Execute Access Forbidden	Execution attempted from a directory that does not allow programs to be executed.
404 File Not Found	Cannot find the file or script asked for.
500 Internal Server Error	Server is incapable of performing the request.
501 Not Implemented	Server does not support the functionality required to fulfill the request.
502 Bad Gateway	The server received an invalid response from an upstream server.

Common ODBC errors:

Data Source Name Not Found	The global.asa may not be in a directory that has Execute permissions, or the DSN may not be configured correctly.
Logon Failed	The account for the SQL database is incorrect.
General Network Error	The DSN is not able to access the database, possibly because the server has been renamed.

Certification Insider™ Press

MCSE
IIS 4
Adaptive Testing Edition

James Michael Stewart
Libby Chovanec
Ramesh Chandak

The Coriolis Group, LLC
14455 N. Hayden Road, Suite 220
Scottsdale, Arizona 85260

480/483-0192
FAX 480/483-0193
http://www.coriolis.com

Library of Congress Cataloging-in-Publication Data
Chovanec, Libby.
    MCSE IIS 4 exam cram adaptive testing edition/ by James Michael Stewart, Libby Chovanec, and Ramesh Chandak.
        p.   cm.
    Includes index.
    ISBN 1-57610-488-5
    1. Electronic data processing personnel--Certification.
2. Microsoft software--Examinations Study guides.   3. Microsoft Internet information server.   I. Stewart, James Michael.   II. Chandak, Ramesh.   III. Title.
QA76.3.C46   1999
005.7'13769--dc21   99-32321
                                                      CIP

Printed in the United States of America
10 9 8 7 6 5 4 3

Publisher
Keith Weiskamp

Acquisitions Editor
Shari Jo Hehr

Marketing Specialist
Cynthia Caldwell

Project Editor
Greg Balas

Technical Reviewer
Jeff Greer

Production Coordinator
Wendy Littley

Cover Design
Jesse Dunn

Layout Design
April Nielsen

CD-ROM Developer
Robert Clarfield

14455 North Hayden Road, Suite 220 • Scottsdale, Arizona 85260

Coriolis: The Training And Certification Destination™

Thank you for purchasing one of our innovative certification study guides, just one of the many members of the Coriolis family of certification products.

Certification Insider Press™ has long believed that achieving your IT certification is more of a road trip than anything else. This is why most of our readers consider us their *Training And Certification Destination*. By providing a one-stop shop for the most innovative and unique training materials, our readers know we are the first place to look when it comes to achieving their certification. As one reader put it, "I plan on using your books for all of the exams I take."

To help you reach your goals, we've listened to others like you, and we've designed our entire product line around you and the way you like to study, learn, and master challenging subjects. Our approach is *The Smartest Way To Get Certified™*.

In addition to our highly popular *Exam Cram* and *Exam Prep* guides, we have a number of new products. We recently launched Exam Cram Live!, two-day seminars based on *Exam Cram* material. We've also developed a new series of books and study aides—*Practice Tests Exam Crams* and *Exam Cram Flash Cards*—designed to make your studying fun, as well as productive.

Our commitment to being the *Training And Certification Destination* does not stop there. We just introduced *Exam Cram Insider*, a biweekly newsletter containing the latest in certification news, study tips, and announcements from Certification Insider Press. (To subscribe, send an email to **eci@coriolis.com** and type "subscribe insider" in the body of the email.) We also recently announced the launch of the Certified Crammer Society and the Coriolis Help Center—two new additions to the Certification Insider Press family.

We'd like to hear from you. Help us continue to provide the very best certification study materials possible. Write us or email us at **cipq@coriolis.com** and let us know how our books have helped you study, or tell us about new features that you'd like us to add. If you send us a story about how we've helped you, and we use it in one of our books, we'll send you an official Coriolis shirt for your efforts.

Good luck with your certification exam and your career. Thank you for allowing us to help you achieve your goals.

Keith Weiskamp
Publisher, Certification Insider Press

About The Authors

James Michael Stewart is a full-time writer focusing on Windows NT and Internet topics. Most recently, he has worked on several titles in the *Exam Cram* and *Exam Prep* series. Michael has written articles for numerous print and online publications, including *C\Net, Computer Currents, InfoWorld, Windows NT Magazine,* and *Datamation.* He is also a regular speaker at Networld+Interop, and TISC.

Michael has been with LANWrights, Inc. developing Windows NT 4 MCSE-level courseware and training materials for several years, including both print and online publications, as well as classroom presentation of NT training materials. He has been an MCSE since 1997, with a focus on Windows NT 4.

Michael graduated in 1992 from the University of Texas at Austin with a bachelor's degree in Philosophy. Despite his degree, his computer knowledge is self-acquired, based on over 15 years of hands-on experience. Michael has been active on the Internet for quite some time, where most people know him by his "nomme de wire" as McIntyre. He spends his spare time learning to do everything, one hobby at a time.

You can reach Michael by e-mail at **michael@lanw.com**, or through his Web page at **www.lanw.com/jmsbio.htm.**

Libby Chovanec, MCSE and MCP+I, has helped write and tech-edit several *Exam Cram* books. She currently works as a technical analyst at Compaq Computer Corporation, where she manages several enterprise-wide Internet infrastructure and e-commerce projects. She graduated from the University of Houston in 1996 with a Bachelor's degree in MIS.

Ramesh Chandak is a graduate with a Fellowship in Advanced Engineering Study from MIT (Cambridge, MA). Ramesh has a total of eight years of work experience in the IT industry. Ramesh has worked extensively with Internet, Microsoft, Sybase, PowerSoft, and Java technologies. In addition, Ramesh has authored 14 books, tech edited 13 books, and written over 25 technical articles for several leading publishers on client/server, database, multimedia, and Internet technologies.

Acknowledgments

Thanks to my boss, Ed Tittel, for including me in this book series. To my parents, Dave and Sue, thanks for your love and consistent support. To Mark, congratulations on graduation! To HERbert, your feline friendship is a wonderful thing. And finally, as always, to Elvis—come back soon, baby, come back soon.

—*James Michael Stewart*

I'd first like to say thanks to John Cook for getting me started, to Dawn Rader for patiently working with me, and to Ed Tittel for including me in this project. Thanks for your support and care to all my coworkers and friends: Chris, John, Shannon, Gary, Richard, Peter, Nick, Jeff, Lorraine, Larry, Chuck, Mike, Greg, Scott, Michelle, Katherine, Bonnie, "Mississippi," et al! To my family, thank you for believing I could do anything and for sticking by me through thick and thin. Finally, thank you to my wonderful daughter Sarah for just being you, you inspire me more than you can imagine.

—*Libby Chovanec*

Thanks to the Big B (Amitabh Bachchan) for being my inspiration and role model throughout my life. Thanks, Dad, for your love, care, blessings, and more. Thanks, Mom, for being the *best* mom in this world.

—*Ramesh Chandak*

Contents At
A Glance

Table Of Contents

Introduction

Welcome to *MCSE IIS 4 Exam Cram, Adaptive Testing Edition*! This book aims to help you get ready to take—and pass—the Microsoft certification Exam 70-087, titled "Implementing and Supporting Microsoft Internet Information Server 4." This Introduction explains Microsoft's certification programs in general and talks about how the *Exam Cram* series can help you prepare for Microsoft's certification exams.

Exam Cram books help you understand and appreciate the subjects and materials you need to pass Microsoft certification exams. *Exam Cram* books are aimed strictly at test preparation and review. They do not teach you everything you need to know about a topic (such as the ins and outs of managing an IIS server, or all the nitty-gritty details involved in using the WWW and FTP services). Instead, we (the authors) present and dissect the questions and problems we've found that you're likely to encounter on a test. We've worked from Microsoft's own training materials, preparation guides, and tests, and from a battery of third-party test preparation tools. Our aim is to bring together as much information as possible about Microsoft certification exams.

Nevertheless, to prepare yourself completely for any Microsoft test, we recommend that you begin by taking the Self-Assessment included in this book immediately following this Introduction. This tool will help you evaluate your knowledge base against the requirements for an MCSE under both ideal and real circumstances.

Based on what you learn from that exercise, you might decide to begin your studies with some classroom training or some background reading. On the other hand, you might decide to pick up and read one of the many study guides available from Microsoft or third-party vendors on certain topics, including The Coriolis Group's *Exam Prep* series (for which a title on IIS 4 is also available).

We also strongly recommend that you install, configure, and fool around with the software that you'll be tested on, because nothing beats hands-on experience and familiarity when it comes to understanding the questions you're likely to encounter on a certification test. Book learning is essential, but hands-on experience is the best teacher of all!

The Microsoft Certified Professional (MCP) Program

The MCP Program currently includes seven separate tracks, each of which boasts its own special acronym (as a would-be certificant, you need to have a high tolerance for alphabet soup of all kinds):

➤ **MCP (Microsoft Certified Professional)** This is the least prestigious of all the certification tracks from Microsoft. Passing any of the major Microsoft exams (except the Networking Essentials exam) qualifies an individual for MCP credentials. Individuals can demonstrate proficiency with additional Microsoft products by passing additional certification exams.

➤ **MCP+I (Microsoft Certified Professional + Internet)** This midlevel certification is attained by completing three core exams: "Implementing and Supporting Microsoft Windows NT Server 4," "Internetworking Microsoft TCP/IP on Microsoft Windows NT 4," and "Implementing and Supporting Internet Information Server 3 and Microsoft Index Server 1.1" or "Implementing and Supporting Microsoft Internet Information Server 4."

➤ **MCP+SB (Microsoft Certified Professional + Site Building)** This certification program is designed for individuals who are planning, building, managing, and maintaining Web sites. Individuals with the MCP+SB credential will have demonstrated the ability to develop Web sites that include multimedia and searchable content and Web sites that connect to and communicate with a back-end database. It requires one MCP exam, plus two of these three exams: "Designing and Implementing Commerce Solutions with Microsoft Site Server 3, Commerce Edition," "Designing and Implementing Web Sites with Microsoft FrontPage 98," and "Designing and Implementing Web Solutions with Microsoft Visual InterDev 6."

➤ **MCSE (Microsoft Certified Systems Engineer)** Anyone who has a current MCSE is warranted to possess a high level of expertise with Windows NT 4 and other Microsoft operating systems and products. This credential is designed to prepare individuals to plan, implement, maintain, and support information systems and networks built around Microsoft Windows NT and its BackOffice family of products.

To obtain an MCSE, an individual must pass four core operating system exams, plus two elective exams. The operating system exams require individuals to demonstrate competence with desktop and server operating systems and with networking components.

You must pass at least two Windows NT-related exams to obtain an MCSE: "Implementing and Supporting Microsoft Windows NT 4 Server" and "Implementing and Supporting Microsoft Windows NT 4 Server in the Enterprise." These tests are intended to indicate an individual's knowledge of Windows NT in smaller, simpler networks and in larger, more complex, and heterogeneous networks, respectively.

Note: The Windows NT 3.51 version is in the process of being retired by Microsoft.

You must pass two additional tests as well. These tests are related to networking and desktop operating systems. At present, the networking requirement can be satisfied only by passing the Networking Essentials test. The desktop operating system test can be satisfied by passing a Windows 95, Windows NT Workstation (the version must match the Windows NT version for the core tests), or Windows 98 test.

The two remaining exams are elective exams. An elective exam may fall in any number of subject or product areas, primarily BackOffice components. These include tests on Internet Explorer 4, SQL Server, IIS, Proxy Server, SNA Server, Exchange Server, Systems Management Server, and the like. However, it is also possible to test out on electives by taking advanced networking topics like "Internetworking with Microsoft TCP/IP on Microsoft Windows NT 4" (but here again, the version of Windows NT involved must match the version for the core requirements taken). If you are on your way to becoming an MCSE and have already taken some exams, visit **www.microsoft.com/mcp/certstep/ mcse.htm** for information about how to proceed with your MCSE certification.

Whatever mix of tests is completed toward MCSE certification, individuals must pass six tests to meet the MCSE requirements. It's not uncommon for the entire process to take a year or so, and many individuals find that they must take a test more than once to pass. Our primary goal with the *Exam Cram* series is to make it possible, given proper study and preparation, to pass all Microsoft certification tests on the first try. Table 1 shows the required and elective exams for the MCSE certification.

Table 1 MCSE Requirements*

Core

All 3 of these are required	
Exam 70-067	Implementing and Supporting Microsoft Windows NT Server 4.0
Exam 70-068	Implementing and Supporting Microsoft Windows NT Server 4.0 in the Enterprise
Exam 70-058	Networking Essentials
Choose 1 from this group	
Exam 70-064	Implementing and Supporting Microsoft Windows 95
Exam 70-073	Implementing and Supporting Microsoft Windows NT Workstation 4.0
Exam 70-098	Implementing and Supporting Microsoft Windows 98

Elective

Choose 2 from this group	
Exam 70-088	Implementing and Supporting Microsoft Proxy Server 2.0
Exam 70-079	Implementing and Supporting Microsoft Internet Explorer 4.0 by Using the Internet Explorer Administration Kit
Exam 70-087	Implementing and Supporting Microsoft Internet Information Server 4.0
Exam 70-081	Implementing and Supporting Microsoft Exchange Server 5.5
Exam 70-059	Internetworking with Microsoft TCP/IP on Microsoft Windows NT 4.0
Exam 70-028	Administering Microsoft SQL Server 7.0
Exam 70-029	Designing and Implementing Databases on Microsoft SQL Server 7.0
Exam 70-056	Implementing and Supporting Web Sites Using Microsoft Site Server 3.0
Exam 70-086	Implementing and Supporting Microsoft Systems Management Server 2.0
Exam 70-085	Implementing and Supporting Microsoft SNA Server 4.0

* This is not a complete listing—you can still be tested on some earlier versions of these products. However, we have included mainly the most recent versions so that you may test on these versions and thus be certified longer. We have not included any tests that are scheduled to be retired.

➤ **MCSE+I (Microsoft Certified Systems Engineer + Internet)** This is a newer Microsoft certification and focuses not just on Microsoft operating systems, but also on Microsoft's Internet servers and TCP/IP.

To obtain this certification, an individual must pass seven core exams plus two elective exams. The core exams include not only the server operating systems (Windows NT Server and Server in the Enterprise) and a desktop OS (Windows 95, Windows 98, or Windows NT Workstation), but also include Networking Essentials, TCP/IP, Internet Information Server (IIS), and the Internet Explorer Administration Kit (IEAK).

The two remaining exams are elective exams. These elective exams can be in any of four product areas: SQL Server, SNA Server, Exchange Server, or Proxy Server. Table 2 shows the required and elective exams for the MCSE+I certification.

Table 2   MCSE+Internet Requirements*

Core

All 6 of these are required	
Exam 70-067	Implementing and Supporting Microsoft Windows NT Server 4.0
Exam 70-068	Implementing and Supporting Microsoft Windows NT Server 4.0 in the Enterprise
Exam 70-058	Networking Essentials
Exam 70-059	Internetworking with Microsoft TCP/IP on Microsoft Windows NT 4.0
Exam 70-087	Implementing and Supporting Microsoft Internet Information Server 4.0
Exam 70-079	Implementing and Supporting Microsoft Internet Explorer 4.0 by Using the Internet Explorer Administration Kit
Choose 1 from this group	
Exam 70-064	Implementing and Supporting Microsoft Windows 95
Exam 70-073	Implementing and Supporting Microsoft Windows NT Workstation 4.0
Exam 70-098	Implementing and Supporting Microsoft Windows 98

Elective

Choose 2 from this group	
Exam 70-088	Implementing and Supporting Microsoft Proxy Server 2.0
Exam 70-081	Implementing and Supporting Microsoft Exchange Server 5.5
Exam 70-028	Administering Microsoft SQL Server 7.0
Exam 70-029	Designing and Implementing Databases on Microsoft SQL Server 7.0
Exam 70-056	Implementing and Supporting Web Sites Using Microsoft Site Server 3.0
Exam 70-085	Implementing and Supporting Microsoft SNA Server 4.0

*   This is not a complete listing—you can still be tested on some earlier versions of these products. However, we have included mainly the most recent versions so that you may test on these versions and thus be certified longer. We have not included any tests that are scheduled to be retired.

➤ **MCSD (Microsoft Certified Solution Developer)** The MCSD credential reflects the skills required to create multitier, distributed, and COM-based solutions, in addition to desktop and Internet applications, using new technologies. To obtain an MCSD, an individual must demonstrate the ability to analyze and interpret user requirements; select and integrate products, platforms, tools, and technologies; design and implement code and customize applications; and perform necessary software tests and quality assurance operations.

To become an MCSD, you must pass a total of four exams: three core exams and one elective exam. Each candidate must also choose one of these two desktop application exams—"Designing and Implementing Desktop Applications with Microsoft Visual C++ 6" or "Designing and Implementing Desktop Applications with Microsoft Visual Basic 6"—*plus* one of these two distributed application exams—"Designing and Implementing Distributed Applications with Microsoft Visual C++ 6" or "Designing and Implementing Distributed Applications with Microsoft Visual Basic 6."

Note: Microsoft is planning to release desktop application and distributed application exams on Visual J++ and Visual FoxPro in the summer of 1999.

Elective exams cover specific Microsoft applications and languages, including Visual Basic, C++, the Microsoft Foundation Classes, Access, SQL Server, Excel, and more.

➤ **MCDBA (Microsoft Certified Database Administrator)** The MCDBA credential reflects the skills required to implement and administer Microsoft SQL Server databases. To obtain an MCDBA, an individual must demonstrate the ability to derive physical database designs, develop logical data models, create physical databases, create data services by using Transact-SQL, manage and maintain databases, configure and manage security, monitor and optimize databases, and install and configure Microsoft SQL Server.

To become an MCDBA, you must pass a total of five exams: four core exams and one elective exam. The required core exams are "Administering Microsoft SQL Server 7," "Designing and Implementing Databases with Microsoft SQL Server 7," "Implementing and Supporting Microsoft Windows NT Server 4," and "Implementing and Supporting Microsoft Windows NT Server 4 in the Enterprise."

The elective exams that you can choose from cover specific uses of SQL Server and include "Designing and Implementing Distributed Applications with Visual Basic 6," "Designing and Implementing Distributed Applications with Visual C++ 6," "Designing and Implementing Data Warehouses with Microsoft SQL Server 7 and Microsoft Decision Support Services 1," and two exams that relate to Windows NT: "Internetworking with Microsoft TCP/IP on Microsoft Windows NT 4" and "Implementing and Supporting Microsoft Internet Information Server 4."

Note that the exam covered by this book can be used as the elective for the MCDBA certification. Table 3 shows the requirements for the MCDBA certification.

➤ **MCT (Microsoft Certified Trainer)** Microsoft Certified Trainers are individuals who are deemed able to deliver elements of the official Microsoft curriculum, based on technical knowledge and instructional ability. Thus, it is necessary for an individual seeking MCT credentials (which are granted on a course-by-course basis) to pass the related certification exam for a course and complete the official Microsoft training in the subject area, and to demonstrate an ability to teach.

Table 3 MCDBA Requirements

Core

All 4 of these are required	
Exam 70-028	Administering Microsoft SQL Server 7.0
Exam 70-029	Designing and Implementing Databases with Microsoft SQL Server 7.0
Exam 70-067	Implementing and Supporting Microsoft Windows NT Server 4.0
Exam 70-068	Implementing and Supporting Microsoft Windows NT Server 4.0 in the Enterprise

Elective

Choose 1 from this group	
Exam 70-015	Designing and Implementing Distributed Applications with Microsoft Visual C++ 6.0
Exam 70-019	Designing and Implementing Data Warehouses with Microsoft SQL Server 7.0 and Microsoft Decision Support Services 1.0
Exam 70-059	Internetworking with Microsoft TCP/IP on Microsoft Windows NT 4.0
Exam 70-087	Implementing and Supporting Microsoft Internet Information Server 4.0
Exam 70-175	Designing and Implementing Distributed Applications with Microsoft Visual Basic 6.0

This latter criterion may be satisfied by proving that one has already attained training certification from Novell, Banyan, Lotus, the Santa Cruz Operation, or Cisco, or by taking a Microsoft-sanctioned workshop on instruction. Microsoft makes it clear that MCTs are important cogs in the Microsoft training channels. Instructors must be MCTs before Microsoft will allow them to teach in any of its official training channels, including Microsoft's affiliated Certified Technical Education Centers (CTECs) and the Microsoft Online Institute (MOLI).

Certification is an ongoing activity. Once a Microsoft product becomes obsolete, MCPs typically have 12 to 18 months in which they may recertify on current product versions. (If individuals do not recertify within the specified time period, their certifications become invalid.) Because technology keeps changing and new products continually supplant old ones, this should come as no surprise.

The best place to keep tabs on the MCP Program and its various certifications is on the Microsoft Web site. The current root URL for the MCP program is **www.microsoft.com/mcp/**. But Microsoft's Web site changes often, so if this URL doesn't work, try using the Search tool on Microsoft's site with either "MCP" or the quoted phrase "Microsoft Certified Professional Program" as a search string. This will help you find the latest and most accurate information about Microsoft's certification programs.

Taking A Certification Exam

Alas, testing is not free. Each computer-based MCP exam costs $100, and if you don't pass, you may retest for an additional $100 for each additional try. In the United States and Canada, tests are administered by Sylvan Prometric and by Virtual University Enterprises (VUE). Here's how you can contact them:

➤ **Sylvan Prometric** You can sign up for a test through the company's Web site at **www.slspro.com**. Or, you can register by phone at 800-755-3926 (within the United States or Canada) or at 410-843-8000 (outside the United States and Canada).

➤ **Virtual University Enterprises** You can sign up for a test or get the phone numbers for local testing centers through the Web page at **www.microsoft.com/train_cert/mcp/vue_info.htm**.

To sign up for a test, you must possess a valid credit card, or contact either company for mailing instructions to send them a check (in the U.S.). Only when payment is verified, or a check has cleared, can you actually register for a test.

To schedule an exam, call the number or visit either of the Web pages at least one day in advance. To cancel or reschedule an exam, you must call before 7 P.M. pacific standard time the day before the scheduled test time (or you may be charged, even if you don't appear to take the test). When you want to schedule a test, have the following information ready:

➤ Your name, organization, and mailing address.

➤ Your Microsoft Test ID. (Inside the United States, this means your Social Security number; citizens of other nations should call ahead to find out what type of identification number is required to register for a test.)

➤ The name and number of the exam you wish to take.

➤ A method of payment. (As we've already mentioned, a credit card is the most convenient method, but alternate means can be arranged in advance, if necessary.)

Once you sign up for a test, you'll be informed as to when and where the test is scheduled. Try to arrive at least 15 minutes early. You must supply two forms of identification—one of which must be a photo ID—to be admitted into the testing room.

All exams are completely closed-book. In fact, you will not be permitted to take anything with you into the testing area, but you will be furnished with a blank sheet of paper and a pen or, in some cases, an erasable plastic sheet and an erasable pen. We suggest that you immediately write down on that sheet of paper all the information you've memorized for the test. In *Exam Cram* books, this information appears on a tear-out sheet inside the front cover of each book. You will have some time to compose yourself, to record this information, and even to take a sample orientation exam before you begin the real thing. We suggest you take the orientation test before taking your first exam, but because they're all more or less identical in layout, behavior, and controls, you probably won't need to do this more than once.

When you complete a Microsoft certification exam, the software will tell you whether you've passed or failed. Results are broken into several topic areas. Even if you fail, we suggest you ask for—and keep—the detailed report that the test administrator should print for you. You can use this report to help you prepare for another go-round, if needed.

If you need to retake an exam, you'll have to schedule a new test with Sylvan Prometric or VUE and pay another $100.

 The first time you fail a test, you can retake the test the next day. However, if you fail a second time, you must wait 14 days before retaking that test. The 14-day waiting period remains in effect for all retakes after the first failure.

Tracking MCP Status

As soon as you pass any Microsoft exam other than Networking Essentials, you'll attain Microsoft Certified Professional (MCP) status. Microsoft also generates transcripts that indicate which exams you have passed and your corresponding test scores. You can order a transcript by email at any time by sending an email to **mcp@msprograms.com**. You can also obtain a copy of your transcript by downloading the latest version of the MCT Guide from the Web site and consulting the section titled "Key Contacts" for a list of telephone numbers and related contacts.

Once you pass the necessary set of exams (one for MCP, six for MCSE, or nine for MCSE+I), you'll be certified. Official certification normally takes anywhere from four to six weeks, so don't expect to get your credentials overnight. When the package for a qualified certification arrives, it includes a Welcome Kit that contains a number of elements:

➤ A MCP, MCSE, or MCSE+I certificate, suitable for framing, along with a Professional Program Membership card and lapel pin.

➤ A license to use the MCP logo, thereby allowing you to use the logo in advertisements, promotions, and documents, and on letterhead, business cards, and so on. Along with the license comes a MCP logo sheet, which includes camera-ready artwork. (Note: Before using any of the artwork, individuals must sign and return a licensing agreement that indicates they'll abide by its terms and conditions.)

➤ A subscription to *Microsoft Certified Professional Magazine*, which provides ongoing data about testing and certification activities, requirements, and changes to the program.

➤ A one-year subscription to the Microsoft Beta Evaluation program. This subscription will get you all beta products from Microsoft for the next year. (This does not include developer products. You must join the MSDN program or become a MCSD to qualify for developer beta products.)

Many people believe that the benefits of MCP certification go well beyond the perks that Microsoft provides to newly anointed members of this elite group. We're starting to see more job listings that request or require applicants to have an MCP, MCSE, MCSE+I, and so on, and many individuals who complete the program can qualify for increases in pay and/or responsibility. As an official recognition of hard work and broad knowledge, one of the MCP credentials is a badge of honor in many IT organizations.

How To Prepare For An Exam

Preparing for any Windows NT Server-related test (including IIS) requires that you obtain and study materials designed to provide comprehensive information about the product and its capabilities that will appear on the specific exam for which you are preparing. The following list of materials will help you study and prepare:

➤ The Windows NT Server product CD includes comprehensive online documentation and related materials; it should be a primary resource when you are preparing for the test.

➤ The exam prep materials, practice tests, and self-assessment exams on the Microsoft Training And Certification Download page (**www.microsoft.com/train_cert/download/downld.htm**). Find the materials, download them, and use them!

In addition, you'll probably find any or all of the following materials useful in your quest for IIS expertise:

➤ **Microsoft TechNet CD** This monthly CD-based publication delivers numerous electronic titles that include coverage of TCP/IP and related topics on the Technical Information (TechNet) CD. Its offerings include product facts, technical notes, tools and utilities, and information on how to access the Seminars Online training materials for TCP/IP. A subscription to TechNet costs $299 per year, but it is well worth the price. Visit **www.microsoft.com/technet/** and check out the information under the "TechNet Subscription" menu entry for more details.

➤ **Study Guides** Several publishers—including Certification Insider Press—offer IIS titles. The Certification Insider Press series includes:

➤ The *Exam Cram* series These books give you information about the material you need to know to pass the tests.

➤ The *Exam Prep* series These books provide a greater level of detail than the *Exam Cram* books and are designed to teach you every thing you need to know from an exam perspective. *MCSE IIS Exam Prep* is the perfect learning companion to prepare you for Exam 70-097, "Implementing and Supporting Microsoft Internet Informa tion Server 4." Look for this book in your favorite bookstores.

Together, the two series make a perfect pair.

➤ **Classroom Training** CTECs, MOLI, and unlicensed third-party training companies (like Wave Technologies, American Research Group, Learning Tree, Data-Tech, and others) all offer classroom training on IIS. These companies aim to help you prepare to pass the IIS test. Although such training runs upwards of $350 per day in class, most of the individuals lucky enough to partake (including your humble authors, who've even taught such courses) find them to be quite worthwhile.

➤ **Other Publications** You'll find direct references to other publications and resources in this book, but there's no shortage of materials available about IIS. To help you sift through some of the publications out there, we end each chapter with a "Need To Know More?" section that provides pointers to more complete and exhaustive resources covering the chapter's information. This should give you an idea of where we think you should look for further discussion.

By far, this set of required and recommended materials represents a nonpareil collection of sources and resources for IIS and related topics. We anticipate that you'll find that this book belongs in this company. In the section that follows, we explain how this book works, and we give you some good reasons why this book counts as a member of the required and recommended materials list.

About This Book

Each topical *Exam Cram* chapter follows a regular structure, along with graphical cues about important or useful information. Here's the structure of a typical chapter:

> ➤ **Opening Hotlists** Each chapter begins with a list of the terms, tools, and techniques that you must learn and understand before you can be fully conversant with that chapter's subject matter. We follow the hotlists with one or two introductory paragraphs to set the stage for the rest of the chapter.

> ➤ **Topical Coverage** After the opening hotlists, each chapter covers a series of topics related to the chapter's subject title. Throughout this section, we highlight topics or concepts likely to appear on a test using a special Exam Alert layout, like this:

 This is what an Exam Alert looks like. Normally, an Exam Alert stresses concepts, terms, software, or activities that are likely to relate to one or more certification test questions. For that reason, we think any information found offset in Exam Alert format is worthy of unusual attentiveness on your part. Indeed, most of the information that appears on The Cram Sheet appears as Exam Alerts within the text.

Pay close attention to material flagged as an Exam Alert; although all the information in this book pertains to what you need to know to pass the exam, we flag certain items that are really important. You'll find what appears in the meat of each chapter to be worth knowing, too, when preparing for the test. Because this book's material is very condensed, we recommend that you use this book along with other resources to achieve the maximum benefit.

In addition to the Exam Alerts, we have provided tips that will help you build a better foundation for IIS knowledge. Although the information may not be on the exam, it is certainly related and will help you become a better test-taker.

 This is how tips are formatted. Keep your eyes open for these, and you'll become a IIS guru in no time!

➤ **Practice Questions** Although we talk about test questions and topics throughout each chapter, this section presents a series of mock test questions and explanations of both correct and incorrect answers. We also try to point out especially tricky questions by using a special icon, like this:

Ordinarily, this icon flags the presence of a particularly devious inquiry, if not an outright trick question. Trick questions are calculated to be answered incorrectly if not read more than once, and carefully, at that. Although they're not ubiquitous, such questions make regular appearances on the Microsoft exams. That's why we say exam questions are as much about reading comprehension as they are about knowing your material inside out and backwards.

➤ **Details And Resources** Every chapter ends with a section titled "Need To Know More?". This section provides direct pointers to Microsoft and third-party resources offering more details on the chapter's subject. In addition, this section tries to rank or at least rate the quality and thoroughness of the topic's coverage by each resource. If you find a resource you like in this collection, use it, but don't feel compelled to use all the resources. On the other hand, we recommend only resources we use on a regular basis, so none of our recommendations will be a waste of your time or money (but purchasing them all at once probably represents an expense that many network administrators and would-be MCPs, MCSEs, and MCSE+Is might find hard to justify).

➤ Your authors have also prepared an adaptive exam for IIS 4 that is available online. To take this practice exam, which should help you prepare even better for the real thing, visit **www.coriolis.com/cip/ testcenter/** and follow the instructions from there. Pick the IIS 4 book, and when prompted for a password enter the string ISPTOL51069.

The bulk of the book follows this chapter structure slavishly, but there are a few other elements that we'd like to point out. Chapters 13 and 15 each include a sample test that provides a good review of the material presented throughout the book to ensure you're ready for the exam. Chapters 14 and 16 provide answer keys to the sample tests that appear in Chapters 13 and 15, respectively. Additionally, you'll find the Glossary, which explains terms, and an index that you can use to track down terms as they appear in the text.

Finally, the tear-out Cram Sheet attached next to the inside front cover of this *Exam Cram* book represents a condensed and compiled collection of facts and tips that we think you should memorize before taking the test. Because you can dump this information out of your head onto a piece of paper before taking the exam, you can master this information by brute force—you need to remember it only long enough to write it down when you walk into the test room. You might even want to look at it in the car or in the lobby of the testing center just before you walk in to take the test.

How To Use This Book

If you're prepping for a first-time test, we've structured the topics in this book to build on one another. Therefore, some topics in later chapters make more sense after you've read earlier chapters. That's why we suggest you read this book from front to back for your initial test preparation. If you need to brush up on a topic or you have to bone up for a second try, use the index or table of contents to go straight to the topics and questions that you need to study. Beyond helping you prepare for the test, we think you'll find this book useful as a tightly focused reference to some of the most important aspects of IIS.

Given all the book's elements and its specialized focus, we've tried to create a tool that will help you prepare for—and pass—Microsoft Exam 70-087, "Implementing and Supporting Microsoft Internet Information Server 4." Please share your feedback on the book with us, especially if you have ideas about how we can improve it for future test-takers. We'll consider everything you say carefully, and we'll respond to all suggestions.

Send your questions or comments to us at **cipq@coriolis.com**. Our series editor, Ed Tittel, coordinates our efforts and ensures that all questions get answered. Please remember to include the title of the book in your message; otherwise, we'll be forced to guess which book you're writing about. And we don't like to guess—we want to *know*! Also, be sure to check out the Web page at **www.certificationinsider.com**, where you'll find information updates, commentary, and certification information.

Thanks, and enjoy the book!

Self-Assessment

Based on recent statistics from Microsoft, as many as 250,000 individuals are at some stage of the certification process but haven't yet received an MCP or other Microsoft certification. We also know that three or four times that number may be considering whether or not to obtain a Microsoft certification of some kind. That's a huge audience!

The reason we included a Self-Assessment in this *Exam Cram* book is to help you evaluate your readiness to tackle MCSE (and MCSE+I) certification. It should also help you understand what you need to master the topic of this book—namely, Exam 70-087, "Implementing and Supporting Microsoft Internet Information Server 4." But before you tackle this Self-Assessment, let's talk about concerns you may face when pursuing an MCSE, and what an ideal MCSE candidate might look like.

MCSEs In The Real World

In the next section, we describe an ideal MCSE candidate, knowing full well that only a few real candidates will meet this ideal. In fact, our description of that ideal candidate might seem downright scary. But take heart: Although the requirements to obtain an MCSE may seem pretty formidable, they are by no means impossible to meet. However, you should be keenly aware that it does take time, requires some expense, and consumes substantial effort to get through the process.

More than 90,000 MCSEs are already certified, so it's obviously an attainable goal. You can get all the real-world motivation you need from knowing that many others have gone before, so you will be able to follow in their footsteps. If you're willing to tackle the process seriously and do what it takes to obtain the necessary experience and knowledge, you can take—and pass—all the certification tests involved in obtaining an MCSE. In fact, we've designed these *Exam Crams*, and the companion *Exam Preps*, to make it as easy on you as possible to prepare for these exams. But prepare you must!

The same, of course, is true for other Microsoft certifications, including:

➤ MCSE+I, which is like the MCSE certification but requires seven core exams, and two electives drawn from a specific pool of Internet-related topics, for a total of nine exams.

➤ MCSD, which is aimed at software developers and requires one specific exam, two more exams on client and distributed topics, plus a fourth elective exam drawn from a different, but limited, pool of options.

➤ Other Microsoft certifications, whose requirements range from one test (MCP or MCT) to many tests (MCP+I, MCP+SB, MCDBA).

The Ideal MCSE Candidate

Just to give you some idea of what an ideal MCSE candidate is like, here are some relevant statistics about the background and experience such an individual might have. Don't worry if you don't meet these qualifications, or don't come that close—this is a far from ideal world, and where you fall short is simply where you'll have more work to do.

➤ Academic or professional training in network theory, concepts, and operations. This includes everything from networking media and transmission techniques through network operating systems, services, and applications.

➤ Three-plus years of professional networking experience, including experience with Ethernet, token ring, modems, and other networking media. This must include installation, configuration, upgrade, and troubleshooting experience.

➤ Two-plus years in a networked environment that includes hands-on experience with Windows NT Server, Windows NT Workstation, and Windows 95 or Windows 98. A solid understanding of each system's architecture, installation, configuration, maintenance, and troubleshooting is also essential.

➤ A thorough understanding of key networking protocols, addressing, and name resolution, including TCP/IP, IPX/SPX, and NetBEUI.

➤ A thorough understanding of NetBIOS naming, browsing services, and file and print services.

➤ Familiarity with key Windows NT-based TCP/IP-based services, including HTTP (Web servers), DHCP, WINS, DNS, plus familiarity with one or more of the following: Internet Information Server (IIS), Index Server, and Proxy Server.

➤ Working knowledge of NetWare 3.x and 4.x, including IPX/SPX frame formats, NetWare file, print, and directory services, and both Novell and Microsoft client software. Working knowledge of Microsoft's Client Service for NetWare (CSNW), Gateway Service for NetWare (GSNW), the NetWare Migration Tool (NWCONV), and the NetWare Client for Windows (NT, 95, and 98) is essential.

Fundamentally, this boils down to a bachelor's degree in computer science, plus three years of work experience in a technical position involving network design, installation, configuration, and maintenance. We believe that well under half of all certification candidates meet these requirements, and that, in fact, most meet less than half of these requirements—at least, when they begin the certification process. But because all 90,000 people who already have been certified have survived this ordeal, you can survive it too—especially if you heed what our Self-Assessment can tell you about what you already know and what you need to learn.

Put Yourself To The Test

The following series of questions and observations is designed to help you figure out how much work you must do to pursue Microsoft certification and what kinds of resources you may consult on your quest. Be absolutely honest in your answers, or you'll end up wasting money on exams you're not yet ready to take. There are no right or wrong answers, only steps along the path to certification. Only you can decide where you really belong in the broad spectrum of aspiring candidates.

Two things should be clear from the outset, however:

➤ Even a modest background in computer science will be helpful.

➤ Hands-on experience with Microsoft products and technologies is an essential ingredient to certification success.

Educational Background

Educational background should also be taken into consideration:

1. Have you ever taken any computer-related classes? [Yes or No]

   If Yes, proceed to question 2; if No, proceed to question 4.

2. Have you taken any classes on computer operating systems? [Yes or No]

   If Yes, you will probably be able to handle Microsoft's architecture and system component discussions. If you're rusty, brush up on basic operating system concepts, especially virtual memory, multitasking regimes, user mode versus kernel mode operation, and general computer security topics.

If No, consider some basic reading in this area. We strongly recommend a good general operating systems book, such as *Operating System Concepts*, by Abraham Silberschatz and Peter Baer Galvin (Addison-Wesley, 1997, ISBN 0-201-59113-8). If this title doesn't appeal to you, check out reviews for other, similar titles at your favorite online bookstore.

3. Have you taken any networking concepts or technologies classes? [Yes or No]

If Yes, you will probably be able to handle Microsoft's networking terminology, concepts, and technologies (brace yourself for frequent departures from normal usage). If you're rusty, brush up on basic networking concepts and terminology, especially networking media, transmission types, the OSI Reference model, and networking technologies such as Ethernet, token ring, FDDI, and WAN links.

If No, you might want to read one or two books in this topic area. The two best books that we know of are *Computer Networks, 3rd Edition*, by Andrew S. Tanenbaum (Prentice-Hall, 1996, ISBN 0-13-349945-6) and *Computer Networks and Internets*, by Douglas E. Comer (Prentice-Hall, 1997, ISBN 0-13-239070-1).

Skip to the next section, "Hands-On Experience."

4. Have you done any reading on operating systems or networks? [Yes or No]

If Yes, review the requirements stated in the first paragraphs after questions 2 and 3. If you meet those requirements, move on to the next section, "Hands-On Experience." If No, consult the recommended reading for both topics. A strong background will help you prepare for the Microsoft exams better than just about anything else.

Hands-On Experience

The most important key to success on all of the Microsoft tests is hands-on experience, especially with Windows NT Server and Workstation, plus the many add-on services and BackOffice components around which so many of the Microsoft certification exams revolve. If we leave you with only one realization after taking this Self-Assessment, it should be that there's no substitute for time spent installing, configuring, and using the various Microsoft products upon which you'll be tested repeatedly and in depth.

5. Have you installed, configured, and worked with:

   ➤ Windows NT Server? [Yes or No]

   If Yes, make sure you understand basic concepts as covered in Exam 70-067 and advanced concepts as covered in Exam 70-068. You should also study the IIS interfaces, utilities, and services for this test, Exam 70-087, plus the ins and outs of TCP/IP for Exam 70-059.

 You can download objectives, practice exams, and other information about Microsoft exams from the company's Training and Certification page on the Web at **www.microsoft.com/ train_cert/**. Use the "Find Exam" link to get specific exam info.

   If you haven't worked with Windows NT Server, TCP/IP, and IIS (or whatever product you choose for your final elective), you must obtain one or two machines and a copy of Windows NT Server. Then, learn the operating system, and do the same for TCP/IP and whatever other software components on which you'll also be tested.

   In fact, we recommend that you obtain two computers, each with a network interface, and set up a two-node network on which to practice. With decent Windows NT-capable computers selling for about $500 to $600 apiece these days, this shouldn't be too much of a financial hardship. You can order a BackOffice Trial Kit from Microsoft, which includes evaluation copies of both Workstation and Server, for under $50 from **www.backoffice.microsoft.com/ downtrial/**.

   ➤ Windows NT Workstation? [Yes or No]

   If Yes, make sure you understand the concepts covered in Exam 70-073.

   If No, you will want to obtain a copy of Windows NT Workstation and learn how to install, configure, and maintain it. You can use *MCSE NT Workstation 4 Exam Cram* to guide your activities and studies, or work straight from Microsoft's test objectives if you prefer.

For any and all of these Microsoft exams, the Resource Kits for the topics involved are a good study resource. You can purchase softcover Resource Kits from Microsoft Press (search for them at **http://mspress.microsoft.com/**), but they're also included on the TechNet CD subscription (**www.microsoft.com/technet**). We believe that Resource Kits are among the best preparation tools available, along with the *Exam Crams* and *Exam Preps*, that you can use to get ready for Microsoft exams.

You have the option of taking the Window 95 (70-064) exam or the Windows 98 (70-098) exam, instead of Exam 70-073, to fulfill your desktop operating system requirement for the MCSE. Although we don't recommend these others (because studying for Workstation helps you prepare for the Server exams), we do recommend that you obtain Resource Kits and other tools to help you prepare for those exams if you decide to take one or both of them for your own reasons.

6. For any specific Microsoft product that is not itself an operating system (for example, FrontPage 98, SQL Server, and so on), have you installed, configured, used, and upgraded this software? [Yes or No]

If the answer is Yes, skip to the next section, "Testing Your Exam-Readiness." If it's No, you must get some experience. Read on for suggestions on how to do this.

Experience is a must with any Microsoft product exam, be it something as simple as FrontPage 98 or as challenging as Exchange 5.5 or SQL Server 7. You can grab a download of BackOffice at **www.backoffice. microsoft.com/downtrial/**; for trial copies of other software, search Microsoft's Web site using the name of the product as your search term.

If you have the funds, or your employer will pay your way, consider taking a class at a Certified Training and Education Center (CTEC) or at an Authorized Academic Training Partner (AATP). In addition to classroom exposure to the topic of your choice, you get a copy of the software that is the focus of your course, along with a trial version of whatever operating system it needs (usually, NT Server), with the training materials for that class.

Before you even think about taking any Microsoft exam, make sure you've spent enough time with the related software to understand how it may be installed and configured, how to maintain such an installation, and how to troubleshoot that software when things go wrong. This will help you in the exam, and in real life!

Testing Your Exam-Readiness

Whether you attend a formal class on a specific topic to get ready for an exam or use written materials to study on your own, some preparation for the Microsoft certification exams is essential. At $100 a try, pass or fail, you want to do everything you can to pass on your first try. That's where studying comes in.

We have included two practice exams in this book, so if you don't score that well on the first test, you can study more and then tackle the second test. We also have built an adaptive exam that you can take online through the Coriolis Web site at **www.coriolis.com/cip/testcenter/** (password: ISPTOL51069). If you still don't hit a score of at least 70 percent after these tests, you'll want to investigate the other practice test resources we mention in this section.

For any given subject, consider taking a class if you've tackled self-study materials, taken the test, and failed anyway. The opportunity to interact with an instructor and fellow students can make all the difference in the world, if you can afford that privilege. For information about Microsoft classes, visit the Training and Certification page at **www.microsoft.com/train_cert/** (use the "Find a Course" link).

If you can't afford to take a class, visit the Training and Certification page anyway, because it also includes pointers to free practice exams and to Microsoft Certified Professional Approved Study Guides and other self-study tools. And even if you can't afford to spend much at all, you should still invest in some low-cost practice exams from commercial vendors, because they can help you assess your readiness to pass a test better than any other tool. All of the following Web sites offer practice exams online for less than $100 apiece (some for significantly less than that):

➤ Beachfront Quizzer at **www.bfq.com/**

➤ CramSession at **www.cramsession.com/**

➤ Hardcore MCSE at **www.hardcoremcse.com/**

➤ LANWrights at **www.lanw.com/books/examcram/order.htm**

➤ MeasureUp at **www.measureup.com/**

7. Have you taken a practice exam on your chosen test subject? [Yes or No]

   If Yes, and you scored 70 percent or better, you're probably ready to tackle the real thing. If your score isn't above that crucial threshold, keep at it until you break that barrier.

If No, obtain all the free and low-budget practice tests you can find (see the list above) and get to work. Keep at it until you can break the passing threshold comfortably.

 When it comes to assessing your test readiness, there is no better way than to take a good-quality practice exam and pass with a score of 70 percent or better. When we're preparing ourselves, we shoot for 80-plus percent, just to leave room for the "weirdness factor" that sometimes shows up on Microsoft exams.

Assessing Readiness For Exam 70-087

In addition to the general exam-readiness information in the previous section, there are several things you can do to prepare for the IIS exam. As you're getting ready for Exam 70-087, visit the MCSE mailing list. Sign up at www.sunbelt-software.com (look for the "Subscribe to..." button). You will also find a great source of questions and related information at the CramSession site at www.cramsession.com. These are great places to ask questions and get good answers, or simply to watch the questions that others ask (along with the answers, of course).

You should also cruise the Web looking for "braindumps" (recollections of test topics and experiences recorded by others) to help you anticipate topics you're likely to encounter on the test. The MCSE mailing list is a good place to ask where the useful braindumps are, or you can check Shawn Gamble's list at www.commandcentral.com or Herb Martin's Braindump Heaven at http://209.207.167.177/.

 When using any braindump, it's Okay to pay attention to information about questions. But you can't always be sure that a braindump's author will also be able to provide correct answers. Thus, use the questions to guide your studies, but don't rely on the answers in a braindump to lead you to the truth. Double-check everything you find in any braindump.

Microsoft exam mavens also recommend checking the Microsoft Knowledge Base (available on its own CD as part of the TechNet collection, or on the Microsoft Web site at http://support.microsoft.com/support/) for "meaningful technical support issues" that relate to your exam's topics. Although we're not sure exactly what the quoted phrase means, we have also noticed some overlap between technical support questions on particular products and trouble-shooting questions on the exams for those products.

For IIS preparation in particular, we'd also like to recommend that you check out one or more of these resources as you prepare to take Exam 70-087:

➤ Sheldon, Tom and John Muller: *Microsoft Internet Information Server 4: The Complete Reference.* Osborne McGraw-Hill, Berkeley, CA, 1998. ISBN: 0-07882-457-5.

➤ Dyson, Peter: *Mastering Microsoft Internet Information Server 4.* Sybex, Alameda, CA, 1997. ISBN: 0-78212-080-6.

➤ Stewart, Michael: *MCSE IIS Exam Prep*, Certification Insider Press, Scottsdale, AZ, 1998. ISBN: 1-57610-267-X.

➤ Microsoft Corporation: *Microsoft Internet Information Server Resource Kit.* Microsoft Press, Redmond, WA, 1998. ISBN: 1-57231-638-1.

➤ Oliver, Robert, Christian Plazas, John Desborough, and David Gulbransen: *Building a Windows NT 4 Internet Server.* New Riders Publishing, Indianapolis, IN, 1997. ISBN: 1-56205-680-8.

➤ Buyens, Jim: *Building Net Sites with Windows NT: An Internet Service Handbook.* Addison-Wesley Publishing Company, Reading, MA, 1996. ISBN: 0-20147-949-4.

Stop by your favorite bookstore or online bookseller to check out one or more of these resources. We believe the first two are the best general all-around references on TCP/IP available, and the second two complement the contents of this *Exam Cram* for test preparation very nicely.

One last note: Hopefully, it makes sense to stress the importance of hands-on experience in the context of the IIS exam. As you review the material for that exam, you'll realize that hands-on experience with IIS services, tools, and utilities is invaluable.

Onward, Through The Fog!

Once you've assessed your readiness, undertaken the right background studies, obtained the hands-on experience that will help you understand the products zand technologies at work, and reviewed the many sources of information to help you prepare for a test, you'll be ready to take a round of practice tests. When your scores come back positive enough to get you through the exam, you're ready to go after the real thing. If you follow our assessment regime, you'll not only know what you need to study, but when you're ready to make a test date at Sylvan or VUE. Good luck!

Microsoft Certification Exams

Terms you'll need to understand:

√ Radio button

√ Checkbox

√ Exhibit

√ Multiple-choice question formats

√ Careful reading

√ Process of elimination

√ Fixed-length tests

√ Adaptive tests

√ Short-form tests

√ Combination tests

√ Simulations

Techniques you'll need to master:

√ Assessing your exam-readiness

√ Preparing to take a certification exam

√ Practicing (to make perfect)

√ Making the best use of the testing software

√ Budgeting your time

√ Guessing (as a last resort)

Exam taking is not something that most people anticipate eagerly, no matter how well prepared they may be. In most cases, familiarity helps offset test anxiety. In plain English, this means you probably won't be as nervous when you take your fourth or fifth Microsoft certification exam as you'll be when you take your first one.

Whether it's your first exam or your tenth, understanding the details of exam taking (how much time to spend on questions, the environment you'll be in, and so on) and the exam software will help you concentrate on the material rather than on the setting. Likewise, mastering a few basic exam-taking skills should help you recognize—and perhaps even outfox—some of the tricks and snares you're bound to find in some of the exam questions.

This chapter, besides explaining the exam environment and software, describes some proven exam-taking strategies that you should be able to use to your advantage.

Assessing Exam-Readiness

Before you take any Microsoft exam, we strongly recommend that you read through and take the Self-Assessment included with this book (it appears just before this chapter, in fact). This will help you compare your knowledge base to the requirements for obtaining an MCSE, and it will also help you identify parts of your background or experience that may be in need of improvement, enhancement, or further learning. If you get the right set of basics under your belt, obtaining Microsoft certification will be that much easier.

Once you've gone through the Self-Assessment, you can remedy those topical areas where your background or experience may not measure up to an ideal certification candidate. But you can also tackle subject matter for individual tests at the same time, so you can continue making progress while you're catching up in some areas.

Once you've worked through an *Exam Cram*, have read the supplementary materials, and have taken the practice tests, you'll have a pretty clear idea of when you should be ready to take the real exam. Although we strongly recommend that you keep practicing until your scores top the 70 percent mark, 75 percent would be a good goal to give yourself some margin for error in a real exam situation (where stress will play more of a role than when you practice). Once you hit that point, you should be ready to go. But if you get through both practice exams in this book and the sample adaptive online exam (discussed in the Self-Assessment, the Introduction, and later in this chapter) without attaining that score, you should keep taking practice tests and studying the materials until you get there. You'll find more information about other practice test vendors in the Self-Assessment, along with even more pointers on how to study and prepare. But now, on to the exam itself!

The Exam Situation

When you arrive at the testing center where you scheduled your exam, you'll need to sign in with an exam coordinator. He or she will ask you to show two forms of identification, one of which must be a photo ID. After you've signed in and your time slot arrives, you'll be asked to deposit any books, bags, or other items you brought with you. Then, you'll be escorted into a closed room. Typically, the room will be furnished with anywhere from one to half a dozen computers, and each workstation will be separated from the others by dividers designed to keep you from seeing what's happening on someone else's computer.

You'll be furnished with a pen or pencil and a blank sheet of paper, or, in some cases, an erasable plastic sheet and an erasable pen. You're allowed to write down anything you want on both sides of this sheet. Before the exam, you should memorize as much of the material that appears on The Cram Sheet (in the front of this book) as you can, so you can write that information on the blank sheet as soon as you are seated in front of the computer. You can refer to your rendition of The Cram Sheet anytime you like during the test, but you'll have to surrender the sheet when you leave the room.

Most test rooms feature a wall with a large picture window. This permits the exam coordinator to monitor the room, to prevent exam-takers from talking to one another, and to observe anything out of the ordinary that might go on. The exam coordinator will have preloaded the appropriate Microsoft certification exam—for this book, that's Exam 70-087—and you'll be permitted to start as soon as you're seated in front of the computer.

All Microsoft certification exams allow a certain maximum amount of time in which to complete your work (this time is indicated on the exam by an on-screen counter/clock, so you can check the time remaining whenever you like). All Microsoft certification exams are computer generated and most use a multiple-choice format. Although this may sound quite simple, the questions are constructed not only to check your mastery of basic facts and figures about IIS, but they also require you to evaluate one or more sets of circumstances or requirements. Often, you'll be asked to give more than one answer to a question. Likewise, you might be asked to select the best or most effective solution to a problem from a range of choices, all of which are technically correct. Taking the exam is quite an adventure, and it involves real thinking. This book shows you what to expect and how to deal with the potential problems, puzzles, and predicaments.

In the next section, you'll learn more about how Microsoft test questions look and how they must be answered.

Exam Layout And Design

Some exam questions require you to select a single answer, whereas others ask you to select one or more correct answers. The following multiple-choice question requires you to select a single correct answer. Following the question is a brief summary of each potential answer and why it is either right or wrong.

Question 1

Clients attempting to access a Web site hosted on IIS receive HTTP error 403. What could cause this error?

○ a. Write access is enabled.

○ b. Read access is not enabled.

○ c. That client's domain is restricted from the Web site.

○ d. Resources are located on a share.

Answer b is correct. A 403 error occurs if the Web site does not have Read access enabled. Enabling Write access has no effect on Read access. Therefore, answer a is incorrect. If the client was restricted from the Web site, an "Access denied" error would be issued instead of a "Read access forbidden" error. Therefore, answer c is incorrect. Pulling resources from a share has no effect on the read error. Therefore, answer d is incorrect.

This sample question format corresponds closely to the Microsoft certification exam format—the only difference on the exam is that questions are not followed by answer keys. To select an answer, you would position the cursor over the radio button next to the answer. Then, you would click the mouse button to select the answer.

Let's examine a question where one or more answers are possible. This type of question provides checkboxes rather than radio buttons for marking all appropriate selections.

Question 2

> The IIS SMTP and NNTP services can be administered and managed through which utilities or interfaces? [Check all correct answers]
>
> ❏ a. Server Manager
>
> ❏ b. IIS's MMC snap-in
>
> ❏ c. Network Monitor
>
> ❏ d. An HTML interface

Answers b and d are correct. The IIS SMTP and NNTP services can be administered through the IIS MMC snap-in or through separate HTML interfaces. Server Manager and Network Monitor are not used to administer these services. Therefore, answers a and c are incorrect.

For this particular question, two answers are required. As far as the authors can tell (and Microsoft won't comment), such questions are scored as wrong unless all the required selections are chosen. In other words, a partially correct answer does not result in partial credit when the test is scored. For Question 2, you have to check the boxes next to items b and d to obtain credit for a correct answer. Notice that picking the right answers also means knowing why the other answers are wrong!

Although these two basic types of questions can appear in many forms, they constitute the foundation on which all the Microsoft certification exam questions rest. More complex questions include exhibits, which are usually screenshots of any of the commands, tools, or utilities related to the IIS environment.

For some of these questions, you'll be asked to make a selection by clicking on a checkbox or radio button on the screenshot itself. For others, you'll be expected to use the information displayed therein to guide your answer to the question. Familiarity with the underlying utility is your key to choosing the correct answer(s).

Other questions involving exhibits use charts or network diagrams to help document a workplace scenario that you'll be asked to troubleshoot or configure. Careful attention to such exhibits is the key to success. Be prepared to toggle frequently between the exhibit and the question as you work.

Microsoft's Testing Formats

Currently, Microsoft uses four different testing formats:

➤ Fixed-length

➤ Adaptive

➤ Short-form

➤ Combination

Some Microsoft exams employ more advanced testing capabilities than might immediately meet the eye. Although the questions that appear are still multiple choice, the logic that drives them is more complex than older Microsoft tests, which use a fixed sequence of questions, called a fixed-length test. Other exams employ a sophisticated user interface, which Microsoft calls a simulation, to test your knowledge of the software and systems under consideration in a more or less "live" environment that behaves just like the original.

For many upcoming exams, Microsoft is turning to a well-known technique, called adaptive testing, to establish a test-taker's level of knowledge and product competence. Adaptive exams look the same as fixed-length exams, but they discover the level of difficulty at which an individual test-taker can correctly answer questions. At the same time, Microsoft is in the process of converting some of its older fixed-length exams into adaptive exams as well. Test-takers with differing levels of knowledge or ability therefore see different sets of questions; individuals with high levels of knowledge or ability are presented with a smaller set of more difficult questions, whereas individuals with lower levels of knowledge are presented with a larger set of easier questions. Two individuals may answer the same percentage of questions correctly, but the test-taker with a higher knowledge or ability level will score higher because his or her questions are worth more.

Also, the lower-level test-taker will probably answer more questions than his or her more-knowledgeable colleague. This explains why adaptive tests use ranges of values to define the number of questions and the amount of time it takes to complete the test.

Adaptive tests work by evaluating the test-taker's most recent answer. A correct answer leads to a more difficult question (and the test software's estimate of the test-taker's knowledge and ability level is raised). An incorrect answer leads to a less difficult question (and the test software's estimate of the test-taker's knowledge and ability level is lowered). This process continues until the test targets the test-taker's true ability level. The exam ends when the test-taker's level of accuracy meets a statistically acceptable value (in other words, when his or her performance demonstrates an acceptable level of knowledge and ability) or when the maximum number of items has been presented (in which case, the test-taker is almost certain to fail).

Microsoft has recently introduced the short-form test for its most popular tests (as of this writing, only Networking Essentials [70-058] and TCP/IP [70-059] have appeared in this format). This test delivers exactly 30 questions to its takers, giving them exactly 60 minutes to complete the exam. This type of exam is similar to a fixed-length test, in that it allows readers to jump ahead or return to earlier questions, and to cycle through the questions until the test is done. Microsoft does not use adaptive logic in this test, but claims that statistical analysis of the question pool is such that the 30 questions delivered during a short-form exam will conclusively measure a test-taker's knowledge of the subject matter in much the same way as an adaptive test will. You can think of the short-form test as a kind of "greatest hits" (that is, most important questions) version of the adaptive exam on the same topic.

A fourth kind of test you could encounter is what we've dubbed the combination exam. Several test-takers have reported that some of the Microsoft exams, including Windows NT Server (70-067), Windows NT Server in the Enterprise (70-068), and Windows NT Workstation (70-073), can appear as combination exams. Such exams begin with a set of 15 to 25 adaptive questions, followed by 10 fixed-length questions. In fact, many test-takers have reported that although some combination tests claim that they will present both adaptive and fixed-length portions, when the test-taker has finished the adaptive portion (usually in exactly 15 questions), the test ends there. Because such users have all attained passing scores, it may be that a high enough passing score on the adaptive portion of a combination test obviates the fixed-length portion, but we're not completely sure about this, and Microsoft won't comment. Most combination exams allow a maximum of 60 minutes for the testing period.

Microsoft tests can come in any one of these forms. Whatever you encounter, you must take the test in whichever form it appears; you can't choose one form over another. Currently, the IIS exam may be adaptive, in which case you'll have 90 minutes to answer between 15 and 30 questions (on average), or short-form, in which case you'll get 60 minutes to answer exactly 30 questions. If anything, it pays off even more to prepare thoroughly for an adaptive or combination exam than for a fixed-length or a short-form exam: The penalties for answering incorrectly are built into the test itself on an adaptive exam or the first part of a combination exam, whereas the layout remains the same for a fixed-length or short-form test, no matter how many questions you answer incorrectly.

The biggest difference between an adaptive test and a fixed-length or short-form test is that on a fixed-length or short-form test, you can revisit questions after you've read them over one or more times. On an adaptive test, you must answer the question when it's presented and will have no opportunities to revisit that question thereafter.

Strategies For Different Testing Formats

Before you can choose a test-taking strategy, you need to know if your test is fixed-length, short-form, adaptive, or combination. When you begin your exam, the software will tell you the test is adaptive, if in fact the version you're taking is presented as an adaptive test. If your introductory materials fail to mention this, you're probably taking a fixed-length test. If the total number of questions involved is exactly 30, then you're taking a short-form test. Combination tests announce themselves by indicating that they will start with a set of adaptive questions, followed by fixed-length questions, but don't actually call themselves "combination tests" or "combination exams," we've adopted this nomenclature for descriptive reasons.

 You'll be able to tell for sure if you are taking an adaptive, fixed-length, short-form, or combination test by the first question. If it includes a checkbox that lets you mark the question for later review, you're taking a fixed-length or short-form test. If the total number of questions is 30, it's a short-form test; if more than 30, it's a fixed-length test. Adaptive test questions (and the first set of questions on a combination test) can be visited (and answered) only once, and they include no such checkbox.

The Fixed-Length And Short-Form Exam Strategy

A well-known principle when taking fixed-length or short-form exams is to first read over the entire exam from start to finish while answering only those questions you feel absolutely sure of. On subsequent passes, you can dive into more complex questions more deeply, knowing how many such questions you have left.

Fortunately, the Microsoft exam software for fixed-length and short-form tests makes the multiple-visit approach easy to implement. At the top-left corner of each question is a checkbox that permits you to mark that question for a later visit.

Note: *Marking questions makes review easier, but you can return to any question by clicking the Forward or Back button repeatedly.*

As you read each question, if you answer only those you're sure of and mark for review those that you're not sure of, you can keep working through a decreasing list of questions as you answer the trickier ones in order.

 There's at least one potential benefit to reading the exam over completely before answering the trickier questions: Sometimes, information supplied in later questions will shed more light on earlier questions. Other times, information you read in later questions might jog your memory about IIS 4 facts, figures, or behavior that will help with earlier questions. Either way, you'll come out ahead if you defer those questions about which you're not absolutely sure.

Here are some question-handling strategies that apply to fixed-length and short-form tests. Use them if you have the chance:

➤ When returning to a question after your initial read-through, read every word again—otherwise, your mind can fall quickly into a rut. Sometimes, revisiting a question after turning your attention elsewhere lets you see something you missed, but the strong tendency is to see what you've seen before. Try to avoid that tendency at all costs.

➤ If you return to a question more than twice, try to articulate to yourself what you don't understand about the question, why the answers don't appear to make sense, or what appears to be missing. If you chew on the subject for awhile, your subconscious might provide the details that are lacking or you might notice a "trick" that will point to the right answer.

As you work your way through the exam, another counter that Microsoft provides will come in handy—the number of questions completed and questions outstanding. For fixed-length and short-form tests, it's wise to budget your time by making sure that you've completed one-quarter of the questions one-quarter of the way through the exam period. For a short-form test, as you may experience with the IIS exam, this means you must complete one-quarter of the questions one-quarter of the way through (the first 8 questions in the first 15 minutes) and three-quarters of the questions three-quarters of the way through (24 questions in 45 minutes).

If you're not finished when only five minutes remain, use that time to guess your way through any remaining questions. Remember, guessing is potentially more valuable than not answering, because blank answers are always wrong, but a guess may turn out to be right. If you don't have a clue about any of the remaining questions, pick answers at random, or choose all a's, b's, and so on. The important thing is to submit an exam for scoring that has an answer for every question.

At the very end of your exam period, you're better off guessing than leaving questions unanswered.

The Adaptive Exam Strategy

If there's one principle that applies to taking an adaptive test, it could be summed up as "Get it right the first time." You cannot elect to skip a question and move on to the next one when taking an adaptive test, because the testing software uses your answer to the current question to select whatever question it plans to present next. Nor can you return to a question once you've moved on, because the software gives you only one chance to answer the question. You can, however, take notes, because sometimes information supplied in earlier questions will shed more light on later questions.

Also, when you answer a question correctly, you are presented with a more difficult question next, to help the software gauge your level of skill and ability. When you answer a question incorrectly, you are presented with a less difficult question, and the software lowers its current estimate of your skill and ability. This continues until the program settles into a reasonably accurate estimate of what you know and can do, and takes you on average through somewhere between 15 and 30 questions as you complete the test.

The good news is that if you know your stuff, you'll probably finish most adaptive tests in 30 minutes or so. The bad news is that you must really, really know your stuff to do your best on an adaptive test. That's because some questions are so convoluted, complex, or hard to follow that you're bound to miss one or two, at a minimum, even if you do know your stuff. So the more you know, the better you'll do on an adaptive test, even accounting for the occasionally weird or unfathomable questions that appear on these exams.

Because you can't tell in advance if a test is fixed-length, short-form, adaptive, or combination, you will be best served by preparing for the exam as if it were adaptive. That way, you should be prepared to pass no matter what kind of test you take. But if you do take a fixed-length or short-form test, remember our tips from the preceding section. They should help you improve on what you could do on an adaptive test.

If you encounter a question on an adaptive test that you can't answer, you must guess an answer immediately. Because of the way the software works, you may suffer for your guess on the next question if you guess right, because you'll get a more difficult question next!

The Combination Exam Strategy

When it comes to studying for a combination test, your best bet is to approach it as a slightly longer adaptive exam, and to study as if the exam were adaptive only. Because the adaptive approach doesn't rely on rereading questions, and suggests that you take notes while reading useful information on test questions, it's hard to go wrong with this strategy when taking any kind of Microsoft certification test.

Exam-Taking Basics

The most important advice about taking any exam is this: Read each question carefully. Some questions are deliberately ambiguous, some use double negatives, and others use terminology in incredibly precise ways. The authors have taken numerous exams—both practice and live—and in nearly every one have missed at least one question because they didn't read it closely or carefully enough.

Here are some suggestions on how to deal with the tendency to jump to an answer too quickly:

➤ Make sure you read every word in the question. If you find yourself jumping ahead impatiently, go back and start over.

➤ As you read, try to restate the question in your own terms. If you can do this, you should be able to pick the correct answer(s) much more easily.

Above all, try to deal with each question by thinking through what you know about HTTP, FTP, TCP/IP, and the various IIS services—the characteristics, behaviors, facts, and figures involved. By reviewing what you know (and what you've written down on your information sheet), you'll often recall or understand things sufficiently to determine the answer to the question.

Question-Handling Strategies

Based on exams we have taken, some interesting trends have become apparent. For those questions that take only a single answer, usually two or three of the answers will be obviously incorrect, and two of the answers will be plausible— of course, only one can be correct. Unless the answer leaps out at you (if it does, reread the question to look for a trick; sometimes those are the ones you're most likely to get wrong), begin the process of answering by eliminating those answers that are most obviously wrong.

Things to look for in obviously wrong answers include spurious menu choices or utility names, nonexistent software options, and terminology you've never seen. If you've done your homework for an exam, no valid information should be completely new to you. In that case, unfamiliar or bizarre terminology probably indicates a totally bogus answer.

Numerous questions assume that the default behavior of a particular utility is in effect. If you know the defaults and understand what they mean, this knowledge will help you cut through many Gordian knots.

Mastering The Inner Game

In the final analysis, knowledge breeds confidence, and confidence breeds success. If you study the materials in this book carefully and review all the practice questions at the end of each chapter, you should become aware of those areas where additional learning and study are required.

Next, follow up by reading some or all of the materials recommended in the "Need To Know More?" section at the end of each chapter. The idea is to become familiar enough with the concepts and situations you find in the sample questions that you can reason your way through similar situations on a real exam. If you know the material, you have every right to be confident that you can pass the exam.

After you've worked your way through the book, take the practice exams in Chapters 13 and 15. This will provide a reality check and help you identify areas to study further. Make sure you follow up and review materials related to the questions you miss on the practice exam before scheduling a real exam. Only when you've covered all the ground and feel comfortable with the whole scope of the practice exam should you take the online exam. Only if you score 75 percent or better should you proceed to the real thing (otherwise, obtain some additional practice tests so you can keep trying until you hit this magic number).

As a special bonus to readers of this book, your authors have created an adaptive practice exam on IIS. Coriolis offers this practice exam on its Web site at **www.coriolis.com/cip/testcenter** (the password is ISPTOL51069; consult the Introduction for more information about how to find and take this practice exam).

Armed with the information in this book and with the determination to augment your knowledge, you should be able to pass the certification exam. However, you need to work at it, or you'll spend the exam fee more than once before you finally pass. If you prepare seriously, you should do well. Good luck!

Additional Resources

A good source of information about Microsoft certification exams comes from Microsoft itself. Because its products and technologies—and the exams that go with them—change frequently, the best place to go for exam-related information is online.

If you haven't already visited the Microsoft Certified Professional site, do so right now. The MCP home page resides at **www.microsoft.com/mcp** (see Figure 1.1).

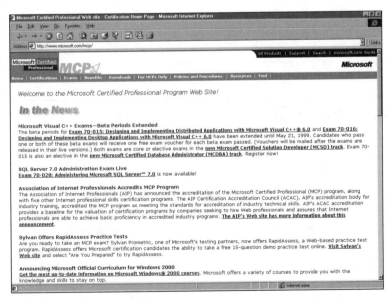

Figure 1.1   The Microsoft Certified Professional home page.

Note: This page might not be there by the time you read this, or it may be replaced by something new and different, because things change regularly on the Microsoft site. Should this happen, please read the sidebar titled "Coping With Change On The Web."

The menu options on the top row of the home page point to the most important sources of information in the MCP pages. Here's what to check out:

➤ **Certifications** Use this menu entry to read about the various certification programs that Microsoft offers.

➤ **Exams** Use this menu entry to pull up the latest information on all Microsoft exams, including new exams, beta exams, and exams that are under development.

➤ **Benefits** Use this menu entry to read about the various benefits that accompany MCP status both for individuals and organizations.

➤ **Downloads** Use this menu entry to find a list of the files and practice exams that Microsoft makes available to the public. These include several items worth downloading, especially the Certification Update, the Personal Exam Prep (PEP) exams, various assessment exams, and a general exam study guide. Try to make time to peruse these materials before taking your first exam.

These are just the high points of what's available in the Microsoft Certified Professional pages. As you browse through them—and we strongly recommend that you do—you'll probably find other informational tidbits mentioned that are every bit as interesting and compelling.

Coping With Change On The Web

Sooner or later, all the information we've shared with you about the Microsoft Certified Professional pages and the other Web-based resources mentioned throughout the rest of this book will go stale or be replaced by newer information. In some cases, the URLs you find here might lead you to their replacements; in other cases, the URLs will go nowhere, leaving you with the dreaded "404 File not found" error message. When that happens, don't give up.

There's always a way to find what you want on the Web if you're willing to invest some time and energy. Most large or complex Web sites—and Microsoft's qualifies on both counts—offer a search engine. On all of Microsoft's Web pages, a Search button appears along the top edge of the page. As long as you can get to Microsoft's site (it should stay at www.microsoft.com for a long time), use this tool to help you find what you need.

The more focused you can make a search request, the more likely the results will include information you can use. For example, you can search for the string

```
"training and certification"
```

to produce a lot of data about the subject in general, but if you're looking for the preparation guide for Exam 70-087, "Implementing and Supporting Microsoft Internet Information Server 4," you'll be more likely to get there quickly if you use a search string similar to the following:

```
"Exam 70-087" AND "preparation guide"
```

Likewise, if you want to find the Training and Certification downloads, try a search string such as this:

```
"training and certification" AND "download page"
```

Finally, feel free to use general search tools—such as www.search.com, www.altavista.com, and www.excite.com—to look for related information. Although Microsoft offers great information about its certification exams online, there are plenty of third-party sources of information and assistance that need not follow Microsoft's party line. Therefore, if you can't find something where this book says it lives, start looking around. If worse comes to worst, you can always email us. We might just have a clue.

Introduction
To IIS 4

Terms you'll need to understand:

- √ Internet Information Server (IIS)
- √ Simple Mail Transfer Protocol (SMTP) and Network News Transfer Protocol (NNTP) services
- √ Option Pack
- √ Microsoft Transaction Server (MTS)
- √ Index Server
- √ Certificate Server
- √ Site Server Express
- √ Microsoft Message Queue Server (MSMQ)
- √ Internet Connection Services for Microsoft RAS (ICS)

- √ Service Pack
- √ Microsoft Management Console (MMC)
- √ Active Server Pages (ASPs)
- √ Hypertext Transfer Protocol (HTTP)
- √ Pipelining
- √ Persistent connections
- √ Chunked transfers
- √ Host headers
- √ Web/FTP server

Techniques you'll need to master:

- √ Understanding Internet Information Server
- √ Knowing the hardware and software requirements for installing IIS
- √ Installing IIS 4

- √ Examining the basic components of IIS 4
- √ Learning the applications distributed on the Option Pack
- √ Identifying the features of IIS 4

Microsoft Internet Information Server (IIS) 4 is the latest version of the Internet information service publication and management system. This chapter gives you an overview of the software and highlights many of the features found in IIS 4.

Internet Information Server: Explored And Explained

Internet Information Server 4 (referred to as IIS or IIS 4) is a Windows NT Server 4 solution for hosting an Internet or intranet Web site. It supports such services as World Wide Web (WWW), File Transfer Protocol (FTP), Simple Mail Transfer Protocol (SMTP), and Network News Transfer Protocol (NNTP).

WWW Service

IIS 4 provides the ability to host Web sites where content and applications can be shared. IIS enables HTML (Hypertext Markup Language) authors to place Web pages in folders on a Web site so that users can view the pages with a Web browser, such as Internet Explorer. The WWW service can also host Web applications that can perform dynamic functions, such as generating reports based on user input.

FTP Service

FTP (File Transfer Protocol) is a standard protocol used for transferring files between computers. Users can use a browser to download files from an FTP server. However, for more efficient downloading or to upload files, users can use an FTP client, such as WS_FTP or Cute FTP, both of which are available from **www.download.com**.

SMTP Service

IIS 4 includes an SMTP (Simple Mail Transfer Protocol) client service that allows Web applications to send and receive email messages. In addition, Web server events can trigger email notification to administrators. The SMTP service gives the Web server an email message box in which error messages, user feedback, or undelivered messages can be deposited for manual administrator processing.

NNTP Service

IIS, with added NNTP (Network News Transfer Protocol) support, can host single-server discussion groups. These discussion groups can be accessed via a standard Web interface or any of the NNTP-compliant newsreaders. The NNTP service is designed to host private discussion forums and does not support news feeds or message replication from the global Usenet NNTP news services. To add true Usenet NNTP news services to an Internet site, you must purchase and deploy Microsoft Exchange Server 5.5, which has full NNTP service support (including news feeds and message replication).

Integrated Setup

IIS 4 is an integral part of the Windows NT 4 Option Pack. The core components of the Option Pack include IIS 4 (and its subcomponents), Transaction Server 2, Certificate Server, Index Server, Data Access Components, Site Server Express, Message Queue Server, Administration components, and Internet Connection Services for Microsoft RAS.

The integrated Setup wizard for the Option Pack lets you easily install IIS and other components simultaneously. Following are the software requirements for installing IIS 4:

➤ Windows NT Server 4

➤ Internet Explorer 4.01

➤ Service Pack 3

The hardware requirements for IIS 4 are basically the same as those for Windows NT Server 4; however, you should modify them to meet the expected workload. Following are the minimum and recommended hardware configurations needed to install the Option Pack on Windows NT Server 4:

➤ Intel 486 66MHz minimum/Pentium 90MHz recommended

➤ 32MB RAM minimum/64MB RAM recommended

➤ 50MB of free hard disk space for installation

➤ 200MB disk space minimum/2GB disk space recommended for caching

Once the software and hardware requirements have been met, you'll need to obtain the distribution files for the Windows NT 4 Option Pack, which includes IIS 4. You can order the CD-ROM from Microsoft, or you can download the Windows NT Option Pack setup files from Microsoft's Web site at **http://backoffice.microsoft.com/downtrial/optionpack.asp**. Once you have these files, you can install IIS 4 by following these steps:

1. Double-click SETUP.EXE.

2. If the Gopher publishing service exists on your machine, Setup indicates that it will remove it (IIS 4 does not support Gopher).

3. Setup displays a Welcome screen, and then the licensing agreement.

4. After you've accepted the agreement, Setup displays the two installation options: Upgrade Only and Upgrade Plus (as shown in Figure 2.1). The Upgrade Only option simply upgrades IIS. Choose the Upgrade Plus option to upgrade IIS 3, as well as to install a few new components.

5. After you choose the Upgrade Plus installation option, Setup asks you to choose from the list of components to install (see Figure 2.2).

6. Next, Setup asks you to specify the directory for installing IIS and Microsoft Transaction Server (see Figure 2.3). Proceed by accepting the default options.

7. Setup then asks you to choose the type of administration: Local (the default) or Remote (see Figure 2.4). Proceed with the default option.

8. Setup starts copying the files. Upon successful completion, Setup reboots your machine. IIS 4 is now installed.

 If several servers are destined to host IIS 4, an unattended installation script can be built that installs Windows NT Server 4, Service Pack 3, Internet Explorer 4.01, and any or all components of the Option Pack.

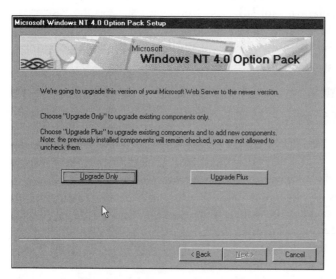

Figure 2.1 The two installation options for IIS.

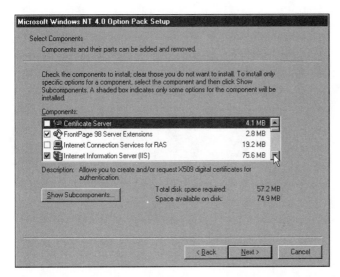

Figure 2.2   Choosing the components you want to install.

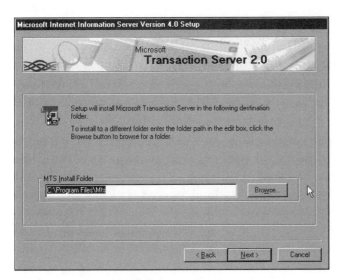

Figure 2.3   Specifying the installation directory for installing Microsoft Transaction Server.

Administration

IIS offers a solid collection of management and administration tools to give you complete control and insight into the operation of your Web server and its related components. In addition, by using the IIS Administration Objects, you can create customized interfaces to meet your particular needs or workflow.

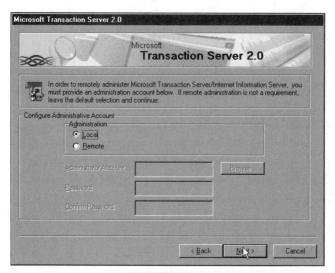

Figure 2.4 Choosing a local type of administration.

Windows-Based Administration

The most obvious change or improvement to IIS 4 is the introduction of the Microsoft Management Console (MMC). MMC is a Windows-based tool that provides total management of all services and applications within a single utility. MMC is also Active Desktop-capable and will eventually be used to access management and control aspects of the entire Windows NT system.

MMC offers you control over every aspect of your Internet site through a single, unified, and standardized interface. Every component of IIS and the Option Pack is managed via an MMC snap-in; this includes WWW, FTP, SMTP, NNTP, Transaction Server, and Index Server services. MMC's Web compatibility provides remote management capabilities in addition to customized console control.

Web-Based Administration

A new and improved Web-based interface for administrative tasks has been added that incorporates Active Server Pages (ASPs) and JavaScript. This interface maximizes your ability to manage your Internet site from a remote browser. This gives the single-site user the freedom to travel; plus, it allows Internet Service Providers (ISPs) or other multisite hosting centers to grant individual customers administrative control over their Web site.

IIS Administration Objects

New IIS Administration Objects (IISAOs) are used to control an entire server programmatically through automated objects. IISAOs enable command-line administration via scripts or command prompts, customized interfaces, and automation of common tasks.

IIS Components

As previously mentioned, IIS 4 is distributed as part of the Windows NT Option Pack. The Option Pack contains seven distinct software components, or applications, that can be installed as an integrated whole to provide Internet publishing and management capabilities. As Microsoft continues to integrate its products, the division line between one product or service and another becomes blurred.

In the following sections, some of the IIS and Option Pack components are discussed briefly. All of these items are dealt with on a more intimate and in-depth basis in subsequent chapters of this book.

Index Server 2

IIS 4 includes an updated and improved Index Server 2. Index Server brings site content indexing and searching to IIS-hosted Web sites. A set of default or customized interface query forms offers users a wide range of search options. With support for ASPs, use of Structured Query Language (SQL) queries, new content filter types, multiple language support, improved performance, fine-tuned scope/range control, updated cache management, and new MMC administration, Index Server 2 is a full-featured content search engine.

Certificate Server 1

Digital certificates can have two purposes—proving the identity of a Web site and proving the identity of a site's user. Web site identity verification is still performed through a contract with a certificate authority. However, until IIS 4 and Certificate Server 1, organizations were unable to use this technology for client/server authentication. Certificate Server gives individual Web servers the ability to issue, revoke, and renew X.509 digital certificates to clients. Such certificates are used to provide the client's identity, to maintain status information, and to circumvent manual user authentication. Certificate Server is also used in the standard sense by supporting SSL and Private Communication Technology (PCT) protocols for authorized secure communications.

Site Server Express 2

A "light" version of Microsoft Site Server, called Site Server Express 2, is included with the IIS 4 Option Pack. This application gives you a wide variety of analysis tools to keep tabs on your Web sites and several publishing utilities to ease content issuance. The Usage Import And Report Writer translates the cryptic IIS log files into easy-to-read documents that contain information such as hits, user information, length of stay, and more. The Content Analysis module creates a visual representation of a Web site and can check for broken links. The Web Publishing wizard can be used by clients to easily post new documents to an IIS-hosted Web site.

Microsoft Transaction Server 2

The integration of Microsoft Transaction Server (MTS) into IIS 4 has brought new robustness, fault tolerance, and programmable extensibility to IIS and Web applications. MTS allows distributed transaction applications to be developed for IIS. MTS simplifies Web application development for multiuser environments by providing much of the basic, low-level system interaction structure. Through MTS, each Web application can be launched as a separate process that can persist beyond a single client request, and its operation and system resources will not interfere with IIS or any other active Web application.

Microsoft Message Queue Server 1

As Web applications developed for distributed deployment become more commonplace, the reliability of applications to communicate with each other and within themselves becomes critical. The Microsoft Message Queue Server (MSMQ) enables applications to communicate via a message queue system, even when remote systems are offline. Called applications are currently nonexecuting, or on nonheterogeneous networks. The range of flexibility and the fault tolerance of distributed Web applications are widened because of MSMQ's integration of MTS, support for ActiveX, and asynchronous communication.

Internet Connection Services For Microsoft RAS 1

Internet Connection Services (ICS) is an extension and upgrade module for Windows NT Server's Remote Access Service (RAS). ICS adds several enhancements to RAS, including customizable client dialers, centrally controlled network phonebooks, new RADIUS authentication support, and improved administration and management tools. ICS was designed to help reduce ISP and connectivity costs, improve and simplify end-user operation, and enable new Internet business solutions. Many of the improvements found in ICS are also found in the Routing And Remote Access Service Update for Windows NT Server.

Data Access And SDK Components

Because IIS supports several standardized data access models and components, Web applications have the widest communication possibilities with database and other information provisioning applications. IIS includes ActiveX Data Objects (ADO), Remote Data Service (RDS), and Open Database Connectivity (ODBC) drivers. In addition, the Software Development Kit (SDK) that comes with IIS 4 contains detailed documentation about developing customized methods and interfaces for existing components to expand and enhance Web applications via ASPs, custom IIS configurations, unique model and object types, logging adaptations, and server extensions. The Microsoft Script Debugger can be used to easily debug ASPs and several types of programming scripts, such as Visual Basic Scripting Edition (VBScript), JScript (Microsoft's JavaScript), and Java, to simplify Web application development.

Microsoft Management Console

As already described, the Microsoft Management Console (MMC) is the management, administration, and control interface for Windows NT. It's added to the Windows NT 4 environment via the installation of IIS 4. It replaces several interfaces and utilities. MMC is able to manage and control all aspects of a network environment—including those services added by IIS—through the use of programmatic controls called *snap-ins*. Every significant component of IIS has a snap-in that gives you administrative control over that component and its related objects. MMC can be accessed through a Web interface, or controlled via command-line instructions by the Windows Scripting Host (WSH), a language-independent scripting host for 32-bit Windows platforms.

IIS Features

IIS 4 has a broad range of features and functions. In the following sections, many of these features are highlighted; however, most of them are also covered in more depth and detail in subsequent chapters.

Support For HTTP 1.1

IIS 4 is fully HTTP (Hypertext Transfer Protocol) 1.1 compliant. HTTP 1.1 offers significant improvements in performance (50 to 100 percent), which results in a more responsive Web experience for users. The performance improvements of HTTP 1.1 and IIS 4 are a result of the following:

➤ **Pipelining** HTTP 1.0 servers processed a single resource request at a time per client. In other words, the client waited for each request to be processed before the next request was sent. HTTP 1.1 uses *pipelining* to allow clients to send multiple requests without waiting for a server's response. Pipelining improves response time and Web display performance.

➤ **Persistent connections** Typically, for each item contained in a single Web document (HTML, GIFs, Java applets, and so on), a separate connection between the client and server must be established. Therefore, if eight items comprise a single document, eight connections are created between the client and server. The overhead for establishing, maintaining, and tearing down these connections is high in comparison to the amount of data sent over them. IIS 4 uses *persistent connections* to send multiple objects over fewer connections. This reduces communication overhead and improves performance.

➤ **Chunked transfers** ASPs vary in size due to their dynamic nature. HTTP 1.0 can have difficulty delivering data when the actual bit size of the resource is unknown at the beginning of the transfer. HTTP 1.1 is able to transmit the variable documents more efficiently through the use of *chunking*. Chunking is the process of breaking a transmission into multiple pieces of different sizes, each with its own header and size indicator. This method greatly increases the efficiency of ASP delivery.

➤ **Proxy support** HTTP 1.1 has caching information built into the protocol itself. This provides servers and proxies with sufficient information to manage cached resources. HTTP 1.1 can provide details, such as expiration dates for resources, without changing the content.

In addition, IIS uses HTTP 1.1's *host headers* as the delivery and communication mechanism to distribute multiple sites using transferred session information. If host headers are not supported, IIS uses a less sophisticated method to "multiplex" Web sites.

 When host headers are in use, the responsibility of tracking the location of a particular browser/client in a Web site is returned to the server instead of with the client. As part of IIS's ability to host multiple Web sites off a single IP address, IIS includes backward-compatible support for older browsers that do not natively support host headers. If an older browser is encountered, IIS simply responds by using the HTTP level supported by the browser.

Support For Robust Web Applications

With the tight integration of several applications from the Option Pack, IIS's ability to support distributed Web applications is greatly improved. Transactional ASPs (Active Server Pages) enrich commerce and business communications by improving script management. ASPs can execute with a transaction. Therefore, if the script fails, the transaction is aborted. This provides for a reliable, more secure, and faster communication link between Web applications and business customers.

Also, launching each application or subprocess in a separate virtual machine isolates each Web site and application from the core IIS system. If any site or application fails or stalls, the rest of the system is not affected. Plus, when a failed application is requested again, IIS restarts the process by creating a new virtual machine. This provides IIS with a system for crash protection and re-covery. Launching each process separately also enables individual components to be loaded and unloaded from memory without restarting the entire IIS system.

Programmers can now also reap the benefits of the built-in Microsoft Script Debugger. This tool gives realtime interactive feedback for designing and troubleshooting Active Server Pages.

Using the clustering services of Windows NT Server Enterprise Edition, IIS can perform server failover. For example, if two sites are hosted on two separate IIS installations and one of the servers fails, the other server automatically takes over by hosting both sites.

 The Microsoft Virtual Machine, which provides Java support, has been updated to improve performance, provide more robust applications, and support server-side component execution.

Security And Authentication

With the addition of the Certificate Server to IIS, organizations are able to establish their own X.509 certificate authorities. This capability improves client/customer recognition and provides for improved certificate/identity authentication.

Improved SSL protocol support grants IIS greater control over secure communications. Server Gated Crypto (SGC) is an extension to SSL, which grants IIS the ability to negotiate a 128-bit encryption session with a client, even if the client does not natively support 128-bit encryption.

Some firewall filtering capabilities, such as refusing service based on the domain of a client, are built into IIS. This feature can be used to block unwanted access or to simply restrict access to a limited number of users.

Improved Documentation

One of the overlooked features of IIS is its documentation. All the IIS documentation can be accessed through a browser, even when the IIS server is not functioning. The Web-based documentation is similar to the standard Help system found in Windows. The documentation can be perused on a content/title basis, keyword basis, or via a full-text search. With several multimedia enhancements, step-by-step walkthroughs, and interactive tutorials, the documentation for IIS is a marked improvement.

IIS And Windows

IIS 4 is designed for deployment on Windows NT Server 4. By default, IIS 4 does not limit the number of simultaneous Internet/intranet Web users. However, your network and Internet communication media and hardware robustness can restrict access for high-traffic high-volume sites.

For Windows NT Workstation 4, Windows 95, and Windows 98 users, Microsoft has also released Peer Web Services (PWS) 4, which reflects most of the improvements found in IIS 4. However, it does not include Site Server Express, Index Server, or Certificate Server. Also, it isn't designed to be a high-volume, multiuser Web server; instead, it's limited by the license agreement to support only 10 simultaneous connections. Its primary purpose is to simply provide content sharing within an intranet or with friends or coworkers over the Internet.

Practice Questions

Question 1

What feature of HTTP 1.1, which is supported by IIS 4, allows multiple Web sites to be easily supported over a single IP address?

○ a. Chunked transfers

○ b. Pipelining

○ c. Persistent connections

○ d. Host headers

Answer d is correct. Host headers are the primary means by which IIS 4 hosts multiple Web sites over a single IP address to clients. A chunked transfer is a delivery method to speed and improve ASPs. Therefore, answer a is incorrect. Pipelining is the process of handling multiple client requests without requiring the client to wait for a server response. Therefore, answer b is incorrect. A persistent connection is a communication feature in which a single connection between the server and client is maintained to transfer multiple resources. Therefore, answer c is incorrect.

Question 2

Which of the following applications are found on the Option Pack and can be installed along with IIS 4? [Check all correct answers]

❑ a. Transaction Server 2

❑ b. Site Server Express

❑ c. Message Queue Server Standard Edition

❑ d. Routing And Remote Access Service Update

Answers a, b, and c are correct. Transaction Server 2, Site Server Express, and Message Queue Server Standard Edition are all included on the Option Pack. The Routing And Remote Access Service Update is not part of the Option Pack. Therefore, answer d is incorrect.

Question 3

Which of the following are requirements for the installation of IIS 4.0? [Check all correct answers]

❑ a.   Service Pack 3 for Windows NT 4

❑ b.   NetBEUI

❑ c.   Internet Explorer 4.01

❑ d.   Windows NT 4 Workstation

Answers a and c are correct. Service Pack 3 for Windows NT and Internet Explorer 4.01 are installation requirements for IIS 4. NetBEUI is not a requirement of IIS 4. Therefore, answer b is incorrect. Windows NT Workstation 4 is not a requirement of IIS 4. In fact, IIS is not supported on Windows NT Workstation. Therefore, answer d is incorrect.

Question 4

What is the new administration feature/utility installed with IIS 4?

○ a.   Microsoft Management Console

○ b.   Microsoft Transaction Server

○ c.   Microsoft Message Queue Server

○ d.   Microsoft Administration System

Answer a is correct. Microsoft Management Console is the new administration feature/utility installed with IIS 4 that will be a standard component of Windows NT 5. Microsoft Transaction Server and Microsoft Message Queue Server are not administration utilities. Therefore, answers b and c are incorrect. Microsoft Administration System is fictitious. Therefore, answer d is incorrect.

Question 5

> IIS 4 uses the Microsoft Virtual Machine to provide support for Java and server-side component execution.
>
> ○ a. True
>
> ○ b. False

True, the Microsoft Virtual Machine provides Java support, and has been updated to improve performance, provide more robust applications, and support server-side component execution. Therefore, answer a is correct.

Question 6

> Which of the following services cannot be installed as part of IIS 4? [Check all correct answers]
>
> ❑ a. WWW
>
> ❑ b. FTP
>
> ❑ c. Gopher
>
> ❑ d. RAS

Answers c and d are correct. IIS 4 does not support Gopher. You can implement Gopher functionality by using the Index Server with IIS. IIS does not directly support RAS; that is a separate service of Windows NT. IIS 4 supports the other two services: WWW and FTP. Therefore, answers a and b are incorrect.

Question 7

> Which of the following are true statements about IIS 4 and its support services and applications? [Check all correct answers]
>
> ❑ a. HTML, text, Microsoft Office, and Adobe PDF documents can be searched.
>
> ❑ b. Client identities can be tracked and verified.
>
> ❑ c. A single Web server can be duplicated to three or more other servers simultaneously.
>
> ❑ d. Applications can communicate even if network connections are broken.

Answers a, b, and d are correct. Answer a refers to Index Server, answer b refers to Certificate Server, and answer d refers to Message Queue Server. Site Server Express can only replicate one server to one server. Only the full Enterprise version of Site Server can replicate one server to multiple servers. Therefore, answer c is incorrect.

Question 8

> When IIS 4 is installed over an existing installation of IIS 3, all configurations for virtual directories must be completely redefined.
>
> ○ a. True
>
> ○ b. False

Answer b is correct. This is a false statement. IIS 4 provides a smooth upgrade from IIS 3 that retains all existing configuration settings. Therefore, answer a is incorrect.

Question 9

> On which operating systems does Internet Information Server 4 run? [Check all correct answers]
>
> ❏ a. Windows NT Server 4
>
> ❏ b. Windows For Workgroups 3.11
>
> ❏ c. Windows 95
>
> ❏ d. Windows NT Workstation 4

Answer a is correct. IIS 4 is supported only on Windows NT Server 4. Windows NT Workstation, Windows 95, and Windows 98 can use scaled-down versions of IIS, called Peer Web Services and Personal Web Server. Therefore, answers b, c, and d are incorrect.

Question 10

The new documentation for IIS 4 allows which of the following functions? [Check all correct answers]

❑ a. Listing by keyword

❑ b. Listing by topic

❑ c. Interactive tutorials

❑ d. Full-text searching

Answers a, b, c, and d are correct. The IIS documentation can be listed by keyword, listed by topic, or full-text searched; plus, it contains interactive tutorials.

Question 11

Which of the following are needed to install Internet Information Server? [Check all correct answers]

❑ a. A local network connection

❑ b. An NTFS partition

❑ c. A computer with at least the minimum hardware required to support Windows NT Server 4

❑ d. TCP/IP protocol installed

❑ e. Access to the Option Pack distribution files

Answers c, d, and e are correct. You need a machine that supports the minimum hardware requirements to install Windows NT Server 4. The TCP/IP protocol is also required for IIS. Access to the Option Pack distribution files can be via an Internet connection to the Microsoft Web site or on a CD-ROM. You don't need a local network connection (because IIS can be an isolated or standalone machine) or an NTFS partition (recommended, but not required) for installing IIS. Therefore, answers a and b are incorrect.

Need To Know More?

 The best overview information for Internet Information Server 4 can be found in the Reviewer's Guide for IIS 4. This document can be found on the TechNet CD-ROM or online via the following IIS Web area: **www.microsoft.com/ntserver/web/**.

Configuring
The WWW
And FTP Services

....

Terms you'll need to understand:

√ Microsoft Management Console (MMC)

√ Transmission Control Protocol (TCP) port

√ Connections

√ Connection timeout

√ Event logging

√ Performance tuning

√ Bandwidth throttling

√ ISAPI filter

√ Default document

√ Secure communication

√ HTTP headers

√ Multipurpose Internet Mail Extensions (MIME) map

√ Custom error

√ Automatic password synchronization

√ Maximum connections message

√ Unix- and MS-DOS-style directory listings

√ Directory security

Techniques you'll need to master:

√ Configuring the WWW service

√ Configuring the FTP service

In these days of electronic media, providing access to electronic versions of information is increasingly important. Two of the most common forms of providing access to this type of information over the Internet are over the World Wide Web (WWW or Web) and via the File Transfer Protocol (FTP). This chapter explains how to configure the two basic publishing services in IIS: WWW and FTP. In addition, we discuss what these publishing services do and the options they have.

 It is important to understand how to make particular IIS configuration changes. The Web and FTP Properties sections of the MMC are where you'll adjust most configurations. From within the Properties screen, depending on the task you must perform, you then click the appropriate tab. This chapter describes each of the configurable settings under each of these tabs. To save your changes, click the OK button at the bottom of the Properties sheet. Finally, choose File|Close.

Configuring The WWW Service

To configure the WWW service, click Start|Programs|Windows NT Option Pack|Microsoft Internet Information Server|Internet Service Manager. Windows NT, in turn, starts the Microsoft Management Console 1, as shown in Figure 3.1.

Double-click Internet Information Server, double-click the computer name, and then right-click Default Web Site and select Properties from the pop-up

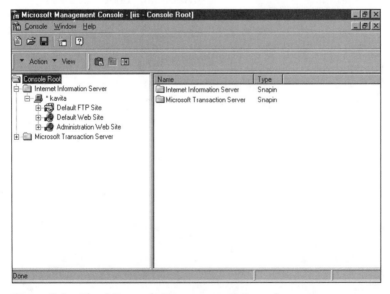

Figure 3.1 The Microsoft Management Console.

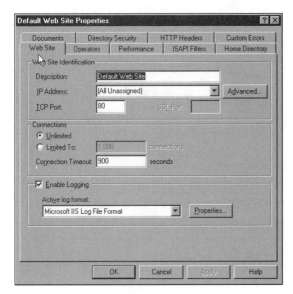

Figure 3.2   The Web Site tab of the Default Web Site Properties dialog box.

menu. Microsoft Management Console 1, in turn, displays the Default Web Site Properties dialog box, as shown in Figure 3.2.

The WWW service has nine items to configure under the Web Site tab. These are discussed in detail in the following sections.

General Properties

Configuring the WWW service's general properties under the Web Site tab includes specifying the following items:

➤ **Description** In the Description text box, type the site's name. The default name is "Default Web Site." You can change the default to something that's more representative of the information contained on your site.

➤ **IP Address** Choose the Internet Protocol (IP) address from the drop-down list box.

➤ **Transmission Control Protocol (TCP) Port** A TCP port represents a data stream. Multiple ports on the same machine represent multiple data streams in a single IP connection.

    In the TCP Port text box, you can specify the port number on which the WWW service runs. The default is port 80. If you assign a different port number, clients will not be able to access the site without specifying the port number in the Uniform Resource Locator (URL).

➤ **Connections** To allow unlimited connections, click Unlimited. To limit the number of connections, specify the number in the Limited To text box. The default is 1,000. The fewer connections you allow, the better your site's overall performance will be. More connections may hamper your site's overall performance. In such cases, you may need to add more memory and hard disk space.

➤ **Connection Timeout** In the Connection Timeout text box, specify the maximum time a client connection can exist without any activity. The default is 900 seconds (or 15 minutes). Use the Connection Timeout parameter to improve your server's efficiency. Change the default value, if necessary, to a value that best suits your site's usage and performance. You can use this parameter to eliminate the unused connections from the server, thus improving your server's overall response time. On the other hand, if the users are in a low bandwidth area, use a higher Connection Timeout value.

➤ **Enable Logging** By logging the activities at your Web site, you can evaluate the WWW service's performance. Logging is also beneficial for security reasons. You can determine which users are allowed to access your site and what they may do once they are there. In addition, you can track activities, such as maximum connections reached and connection timeouts. You can configure the Web server to create logs at different time periods, including daily, weekly, monthly, and so on.

To enable event logging, click Enable Logging and choose the format for the log file from the Active Log Format drop-down list.

To specify additional properties for logging, click Properties. The Microsoft Management Console, in turn, displays the Microsoft Logging Properties dialog box, as shown in Figure 3.3.

In the dialog box, choose the time period option for creating the log file: Daily, Weekly, Monthly, Unlimited File Size, or When File Size Reaches (the server creates a new log file when file size reaches a number specified here).

In addition, in the Log File Directory text box, specify the directory where the Web server should place the log file. The default log file directory is C:\Winnt\System32\Logfiles.

Operators

In the Operators tab, you can specify the Windows NT user accounts for which you want to grant the operator privileges for the Web site (see Figure 3.4).

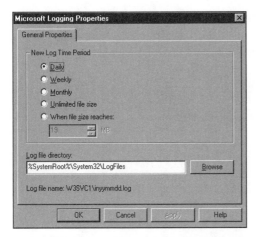

Figure 3.3 Specifying additional properties for logging.

Figure 3.4 The Operators tab.

Performance Tuning

In the Performance tab, you can specify the number of hits you expect per day on your IIS server (see Figure 3.5). The range is from Fewer Than 10,000 to Fewer Than 100,000 (default) to More Than 100,000. The server allocates memory for the number of connections you specify. The more connections you specify, the more memory the server allocates. Therefore, if the actual number of connections is much lower than the allocated number, the server memory is

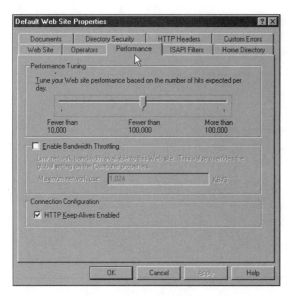

Figure 3.5   The Performance tab.

wasted. Monitor the site regularly so you can adjust this number based on the actual site usage. This improves the server's overall performance.

To limit the amount of bandwidth your Web site uses, check Enable Bandwidth Throttling. You can specify the maximum network size in kilobytes.

By default, HTTP Keep-Alives Enabled is checked. This means the server does not create a new HTTP connection for every client request. This is an efficient use of the server resources, and it therefore improves the overall performance.

ISAPI Filters

An ISAPI filter is a memory-resident program that responds to the events during an HTTP request's processing. They are typically DLL (dynamic link library) files. An example of an ISAPI filter is the SSL ISAPI filter, which encrypts and decrypts Web server data.

The ISAPI Filters tab, shown in Figure 3.6, indicates each filter's name, status (loaded, unloaded, or disabled), and priority (high, medium, or low). IIS will execute the filters in the order listed here.

To add a new filter, click Add. Microsoft Management Console, in turn, displays the Filter Properties dialog box, as shown in Figure 3.7.

Specify the filter's name in the Filter Name text box. In addition, specify the DLL file.

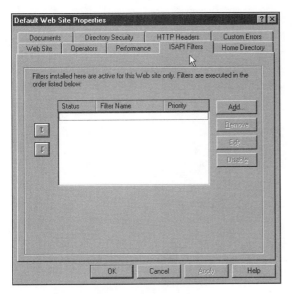

Figure 3.6   The ISAPI Filters tab.

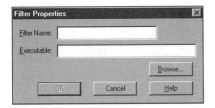

Figure 3.7   The Filter Properties dialog box.

Home Directory

To change your site's home directory or the home directory's characteristics, use the Home Directory tab (see Figure 3.8). During IIS installation, the installation program creates a default home directory called "Wwwroot" (the default path is C:\InetPub\Wwwroot).

You can change the home directory's location to one of the following:

➤ A Directory Located On This (local) Computer (default)

➤ A Share Located On Another Computer

➤ A Redirection To A URL

Depending on your choice, type the path of the directory on the same (or another) computer or the URL in the Local Path text box. For a local directory, specify the full path. For a network share, specify the Universal Naming Convention (UNC) and the name of the share (for example, \\Iis\Htmlfiles).

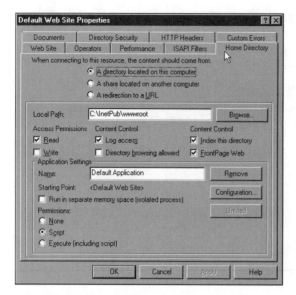

Figure 3.8 The Home Directory tab.

In the Home Directory tab, you can modify access permissions, content control, and application settings:

➤ **Access Permissions** This section of the tab allows you to choose Read or Write access for a local directory or network share. Read access lets the Web clients download or read files in a home or virtual directory. Write access lets the Web clients upload files or change content in the write-enabled files.

 Grant Read access to the files you publish (for example, HTML files). Deny Read access to application files such as CGI programs (scripts or executables) and ISAPI filters.

➤ **Content Control** To record access to the directory in a log file, click Log Access. To let the user navigate through the directory structure on your IIS server, click Directory Browsing Allowed. To direct Microsoft Index Server to include the directory in a full-text index of your site, click Index This Directory. To create a FrontPage Web for the site, click FrontPage Web.

➤ **Application Settings** Per the IIS documentation, an *application* is a collection of all the directories and files contained in a directory that is marked as an application starting point. In the Home Directory tab, you can configure your home directory as the application starting point. You specify the application's name in the Name text box. To configure the application's properties, click Configuration.

To direct the server to run the application in a memory space isolated from the Web server, check Run In Separate Memory Space. The benefit is that if the application fails, the Web server and other applications still continue to run.

You can specify the following three types of permissions for executables or scripts in the home directory:

➤ **None** Do not allow any programs or scripts to run in this directory.

➤ **Script** Allow only scripts to run in this directory, no executables.

➤ **Execute (including script)** Allow both scripts and executables to run in this directory.

Documents

You can configure the Web server to load a default document, typically your site's home page, when a user connects to your site. Using the home page as your site's default document provides the users with a method for navigating the site. The Documents tab is shown in Figure 3.9.

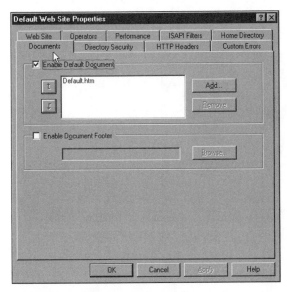

Figure 3.9   The Documents tab.

To specify that the default document IIS loads when a user connects to the server, click Enable Default Document. To specify the document, click Add. Multiple default document names can be listed. The WWW service will look for and display the appropriate default page based on the order specified in this section.

To specify the default document footer, click Enable Document Footer. Specify the document footer file in the resulting text box.

Note: A document footer is an HTML-formatted file the server adds to the bottom of every Web document sent by the server.

Directory Security

The Directory Security tab lets you configure your server's security (see Figure 3.10). It includes the following three options:

➤ **Anonymous Access And Authentication Control** Click Edit to configure anonymous access and confirm the identity of users before granting access to your server's restricted content.

➤ **Secure Communications** Click Key Manager to create an SSL key pair and server certificate request. By associating an SSL key pair with a server certificate request, you direct the client browser to establish an encrypted link to a directory or file on your IIS server. This enables a secure communication link between the browser and the server.

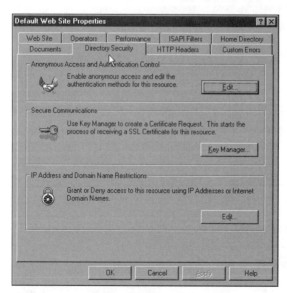

Figure 3.10 The Directory Security tab.

► **IP Address And Domain Name Restrictions** To prevent or allow specific users from accessing your Web site, directory, or file, click Edit. If you click Granted Access, all users will be granted access by default. Click Add to list specific computers that should be denied access. If you click Denied Access, all users will be denied access by default. Click Add to list specific computers that should be granted access.

 | Make sure you're up to date on how to assess an IP network address, and a subnet mask that represent the IP address range you're given to grant or deny a group of users access to the server based on an IP address range.

HTTP Headers

Figure 3.11 shows the HTTP Headers tab. You can add custom information to the HTTP headers; then the Web server sends it to the browser. The HTTP Headers tab lets you configure information such as content expiration, content rating, custom headers, and MIME maps, all of which are discussed here:

► **Enable Content Expiration** Click Enable Content Expiration to include an expiration date in the HTTP header. The browser compares the expiration date to the current date and determines whether it should retrieve the page from the cache or request an updated page from the server.

► **Custom HTTP Headers** You can configure the server to send a custom HTTP header to the client. For example, the server can send a custom

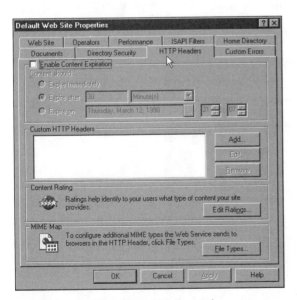

Figure 3.11   The HTTP Headers tab.

header that prevents the proxy server from caching a page but lets the browser cache the page. To configure a custom HTTP header, click Add.

➤ **Content Rating** The Web offers various types of content, some of which certain users may find potentially objectionable. The browser can use the content rating information to help users identify this type of information. You can include descriptive content labels in the HTTP headers. The browser detects these labels, thus helping users identify potentially objectionable content. You can set the content ratings for the Web site, a directory, or a file. To do so, click Edit Ratings.

➤ **MIME Map** To configure the MIME map, click File Types. MIME maps define which applications should be used with specified file types. For example, there may be a MIME map that tells the client to open HTML files with Internet Explorer. The File Types dialog lists the file types registered on the server. To configure additional MIME mappings, click New Type.

Custom Errors

You can customize the errors IIS displays in the event of an error or exception. You can specify the message type and the corresponding HTML file or URL. Figure 3.12 shows the Custom Errors tab.

To edit the error message for an HTTP error, click the HTTP error and then click Edit Properties. Microsoft Management Console, in turn, displays the Error Mapping Properties dialog box, as shown in Figure 3.13.

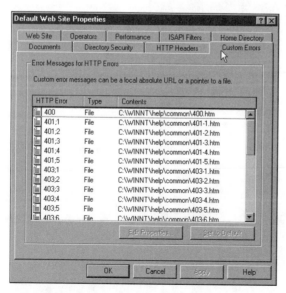

Figure 3.12 The Custom Errors tab.

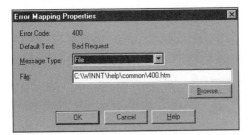

Figure 3.13   The Error Mapping Properties dialog box.

In the dialog box, you can change the message type. In addition, you can specify the HTML file or the URL (depending on the error type).

Configuring The FTP Service

As mentioned previously, FTP is an application and a protocol used for remote file manipulation. To configure the FTP service, click Start|Programs|Windows NT Option Pack|Microsoft Internet Information Server|Internet Service Manager. Windows NT, in turn, starts the Microsoft Management Console 1. Once MMC has launched, double-click IIS and then the computer name. Then, right-click Default FTP Site and select Properties from the pop-up menu. Microsoft Management Console 1.0, in turn, displays the Default FTP Site Properties dialog box, as shown in Figure 3.14.

When configuring the FTP service, you have five tabs to configure. These tabs are discussed in detail in the following sections.

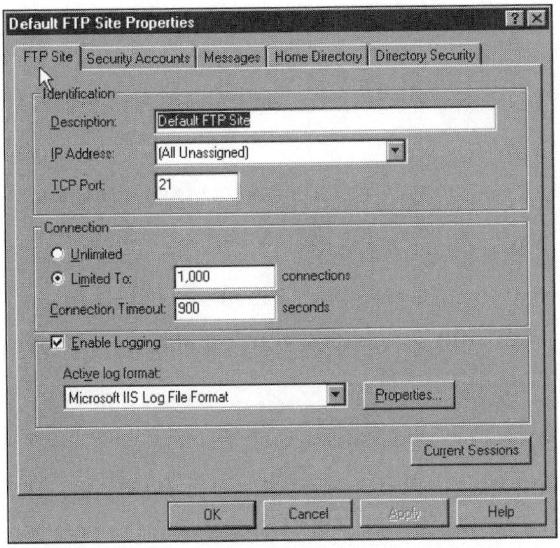

Figure 3.14   The Default FTP Site Properties dialog box.

General Properties

Configuring the FTP service's general properties is very similar to the WWW service configuration, and includes specifying the following items:

➤ **Description** In the Description text box, type the site's name. The default name is "Default FTP Site." You can change the default to something meaningful that's more representative of the information contained in your site.

➤ **IP Address** Choose the IP address from the drop-down list box.

➤ **TCP Port** In the TCP Port text box, you can specify the port number on which the FTP service runs. The default is port 21.

 In the TCP Port text box, you can specify the port number on which the FTP service runs. The default is port 21. If you assign a different port number, clients will not be able to access the site without specifying the port number in the URL.

➤ **Connection** To allow unlimited connections, click Unlimited. To limit the number of connections, specify the number in the Limited To text box. The default is 1,000. The fewer connections you allow, the better your site's overall performance will be. More connections may hamper your site's overall performance. In such cases, you may need to add more memory and hard disk space.

 FTP connections consume more bandwidth than HTTP connections, because FTP connections handle larger file transfers than HTTP connections.

➤ **Connection Timeout** In the Connection Timeout text box, you specify the maximum time a client connection can exist without any activity. The default is 900 seconds (or 15 minutes). Use the Connection Timeout parameter to improve your server's efficiency. Change the default value, if necessary, to a value that best suits your site's usage and performance. You can use this parameter to eliminate the unused connections from the server, thus improving your server's overall response time. On the other hand, if the users are in a low bandwidth area, use a higher Connection Timeout value.

➤ **Logging** By logging the activities at your FTP site, you can evaluate the FTP service's performance. Logging is also beneficial for security reasons. You can determine your site's users and their activities. In addition, you can track activities such as maximum connections reached and connection timeouts. You can configure the FTP server to create logs at different time periods, including daily, weekly, monthly, and so on.

To enable event logging, click Enable Logging and choose the format for the log file from the Active Log Format drop-down list box.

To specify additional properties for Logging, click Properties. The Microsoft Management Console, in turn, displays the Microsoft Logging Properties dialog box, as shown in Figure 3.15.

In the dialog box, choose the time period for creating the log file: Daily, Weekly, Monthly, Unlimited File Size, or When File Size Reaches (the server creates a new log file when file size reaches a number specified here).

In addition, in the Log File Directory text box, specify the directory where the FTP server should place the log file.

➤ **Current Sessions** To display the active users at your FTP site at any given point, click Current Sessions.

Security Accounts

The Security Accounts tab lets you configure access for anonymous users to your FTP site. In addition, you can set up Windows NT user accounts as FTP site operators. Figure 3.16 shows the Security Accounts tab.

By default, anonymous users can connect to the FTP site. In the Username text box, specify the Windows NT user account the FTP service should use for

Figure 3.15   The Microsoft Logging Properties dialog box.

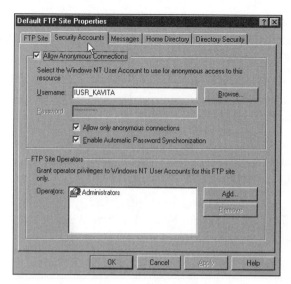

Figure 3.16   The Security Accounts tab.

anonymous access to this service. By default, the user account is "IUSR_ *computername*" (where *computername* is the name of the system on which IIS is installed).

The Password text box specifies the password that goes with the user name in the Username text box. If you change the password here, you must also change the password for the server and domain controller. By default, the password synchronization is automatic. That is, the server automatically synchronizes the FTP site password with the Windows NT password for anonymous users. To disable this feature, deselect Enable Automatic Password Synchronization.

To prevent the anonymous users from connecting and using the FTP site, deselect Allow Anonymous Connections.

 To avoid passing usernames and passwords across the network, both the Allow Anonymous Connections and the Allow Only Anonymous Connections options should be checked.

In the FTP Site Operators group, you can specify the Windows NT user accounts for which you want to grant the operator privileges for the FTP site.

The Messages

You can configure IIS to display an appropriate message when a user connects to the FTP service. IIS displays the following three types of message options in the Messages tab (see Figure 3.17):

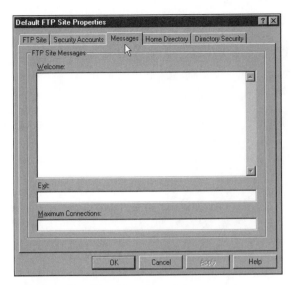

Figure 3.17   The Messages tab.

➤ **Welcome** In the Welcome text box, specify the greeting the users will see when they connect to the FTP site. You can also specify information about your company and the site, as well as display copyright and legal notices.

  Some browsers can't handle more than one line in an FTP site welcome message and may display a 404 error.

➤ **Exit** In the Exit text box, specify the exit message the users will see when they disconnect from the FTP site.

➤ **Maximum Connections** In the Maximum Connections text box, specify the warning message the users will see when they connect to the FTP site and it has already reached the maximum number of connections.

Home Directory

To change your site's home directory or the home directory's characteristics, use the Home Directory tab (see Figure 3.18). During IIS installation, the installation program creates a default home directory called "Ftproot" (the default path is C:\InetPub\Ftproot).

A user connecting to the home directory can see the content coming from a directory located on this computer or a share located on another computer.

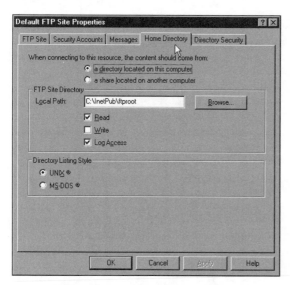

Figure 3.18 The Home Directory tab.

In the Local Path text box, specify the root directory for the FTP service (the default is C:\InetPub\Ftproot). The default access level is Read, which means the users have Read access to the directories on the FTP site. In addition, by default the server logs the access activities at the site. To provide Write access, click Write.

In addition, you can choose the directory listing style—Unix or MS-DOS. Most FTP hosts are Unix machines; therefore, the Unix directory listing style is a logical choice. A DOS directory listing displays the dates, times, sizes, and names of files. A Unix directory listing can display the same information, as well as permission information.

 The Unix Directory Listing Style is recommended because many non-Windows client machines are not able to view the MS-DOS style.

Directory Security

Securing the directories on the server is one of the most important things you should consider when configuring your FTP server. In addition to protecting the site with a password authentication scheme, you can use the Directory Security tab to secure the directories on your FTP server (see Figure 3.19). You can choose to grant or deny access to all or specific directories on your FTP server. As a result, you can prevent unauthorized access to the server. By default, all computers are granted access.

Figure 3.19 The Directory Security tab.

To specify exceptions, click Add. Microsoft Management Console, in turn, displays the Deny Access On (or Grant Access On) dialog box, as shown in Figure 3.20.

In the dialog box, choose whether you want to deny or grant access to a single computer, a group of computers, or an entire domain name.

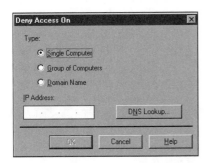

Figure 3.20 The Deny Access On dialog box.

Practice Questions

Question 1

What is the default port for the WWW service?

○ a. 80

○ b. 81

○ c. 82

○ d. 83

Answer a is correct. The default port for the WWW service is 80. Therefore, answers b, c, and d are incorrect.

Question 2

What is the default port for the FTP service?

○ a. 20

○ b. 21

○ c. 22

○ d. 23

Answer b is correct. The default port for the FTP service is 21. Therefore, answers a, c, and d are incorrect.

Question 3

What is the maximum number of Web connections allowed by IIS?

○ a. 1,000

○ b. 10,000

○ c. 100,000

○ d. Unlimited

Answer d is correct. IIS can handle unlimited Web connections. Therefore, answers a, b, and c are incorrect. However, practically speaking, the server is limited by its available resources (RAM and hard disk space).

Question 4

> What is the maximum number of FTP connections allowed by IIS?
>
> ○ a. 1,000
>
> ○ b. 10,000
>
> ○ c. 100,000
>
> ○ d. Unlimited

Answer d is correct. IIS can handle unlimited FTP connections. Therefore, answers a, b, and c are incorrect. However, practically speaking, the server is limited by its available resources (RAM and hard disk space).

Question 5

> What is the maximum connection timeout (in seconds) you can set for the WWW and FTP services?
>
> ○ a. 900
>
> ○ b. 10,000
>
> ○ c. 100,000
>
> ○ d. Unlimited

Answer d is correct. Although the default is 900 seconds, in the Connection Timeout text box you can actually specify any number—there is no limit. Therefore, answers a, b, and c are incorrect.

Question 6

> Your users employ FTP to upload new files to the system. The network begins Experiencing poor performance as use of the corporate intranet Web server increases. Which of the following changes can improve network performance?
>
> ○ a. Enable bandwidth throttling
>
> ○ b. Disable HTTP keep-alives
>
> ○ c. Disable the FTP service
>
> ○ d. Increase the RAM in the IIS host

Answer a is correct. Enabling bandwidth throttling can force the amount of network bandwidth consumed by intranet Web access to a predetermined maximum, which frees the network for other purposes. Disabling HTTP keep-alives will not restore network performance. Therefore, answer b is incorrect. The FTP service should not be disabled. Therefore, answer c is incorrect. Adding more RAM may cause a decrease in performance due to an increase in connections. Therefore, answer d is incorrect.

Question 7

You can run multiple instances of FTP and WWW services on the same IIS.

○ a. True

○ b. False

Answer a is correct. You can add virtual FTP and WWW services on the same IIS. Therefore, answer b is incorrect.

Question 8

The maximum number of FTP connections supported by your IIS server is 1,000, and the server has reached its limit. When the next user connects to the server, what message does IIS display?

○ a. A warning message

○ b. An exit message

○ c. A welcome message

○ d. A welcome message, then a warning message

○ e. A warning message, then an exit message

○ f. A welcome message, then a warning message, then an exit message

Answer a is correct. Because the maximum connections limit is reached, IIS displays a maximum connections warning message (that is, the message you specify in the FTP Site Properties dialog's Messages tab). The server displays a welcome message only if the server lets the user access the site. Therefore, answers c, d, and f are incorrect. The server displays an exit message if a user has already connected to the site and then disconnects from the site. Therefore, answers b and e are incorrect.

Question 9

Which of the following can you configure on the Directory Security tab? [Check all correct answers]

❑ a. Anonymous Access And Authentication Control

❑ b. Active Server Pages with ActiveX controls

❑ c. Secure Communications

❑ d. Windows NT user permissions

❑ e. IP Address And Domain Name Restrictions

Answers a, c, and e are correct. You can configure anonymous access and authentication control, secure communications, and restrictions based on IP address and domain name on the Directory Security tab. You cannot configure Active Server Pages with Active X controls or Windows NT user permissions on the Directory Security tab. Therefore, answers b and d are incorrect.

Question 10

From which sections of the MMC do you make Web and FTP configuration changes? [Check all correct answers]

❑ a. Web Properties

❑ b. Web and FTP snap-in

❑ c. FTP Properties

❑ d. None of the above, you don't use the MMC to make Web and FTP changes

Answers a and c are correct. The Web and FTP Properties sections of the MMC are where you'll adjust most configurations. From within the Properties screen, depending on the task you must perform, you then click the appropriate tab. To save your changes, click the OK button at the bottom of the Properties sheet. There is no Web and FTP snap-in. Therefore, answer b is incorrect. Because answers a and c are correct, answer d is incorrect.

Question 11

You are a consultant. The ISP (Internet Service Provider) asks you to improve the Web server's performance. How would you do this?

○ a. Enable SSL

○ b. Disable SSL

○ c. Disable Gopher

○ d. Disable FTP

Answer b is correct. Disabling the SSL improves performance because the server does not need to go through the additional layer of security check. SSL is CPU-intensive and would therefore decrease the server's performance. Therefore, answer a is incorrect. IIS 4 does not support Gopher. Therefore, answer c is incorrect. Disabling FTP means that the users cannot use the FTP service to transfer the files. Therefore, answer d is incorrect.

Question 12

You recently joined a multinational organization that has Webmasters supporting heterogeneous platforms. The organization supports the growing demands of its employees for downloading popular software by using the FTP service running on IIS. Some of the users complain that they have problems trying to access the directory listing on the FTP site. When investigating this problem, you find that although this is true for some users, others have no problem getting the directory listing. How do you resolve this situation?

○ a. Reinstall IIS with the FTP option.

○ b. Enable directory browsing for FTP.

○ c. Disable Windows NT Challenge/Response.

○ d. Set the directory listing to Unix.

○ e. Set the directory listing to MS-DOS.

Answer d is correct. Because the organization supports heterogeneous platforms, the Unix-style directory listing is appropriate. Reinstalling IIS with the FTP option is not necessary. Therefore, answer a is incorrect. You do not need to enable directory browsing for FTP because some users can already access the directory listing on the FTP site. Therefore, answer b is incorrect. The Windows NT Challenge/Response is a password authentication scheme used with the Web Service only. Therefore, answer c is incorrect. The MS-DOS-style directory listing works only with Windows systems. Therefore, answer e is incorrect.

Question 13

You're working for an accounting firm that has 26 Web administrators. The firm has one Windows NT Server to service all its needs. The firm has a mission-critical application developed with SQL Server as the database back end running on the Windows NT Server. The client front end is in Visual Basic, and it resides on each user's machine. Recently, the firm also installed IIS and created an intranet. The intranet is yet in its nascent stage, where the firm posts all its notices, policies, procedures, and more. After IIS was deployed, the network administrator began to complain that the network is becoming increasingly slower. This, in turn, affects the mission-critical application. How do you handle this request?

○ a. Stop the FTP service on IIS.

○ b. Disable the keep-alive HTTP connection.

○ c. Tune your Web site's performance for fewer than 10,000 hits per day.

○ d. Enable bandwidth throttling.

Answer d is correct. By enabling bandwidth throttling, you can limit the bandwidth your Web site uses. Stopping the FTP service on IIS is not the most viable solution because users may need this feature. You do not want to disable the FTP service. Therefore, answer a is incorrect. Disabling the keep-alive HTTP connection is no solution, either. In fact, keeping the HTTP connection alive helps improve the performance. Therefore, answer b is incorrect. Tuning your Web site's performance to fewer than 10,000 hits per day is not the most efficient solution. Although this may improve performance, your site will not be able to handle larger volume traffic. Therefore, answer c is incorrect.

Question 14

A client is attempting to access a directory called "dirt" on the server called "Webspace," which uses port 81. Which URL should he use from his client machine to access this site?

○ a. **http://localhost/dirt/**

○ b. **http://webspace/inetpub/wwwroot/dirt/**

○ c. **http://webspace:81/dirt/**

○ d. **http://webspace/dirt/**

Answer c is correct. Using "localhost" only applies on the same machine as the host. Therefore, answer a is incorrect. Although the dirt directory probably exists in the server's C:\Inetpub\wwwroot directory, the default configuration in IIS defines that path as the virtual home directory. Therefore, answer b is incorrect. The default port of a Web server is 80, so attempting to access this site without specifying the port number would fail. Therefore, answer d is incorrect.

Question 15

You are the Webmaster of your company's intranet Web site. Many of the Web authors have been naming their HTML pages with a ".HHTW" extension. However, when users try to access these files from their browsers, they are asked whether they want to open or save the file to their disk. What change should you make to have documents with a ".HHTW" extension automatically open up in all users' browsers?

○ a. Change the Web server's MIME type association using RegEdit.

○ b. Change the Web server's MIME type association using the HTTP Headers tab of the Properties sheet in Internet Service Manager.

○ c. Change the Web server's MIME type association using the Home Directory tab of the Properties sheet in Internet Service Manager.

○ d. Change the MIME mappings on each of the client's machines.

Answer b is correct. To change the MIME mappings for documents that are delivered to browsers via IIS, you must make the changes to the metabase, rather than the server's Registry. Therefore, answer a is incorrect. The appropriate tab in Internet Service Manager is the HTTP Headers tab. Therefore, answer c is incorrect. Answer d is incorrect because, although changing the MIME mappings on each client's machine would work, it is not the most efficient method.

Need To Know More?

 Dyson, Peter: *Mastering Microsoft Internet Information Server 4, 2nd edition*. Sybex, Alameda, CA, 1997. ISBN: 0-78212-080-6. This is a nice introductory text on Microsoft's latest Web server technology. In addition, the book contains a lot of background information on Internet technologies and TCP/IP.

 Microsoft Corporation: *Microsoft Internet Information Server Resource Kit*. Microsoft Press, Redmond, WA, 1998. ISBN: 1-57231-638-1. The kit goes deep into the internal workings of IIS and provides valuable clues for successful implementation. The CD-ROM accompanying the book includes a copy of IIS version 4, additional utilities, a sampler of third-party tools, and detailed information on capacity planning and using IIS to set up an Internet Service Provider site.

 Oliver, Robert, Christian Plazas, John Desborough, and David Gulbransen: *Building a Windows NT 4 Internet Server*. New Riders Publishing, Indianapolis, IN, 1997. ISBN: 1-56205-680-8. This is a good book that uses a tutorial-based approach to teach you how to implement and administer an Internet server. The book focuses on several security considerations and configurations for a Windows NT Internet server. The book's CD-ROM includes several software utilities from the *Microsoft Resource Kit* used to build an Internet server on the Windows NT platform.

 Sheldon, Tom and John Muller: *Microsoft Internet Information Server 4: The Complete Reference*. Osborne McGraw-Hill, Berkeley, CA, 1998. ISBN: 0-07882-457-5. This book provides a comprehensive coverage of IIS 4.0. You'll find a lot of information on installation, setup, monitoring, troubleshooting, and more.

 Microsoft TechNet. January, 1998. The technical notes for Microsoft Internet Information Server provide insight into its design and architecture.

 For discussions on Microsoft Management Console, subscribe to the newsgroup **microsoft.public.management.mmc**.

IIS Security

. . . .

Terms you'll need to understand:

√ User authentication and authorization

√ Anonymous account

√ NTLM (*Windows NT Challenge/Response*) authentication

√ New Technology File System (NTFS)

√ Digital certificate

√ Secure Sockets Layer (SSL)

√ Packet filter

√ Firewall

√ Proxy server

√ Directory security

√ Event auditing

√ Home directory

√ Directory browsing

√ Access permission

√ Secure communication

Techniques you'll need to master:

√ Configuring Windows NTFS permissions

√ Configuring IIS security

√ Using event auditing

√ Controlling access by IP address

IIS is tightly integrated with Windows NT. As a result, IIS benefits from and inherits Windows NT's security features. In this chapter, we'll explore the steps necessary to secure your IIS server. In addition to Windows NT, IIS is also tightly integrated with Microsoft Proxy Server, Certificate Server, Site Server, and BackOffice; therefore, we'll examine how security relates to those systems as well.

Basic Security Overview

Because security is such an important issue with IIS, you must fully understand what types of access you can allow on your system. For example, you can configure IIS to grant or deny access to specific IP addresses, and you can enable anonymous access or require a valid Windows NT logon. The following sections cover authentication checks that IIS performs to verify that the user has permission to access a file or directory on a Web site.

User Authentication

The following are the user authentication methods available for IIS:

➤ **Anonymous access** During the IIS installation, the installation program creates anonymous accounts for both Web and FTP services. Neither Windows NT nor IIS authenticates the anonymous access. The anonymous accounts can only access the files and applications for which the system administrator grants permission.

➤ **Basic authentication** You can configure IIS to authenticate the use of files and applications by specific users or groups of users only. That is, the user must provide a valid user name and password before he or she can use the files and applications. Windows NT compares the user name and password to the accounts in the Windows NT Server directory. Note that Windows NT does not encrypt the user name and password in such cases. Authentication that is not encrypted is called basic authentication.

➤ **Windows NT Challenge/Response** Sometimes referred to as NTLM or Microsoft CHAP (Challenge Handshake Authentication Protocol) security, Windows NT Challenge/Response is an authentication technique the browser uses to encrypt and send a password across the network without prompting the user. Microsoft Internet Explorer 3 and higher supports Windows NT Challenge/Response authentication. For other browsers, Microsoft provides the Software Developer's Kit (SDK), which other vendors can use to provide Windows NT Challenge/Response authentication techniques within their browsers and applications.

If browsers that do not support Windows NT Challenge/ Response attempt to access a site in which Windows NT Challenge/Response is the only authentication method available, they will receive an Access Is Denied message.

Permissions

The following are the types of permissions that can be assigned by IIS:

➤ **Web permissions** Read, write, and execute permissions can be assigned in IIS on a per-site, per-directory, or per-file basis.

➤ **NTFS permissions** You should install Windows NT on an NTFS (New Technology File System) partition because it includes built-in security that both Windows NT and IIS can use. Under an NTFS partition, you can configure the access permissions for individual files or an entire directory.

Other Security Features

The other types of security features provided by IIS are as follows:

➤ **Digital certificates** For access control, IIS supports X.509 digital certificates. A digital certificate is like a driver's license: To validate your identity to the authorities, you must present a form of identification, such as the driver's license. Similarly, a client accessing the server's resources must present a valid ID, such as a digital (client) certificate. Just like the state authority that issues driver's licenses, there are trusted certificate authorities, such as VeriSign (**www.verisign.com**), that issue digital certificates. It is not enough to just have a valid digital certificate—a client must also know the password associated with the certificate. The combination of these two things is the key to successful access of a server's resources. A server can also have a certificate, called the server certificate, similar to a client certificate. A client machine can use the server certificate to validate the server's authenticity. The support of both client and server certificates is an important part of the IIS security features.

Note: To issue digital certificates, you can use the Microsoft Certificate Server.

➤ **Secure Sockets Layer (SSL)** SSL encrypts the communication between the browser and server. You can, therefore, send sensitive data, such as credit card information, and so on, within an encrypted line of communication.

Typically, SSL encrypted communication is slower and requires more bandwidth and CPU utilization than nonencrypted communication. It is therefore good practice to enable only SSL encryption on the specific directories that need encryption rather than on the entire Web server.

➤ **Auditing** Both Windows NT and IIS support event logging. You can log the activities on the server to a log file and then use the Crystal Reports engine (which comes with Windows NT) to generate reports of the log file. You can log the following types of activities:

➤ All logons

➤ Failed logon attempts

➤ Activities on the server, including file and directory accesses such as Read and Write operations

Auditing the activities on the server is an important part of configuring its security. If you sense unauthorized use of the server resources, you should enable auditing to track the activities.

You can complement Windows NT's security features by using one or more of the following techniques:

➤ **Packet filter** Think of a packet filter as a security guard. As an example, when you enter a Fortune 500 corporation's office complex, you'll probably notice a security guard in the lobby. The guard's responsibility is to let only authorized personnel into the building. A packet filter's function is similar: A packet filter analyzes the incoming TCP/IP packets. A packet filter resides between the two networks (the Internet and your corporation's LAN) and acts as a security guard. The Internet is the outside world and your corporation's LAN is the intellectual asset you want to protect from intruders and unauthorized users. Based on your specifications, the filter evaluates the validity of the incoming TCP/IP packets. If the incoming packet meets the set of rules, the filter lets the packet pass; otherwise, the filter blocks the packet. A packet filter is faster, but not as secure, as a firewall.

➤ **Firewall** A firewall is a computer that resides between the Internet and your corporation's LAN. Its function is similar to the packet filter. A firewall is typically more secure, but slower, than a packet filter. You can configure a firewall to block the communication between the two networks based on the following criteria:

➤ TCP/IP socket number

➤ Source computer's IP address (or IP network)

➤ Destination computer's IP address (or IP network)

A firewall could, for example, be used to block Internet users from using your server's file and printing services. The firewall blocks access to all services except HTTP and FTP.

➤ **Proxy server** Although a *proxy server's* primary responsibility is to improve browsing response time and efficiency by caching content, it also has some firewall functionality. For example, Microsoft Proxy Server 2 includes a reverse proxy feature that limits the possibilities of an intruder trying to reach the Web server, because the intruder must go through the Proxy server before reaching the Web server.

Windows NT Security

In this section, we'll discuss Windows NT security and cover its features in detail, including setting up group and user accounts, directory sharing, file security, and event auditing. Because IIS is installed on Windows NT, these settings are used on both systems.

User And Group Accounts

When you install Windows NT, by default, the installation program creates two accounts automatically—Administrator and Guest, with the Guest account disabled. The Administrator account is very important because it is the only account you can use to log on to Windows NT immediately after installation. As an administrator, you can add new Windows NT user accounts and create Windows NT group accounts.

For each user, you must create a valid user name and password. When assigning passwords, be careful, yet creative. A simple and easy-to-guess password can be potentially harmful to your system. For example, assigning the user's first name as the user name and the user's last name as the password is easy for any intruder to guess. Typically, to create a password you should use a combination of numbers and uppercase and lowercase letters. For clients accessing sensitive data in certain directories on the server, enable SSL so that the password and other sensitive information the browser sends is encrypted. To learn more about SSL, refer to the section "WWW Service: Directory Security" later in this chapter.

The IIS installation program automatically creates an anonymous account for both the Web and FTP services. The
anonymous account's ID is IUSR_*computername*, where
computername is the name of the machine on which you
install Windows NT and IIS. This Internet guest account is
automatically added to Windows NT's Guest group.

Directory Security

For a directory residing on Windows NT Server, you can configure the
directory's security permissions. To do so, right-click the directory and select
Properties from the pop-up menu. Click the Permissions button. Windows
NT, in turn, displays the dialog box, shown in Figure 4.1.

You can assign the following types of permissions to the NTFS directories:

➤ **No Access** The user can see the directory name but cannot do anything
with the directory.

➤ **Full Control** The user has complete access and control over the directory. The user can read, write, execute, and delete files in the directory.
In addition, the user can delete the directory itself. The user can also
change the permissions for the directory and the files in the directory
(assuming the files themselves do not have prior restrictions on them).

➤ **Read** The user can read and execute the files but cannot make any
changes to the files in the directory.

➤ **Change** The user can read, write, execute, and delete files in the
directory. However, the user cannot change the permissions for either
the directory or the files in the directory.

➤ **Special Access** The user's access is defined by a custom set of permissions.

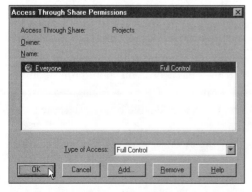

Figure 4.1 The Access Through Share Permissions dialog box.

File Security

For a file residing on a Windows NT Server machine, you can configure the file's security permissions. To do so, right-click the file and select Properties from the pop-up menu. Click the Permissions tab. You can assign the following types of permissions to an NTFS file:

➤ **No Access** The user can see the file but has no control or access over the file.

➤ **Full Control** The user has complete access and control over the file. The user can read, write, execute, and delete the file. The user can also change the permissions for the file.

➤ **Read** The user can read and execute the file but cannot make any changes to the file.

➤ **Change** The user can read, write, execute, and delete the file but cannot change the permissions for the file.

Event Auditing

You can log the activities to access the files and directories on the server with event logging. Note that this is only possible if you have installed Windows NT on an NTFS partition. If you installed Windows NT on a FAT (File Allocation Table) file system, this option is not available because the FAT file system does not provide the built-in security features that NTFS does. By default, both Windows NT and IIS allow event logging. A log file includes the following data, typically in a comma-delimited format:

➤ **Client** The client machine accessing the server.

➤ **User Name** The user ID accessing the server. For anonymous users, the log file includes a hyphen (-).

➤ **Log Date** The log date.

➤ **Log Time** The log time.

➤ **Service** The IIS service that the client machine is accessing.

➤ **Machine** The server's computer name.

➤ **Server IP** The server's IP address.

➤ **Processing Time** The total time for IIS to process the request.

➤ **Bytes Received** The client request's size in bytes.

➤ **Bytes Sent** The server response's size in bytes.

➤ **Service Status** The service's status.

➤ **Win32 Status** The Win32 subsystem's status.

➤ **Operation** The specific client request.

➤ **Target** The client request's target (for example, Web page, FTP directory, and so on).

➤ **Parameters** The parameters for the request.

➤ **Other Info** Any other information.

You can use Windows NT's Event Viewer to view the log files. Alternatively, you can use the built-in Crystal Reports engine to view the log files. By default, the following Crystal Reports are available:

➤ Activity by day of the week

➤ Activity by hour of the day

➤ Most frequently requested pages

➤ Most frequently accessed directories

➤ Most frequently downloaded file types and sizes

➤ Server errors

IIS Security

You can configure the security options for the Web and FTP services by using the Microsoft Management Console. Click Start|Programs|Windows NT Option Pack|Microsoft Internet Information Server|Internet Service Manager. Windows NT, in turn, starts the Microsoft Management Console 1, as shown in Figure 4.2. The various security settings that can be configured for the Web and FTP services are detailed in the following sections.

WWW Service: Home Directory

By right-clicking the site, and selecting Properties, and then the Home Directory tab, you can change some of the permission sets assigned to the root Web Site Directory and its child directories (see Figure 4.3).

Access Permissions

You can configure the access permissions (Read and Write) for a local directory or network share through the Home Directory tab. Read access allows the Web clients to download or read files. Write access allows the Web clients to upload files or change the content in the write-enabled files.

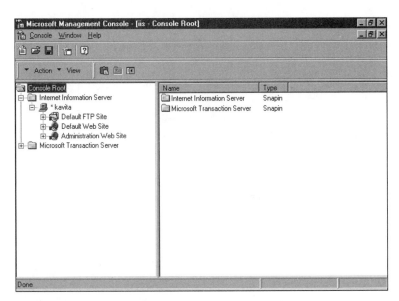

Figure 4.2 The Microsoft Management Console.

Figure 4.3 The Home Directory tab.

Grant Read access to the files you publish (for example, HTML files). Deny Read access to application files, such as Common Gateway Interface (CGI) programs (scripts or executables) and ISAPI filters.

Content Control

In addition to controlling access to IIS, you can also control access to its content. The server offers the following four options:

➤ **Log access** Check this to record access to the directory in a log file.

➤ **Directory browsing allowed** Uncheck this to prevent users from navigating through the directory structure on the IIS server. By default, IIS lets users browse through the directory structure.

 You may want to consider disabling directory browsing. Providing a view of your server's directory structure indicates the type of information available on the server, thus increasing the potential for hacker and intruder attacks. You can disable directory browsing for an entire Web site, but not for a single directory.

➤ **Index this directory** Check this to direct Microsoft Index Server to include the home directory in a full-text index of your site.

➤ **FrontPage Web** Check this to create a FrontPage Web for the site.

Permissions

You can configure the following three types of permissions for executables or scripts in the Home Directory tab:

➤ **None** IIS does not allow any programs or scripts to run in this directory.

➤ **Script** IIS allows only scripts to run in this directory, no executables.

 You must grant script permission for directories containing ASPs. CGI and ISAPI applications should reside in a dedicated directory (to which permissions are assigned).

➤ **Execute (including script)** IIS allows both scripts and executables to run in this directory.

 If there is a reason for users to execute a CGI script or ISAPI DLL, place all such scripts and DLLs in a single directory, grant execute permission on that directory alone, and disable the execute permission for all other directories.

WWW Service: Directory Security

The sections that follow show you how you can use the Directory Security tab to configure your server's security. By using the Directory Security tab, you can perform the following tasks:

➤ Prevent specific users or domains from accessing your Web site

➤ Configure anonymous access to the site

➤ Establish a secure communication link between the browser and the server

Figure 4.4 shows the Directory Security tab.

IP Address And Domain Name Restrictions

To prevent specific users, Web sites, or domains from accessing your Web site, directory, or file, click Edit in the IP Address And Domain Name Restrictions area.

Typically, you know the IP addresses of the machines in your company accessing the intranet. As a result, you can grant access to only those IP addresses and block the rest.

To grant access to the outside users of your company's intranet, first grant access to all and then selectively block the specific IP addresses as you detect potential intruder problems.

Figure 4.4   The Directory Security tab.

Anonymous Access And Authentication Control

To configure anonymous access and confirm the identity of users before granting access to your server's restricted content, click Edit in the Anonymous Access And Authentication Control section. The MMC, in turn, displays the Authentication Methods dialog box, as shown in Figure 4.5.

In this dialog box, choose one or more of the following authentication methods:

➤ **Allow Anonymous Access** No user name and password are required for anonymous access.

➤ **Basic Authentication** A user is prompted for a username and password.

➤ **Windows NT Challenge/Response** The server authenticates the user in the background, so the user is not prompted for a username and password.

Secure Communications

To create an SSL key pair and server certificate request, click Key Manager. By associating an SSL key pair with a server certificate request, you direct the client browser to establish an encrypted link to a directory or file on your IIS server. This enables a secure communication link between the browser and the server. You should establish a secure communication link only if the directory or file contains sensitive information, because a secure communication link is typically slower and requires more bandwidth than a nonencrypted line of communication.

FTP Service: Home Directory

By right-clicking the site and selecting Properties, and then selecting the Home Directory tab, you can change some of the permission sets assigned to the root FTP Site Directory and its child directories.

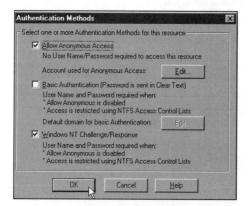

Figure 4.5 The Authentication Methods dialog box.

You can configure the access permissions (Read and Write) for a local directory or network share through the Home Directory tab. You can configure the following three types of permissions for the FTP files on the server:

➤ **Read** Users can read or download files in this directory.

➤ **Write** Users can upload files to this directory.

➤ **Log Access** Check this to record access to the directory in a log file.

 Grant Read access to the FTP directories containing publicly accessible files for download and remove Write access from these directories. Create a separate directory for the users to upload files and grant both Read and Write access to this directory. By default, event logging is enabled for the FTP server. To detect potential unauthorized access or any other misuse, monitor the event log regularly.

FTP Service: Security Accounts

By using the Security Accounts tab, you can configure anonymous access to your FTP site. By default, anonymous users can connect to the FTP site. With this tab, you can also configure Windows NT user accounts as FTP site operators. Figure 4.6 shows the Security Accounts tab.

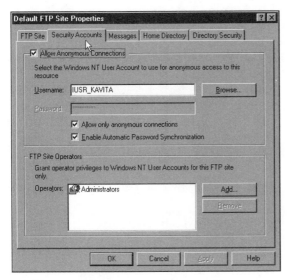

Figure 4.6 The Security Accounts tab.

In the Username text box, specify the Windows NT user account the FTP service should use for anonymous access to this service. By default, the user account is IUSR_*computername*, where *computername* is the name of the system on which IIS is installed.

The Password text box specifies the password that goes with the user name. If you change the password here, the password for the Windows NT IUSR_*computername* account must also be changed. By default, password synchronization is automatic. That is, the server automatically synchronizes the FTP site password with the Windows NT password for anonymous users. To disable this feature, uncheck Enable Automatic Password Synchronization.

In the FTP Site Operators section, you can specify the Windows NT user accounts to whom you want to grant the operator privileges for the FTP site.

FTP Service: Directory Security

Securing the directories on the server is one of the most important things you should consider when configuring your FTP server. In addition to protecting the site with a password authentication scheme, you can use the Directory Security tab to secure the directories on your FTP server (see Figure 4.7). You can choose to grant or deny access to all or specific directories on the server, thus preventing unauthorized access to the server.

Figure 4.7   The Directory Security tab.

By default, the FTP server grants access to all computers.

To specify exceptions, click Add. Microsoft Management Console, in turn, displays the Deny Access On dialog box, as shown in Figure 4.8.

In this dialog box, choose whether you want to deny or grant access to a single computer (IP address), a group of computers (Network ID and subnet mask), or a domain name.

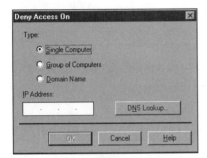

Figure 4.8 The Deny Access On dialog box.

Practice Questions

Question 1

> Windows NT's basic authentication scheme does not perform which of the following actions?
>
> ○ a. Encrypt the password
>
> ○ b. Encrypt the user name
>
> ○ c. Encrypt both the user name and password
>
> ○ d. None of the above

Answer c is correct. The basic authentication scheme is just that, basic. The scheme does not encrypt anything involved in the authentication process. Therefore, answers a, b, and d are incorrect.

Question 2

> Which of the following browsers natively support Windows NT Challenge/Response? [Check all correct answers]
>
> ❑ a. Internet Explorer 3
>
> ❑ b. Internet Explorer 4
>
> ❑ c. Navigator 4
>
> ❑ d. All of the above

Answers a and b are correct. All versions of Internet Explorer 3 and greater support Windows NT Challenge/Response. Netscape Navigator 4 does not support this authentication scheme. Therefore, answer c is incorrect. Because answer c is incorrect, answer d is also incorrect.

Question 3

You can configure IIS to block specific IP addresses from accessing and using which of the following services? [Check all correct answers]

❑ a. WWW

❑ b. FTP

❑ c. Gopher

❑ d. Telnet

Answers a and b are correct. You can configure both WWW and FTP services to block specific IP addresses. IIS 4 does not support Gopher or Telnet. Therefore, answers c and d are incorrect.

Question 4

Which one of the following file systems should you install IIS on so that IIS benefits from its tight integration with Windows NT?

○ a. FAT

○ b. NTFS

○ c. Windows 95

○ d. DOS

Answer b is correct. NTFS is a secure file system. FAT does not have any built-in security. Therefore, answer a is incorrect. Both Windows 95 and DOS are operating systems, not file systems. Therefore, answers c and d are incorrect.

Question 5

Which of the following can you use IIS's auditing services to audit?

○ a. Logons

○ b. Failed logon attempts

○ c. Access activities on the server

○ d. All of the above

Answer d is correct. IIS's event logging capabilities let you record all types of information, including both successful and failed logon attempts. In addition, you can log the different types of access activities, including Web and FTP activities. Because answer d is correct, answers a, b, and c are incorrect.

Question 6

For anonymous access, you can configure IIS so Windows NT automatically synchronizes the Windows NT password with the HTTP or FTP password.

○ a. True

○ b. False

Answer a is correct. Synchronizing the Windows NT password with the HTTP or FTP password is IIS's default configuration.

Question 7

Which is the default account created by the installation program during the IIS installation?

○ a. IUSR_*computername*, where *computername* is the name of the machine on which you installed IIS

○ b. USR_*computername*, where *computername* is the name of the machine on which you installed IIS

○ c. *Computername*, where *computername* is the name of the machine on which you installed IIS

○ d. IUSR_*servername*, where *servername* is IIS's name

Answer a is correct. IUSR_*computername* is, in fact, the default user account. Therefore, answers b, c, and d are incorrect.

Question 8

> If you only have Read access to a file on the FTP server, which of the following operations can you perform? [Check all correct answers]
>
> ❑ a. Download the file
>
> ❑ b. Read the file
>
> ❑ c. Write to the file

Answers a and b are correct. Downloading a file is equivalent to a read operation. Because you have Read access on the file, you can read and download the file. To be able to write to the file, you must have Write access to the file, which is a separate permission from Read and does not rely upon Read access. Therefore, answer c is incorrect.

Question 9

> Netscape distributes the Navigator source code for free. Netscape Navigator does not inherently support the NTLM authentication scheme. How can you build this scheme into Navigator?
>
> ○ a. By using the Software Developer's Kit from Microsoft.
>
> ○ b. By using the Software Developer's Kit from Netscape.
>
> ○ c. By using the Microsoft Windows API.
>
> ○ d. NTLM authentication is Internet Explorer-specific only; you cannot add this functionality into Navigator.

Answer a is correct. You can enhance Navigator by integrating the NTLM authentication scheme. To do so, you must use the Software Developer's Kit from Microsoft. The NTLM authentication scheme originates from Microsoft, so using the Software Developer's Kit from Netscape does no good. The Microsoft Windows API does not include any such scheme, either. Although this scheme originates from Microsoft, the scheme is not Internet Explorer-specific. Microsoft provides a Software Developer's Kit you can use to integrate the scheme within other browsers, including Netscape Navigator. Therefore, answers b, c, and d are incorrect.

Question 10

You have been the IIS administrator for your company for more than a year. The Internet content for your company's Web site has grown, and you are asked to create a proprietary authentication program for the site. As the Web site administrator, you are asked to choose the design technique. What technique would you choose? [Check all correct answers]

❑ a. Create an ISAPI filter to authenticate all the users.

❑ b. Create a CGI script to authenticate all the users.

❑ c. Create a user account on Windows NT for all the users.

Answers a and b are correct. Answer a is the most efficient technique because the approach uses an ISAPI filter. ISAPI implementation consumes fewer server resources compared to a CGI implementation. Answer b is less efficient (but still correct) because an ISAPI solution is faster than a CGI solution. Answer c is not an option because you do not want to create a Windows NT user account for each user. Therefore, answer c is incorrect.

Question 11

Your company has developed a killer software product. The company would like potential customers to download the product's evaluation copy for free from its Web site. As the site's Webmaster, how do you propose to implement this in the best way possible?

○ a. Create a Web form where users register themselves and you mail them a disk with the free software.

○ b. Place the software on the FTP site and set the FTP directory to Read Only. Point the interested users to this site.

○ c. Use Microsoft Merchant Server to configure the download facility.

○ d. Install a proxy server and then use IIS's FTP service to facilitate the download.

Answer b is correct. The FTP service's primary function is to allow users to download and upload files easily. Creating a Web form for users to register themselves and then mailing them a disk is not a state-of-the-art solution. Therefore, answer a is incorrect. You can use the Microsoft Merchant Server to design and build Web storefronts that may include a file download facility, but this is not really necessary because IIS's FTP service suffices. Therefore, answer c is incorrect. The proxy server has no role as far as implementing a download facility is concerned. Therefore, answer d is incorrect.

Need To Know More?

 Buyens, Jim: *Building Net Sites with Windows NT: An Internet Service Handbook*. Addison-Wesley Publishing Company, Reading, MA, 1996. ISBN: 0-20147-949-4. This book provides practical, accessible advice on selecting and installing hardware, operating systems, and application and administrative services. In addition, the book covers IIS. This book also supplies valuable guidance on site planning, security, and ongoing operation of an NT Internet site (information that can be difficult to find).

 Edwards, Mark: *Internet Security With Windows NT*. Duke Communications, Loveland, CO, 1997. ISBN: 1-88241-962-6. In this book, security guru Mark Edwards shares the wisdom he accumulated through his years in the security field to help you protect your network from attack, detect security breaches when they occur, and recover from problems as quickly as possible.

 Rutstein, Charles B.: *Windows NT Security: A Practical Guide to Securing Windows NT Servers and Workstations, 2nd edition*. Osborne McGraw-Hill, Berkeley, CA, 1998. ISBN: 0-78815-680-2. This authoritative guide provides essential information on how to tap the Windows NT operating system's sophisticated security capabilities. You can apply the book's pragmatic advice on designing secure Windows NT networks to small, medium, and large organizations.

 Sheldon, Tom: *Windows NT Security Handbook*. Osborne McGraw-Hill, Berkeley, CA, 1996. ISBN: 0-07882-240-8. Sheldon's guide approaches security from the Windows NT perspective and addresses key issues, such as protective features available in Windows NT, as well as potential security holes. You'll learn how to create defensive strategies and become familiar with the different security protocols.

 Sheldon, Tom and John Muller: *Microsoft Internet Information Server 4: The Complete Reference*. Osborne McGraw-Hill, Berkeley, CA, 1998. ISBN: 0-07882-457-5. This book provides a comprehensive coverage of IIS 4.0. You'll find a lot of information on installation, setup, monitoring, troubleshooting, and more.

Microsoft TechNet. January, 1998. The technical notes for Microsoft Internet Information Server provide insight into its design, architecture, and security. Also search the TechNet CD using the following keywords: "IIS security," "authentication and authorization," "NTLM authentication," "Secure Sockets Layer," "digital certificate," "event auditing," "directory security," "access permission," "firewall," and "packet filtering."

 Browse product documentation locally on your server at **http://localhost/iishelp/misc/default.htm**.

 For timely information about weaknesses in Internet software security, visit **www.cert.org**.

 The Microsoft Web site at **www.microsoft.com/ntserver/web** provides a wealth of information regarding IIS, including datasheets, white papers, system requirements, a downloadable copy of IIS, case studies, tips, tricks, and lots more.

 The BHS Web site at **www.bhs.com** is a valuable resource center for information on Windows NT and tools that are dependent on Windows NT, such as IIS.

Enhanced Security Through Authentication And Encryption

5

Terms you'll need to understand:

√ Encryption/decryption

√ Public key encryption

√ Digital signatures and secure envelopes

√ Certificate authorities (CAs)

√ Certificates

√ Secure Sockets Layer (SSL)

√ https://

√ Certificate Server

√ Public Key Cryptography Standards (PKCS)

√ CryptoAPI

Techniques you'll need to master:

√ Understanding the basics of encryption, keys, and certificates

√ Requesting and obtaining a certificate for IIS 4

√ Understanding how SSL works with IIS 4

√ Using client certificates

√ Using Certificate Server

√ Understanding the purpose of the CryptoAPI

Most Internet services are, by nature, distributed in a clear text format. Therefore, standard service communications can be intercepted anywhere between a server and client. Internet Information Server (IIS) 4 includes native support for secure communications through Secure Sockets Layer (SSL) certificates. This chapter discusses IIS 4's support for SSL and other advanced security features.

Secure Internet Transmission

Secure transmissions over the Internet or an intranet using IIS 4 are possible through the use of encryption. Encryption is simply the process of scrambling data (whether it's a message, streaming multimedia, data files, or whatever) into a form that is unusable and unreadable by anyone except the intended recipient. Decryption is the necessary flip-side of encryption. Decryption is the process of unscrambling the encrypted data.

When data is encrypted, a tool known as an encryption key is used (see Figure 5.1). An encryption key is an electronic mathematical formula used to scramble

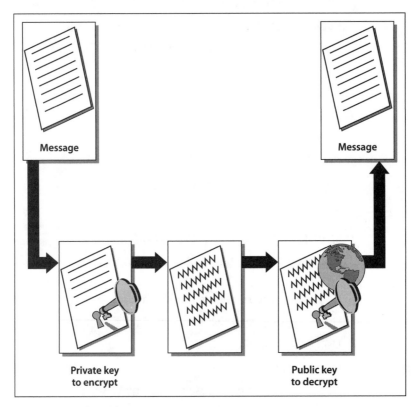

Figure 5.1 Basic key encryption.

data. An encryption key can be thought of like any metal key—once it's used on a door, that door is inaccessible to anyone without the key because it's locked.

When data is decrypted, a tool known as a decryption key is used. A decryption key is the mathematical inverse of the encryption key. The decryption key unscrambles encrypted data to extract the original. Only the decryption key can unlock and restore encrypted data. It's very important to maintain control over the decryption key because anyone with access to it can unscramble any data encrypted by the related encryption key. Granting wide access to the decryption key will, in effect, circumvent the security of encryption.

IIS uses a form of cryptology known as public key encryption. In this system, both the server and the client use two keys—a private key and a public key. The client uses the server's public key and its own private key to encrypt a message; then, the server uses the client's public key and its own private key to decrypt the same message. The same pattern occurs when data is sent from the server to the client. In each case, once the data is locked, only the private key of the recipient combined with the public key of the sender will decrypt the data.

In the public key system, private keys are obviously kept secure and are not distributed. However, the public key is widely distributed. This gives both the sender and the recipient the ability to send and receive messages using the two-key encryption system.

A system related to public key encryption (shown in Figure 5.2) is known collectively as digital signatures and secure envelopes. In this system, the private key of the sender is the digital signature. Its presence verifies the origin and identity of the sender, rather than encrypting the message. The secure envelope is the public key encryption of the sender. This encrypts the message. Once the message is received by the recipient, the recipient's private key is used to decrypt the message from the secure envelope; then, the public key of the sender is used to verify the signature of the message.

The next logical step in the realm of digital signatures is identity verification. Because anyone can claim to be anyone via the anonymity of the Internet, identity verification is extremely important. For instance, you need to know that the Web site you're sending your credit card information to is, in fact, the flower store in San Francisco and not some hacker impersonating it. The scheme used in identity verification is called a certificate. A certificate is a digital signature issued by a third party (called a certificate authority or CA) that claims to have verified the identity of a server or an individual. The presence of a certificate from a CA indicates that some type of offline verification process was used to establish an identity.

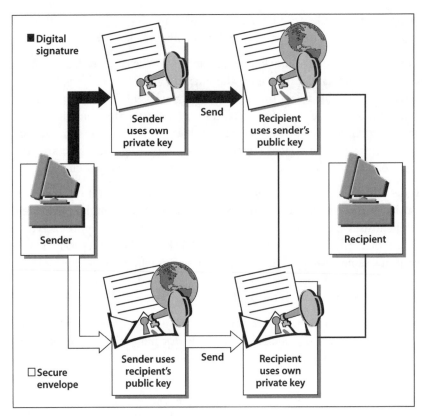

Figure 5.2 An example of encrypted message transmission using digital signatures and secure envelopes.

Certificates are used to create the private signature key for a sender and the public verification key for the recipient. The private signature key is given only to the entity whose identity is verified by the certificate. The public verification key is distributed either by the sender, the CA, or both. This enables a recipient to verify the identity of a communication partner by relying on the word and reputation of the CA.

In addition to issuing certificates, CAs are also responsible for renewing and revoking certificates. Once the life span of a certificate has expired, most organizations want to renew their certificates to continue to offer secure communications. A certificate can be revoked for several reasons, including expiration of life span, improper use of a certificate, and termination of a compromised certificate. A certificate revocation list (CRL) is maintained by the CA, which lists all invalid certificates. This grants servers and clients the ability to determine if an invalid certificate is being used.

SSL 3

SSL (Secure Sockets Layer) is an industry-standard protocol used to establish secure communications between a Web server (or other information service server) and a client. SSL is a dual-layered protocol. The lower layer—SSL Record Protocol—operates just above the Transport Control Protocol (TCP). It encapsulates higher-level protocols, thus making it a flexible and application protocol-independent security scheme. The higher layer—SSL Handshake Protocol—is used to coordinate an encryption algorithm for use between a client and server for secured communications. Figure 5.3 shows SSL in action.

Establishing an SSL session involves the following steps:

1. The client initiates communication by requesting a resource from a server. The request takes the form "https://…".

2. The server responds to indicate that it received the request for a secured resource.

3. The server sends its certificate to the client.

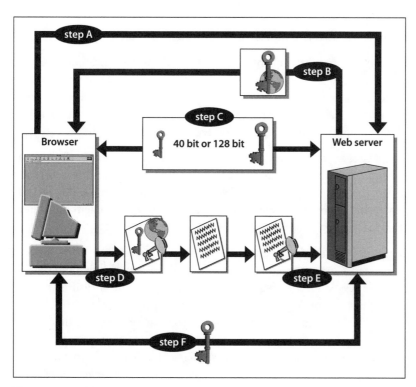

Figure 5.3   SSL in action.

4. If required, the server requests the client's certificate.

5. The server indicates its transmission is complete.

6. The client responds by sending its own certificate to the server, if the server requested the client's certificate.

7. The client attempts to verify the server's certificate using the CA-distributed public key.

8. If the certificate is verified, the client sends the encryption specification it needs to the server. This is typically called a *session key*. It's encrypted using the client's private key.

9. The client indicates its transmission is complete.

10. The server verifies the validity of the client's certificate, if requested.

11. The server receives the session key, decrypts it using the client's public key, and then modifies its (the server's) encryption to match that requested by the client.

12. The server indicates the end of normal transmissions.

13. Secure encrypted communication begins between the client and server.

This process will fail if the client or the server fails to respond to any request for information, or if a response indicates that no such information, data, or certificate is available. The communication link will also be severed if either the server's or the client's certificates are unable to be validated, or if the server is unable to comply with the encryption requirements of the client.

The certificates are used to establish the secure communication between a client and server, to verify the identity of one or both parties, and to secure the session key. It's the encryption technology defined by the session key, not the certificate, that governs the encryption of data between the client and server once the SSL channel has been established.

The session key is the key used by the client and server to encrypt all data communicated between them. The session key can have a range of strength based on its degree of encryption. Encryption degrees are measured in bits. The longer the session key, the stronger the encryption it provides. A 40-bit encryption key is typical and is the current maximum encryption that can be used when communications pass outside of U.S. borders. Within the U.S., 128-bit or more encryption can be used. The strength or bit length of an encryption key also affects the performance of communications: The stronger the encryption, the more complicated the encryption/decryption process becomes. For every additional bit added to a key, you double its effectiveness, as well as the resources required to process it.

 Windows NT Server only supports 40-bit encryption schemes straight out of the box. To add support for 128-bit encryption, you must apply the 128-bit domestic version of Service Pack 3 or 4.

Using SSL With IIS 4

To use SSL with IIS 4, you must obtain a server certificate from a CA such as VeriSign (but any will do). A server certificate is requested by creating a key request file using the Key Manager and sending it to a CA. Once the CA grants you a server certificate, it must be installed on the server.

The Key Manager is accessed by following these steps:

1. Launch the Microsoft Management Console (MMC) by choosing Start|Programs|Windows NT 4 Option Pack|Microsoft Internet Information Server|Internet Service Manager. Figure 5.4 shows MMC.

2. Select a local Web site from within MMC.

3. Select Properties from the Action pull-down menu.

4. Select the Directory Security tab, as shown in Figure 5.5.

5. Click the Key Manager button. The Key Manager is shown in Figure 5.6.

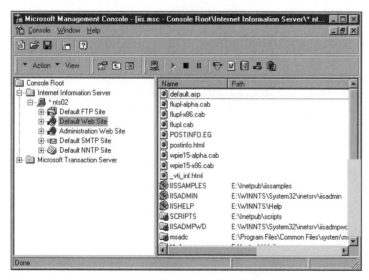

Figure 5.4   The Microsoft Management Console.

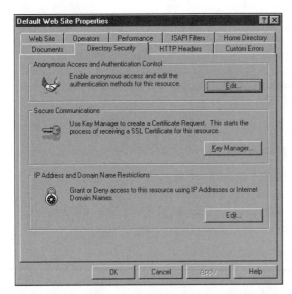

Figure 5.5 MMC's Directory Security tab in the Default Web Site Properties dialog box (precertificate installation).

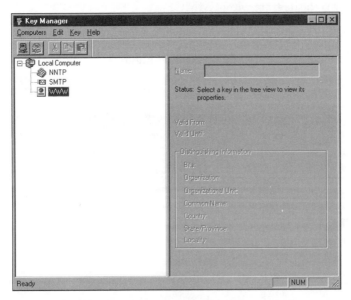

Figure 5.6 The Key Manager.

To create a key request file, perform the following steps:

1. Select the WWW service listed for the local computer within the Key Manager.

2. Select Create New Key from the Key menu. The Create New Key Wizard then appears.

3. The first page of the wizard allows you to select whether to create a request file, which you must send to a CA, or for the wizard to send the request file automatically to a known CA (typically useful only when the Certificate Server is installed). Choose to create a request file, specify the path, and then click Next.

4. Define a key name, a password, and a bit length. The key name is used to identify individual keys. The password is required for later installation of the issued certificate. The bit length determines the strength of the requested certificate. (Note that without the installation of 128-bit Service Pack 3, you do not have a choice of bit length. The only selection is 512. If you have applied the 128-bit Service Pack, you can select from 512, 768, or 1,024, with 1,024 being the default.) Click Next.

The bit length defined here is related only to the certificate and the key request. The bit lengths of 512, 768, or 1,024 are extremely secure and are used to protect identity certificates. Once a certificate is issued and installed, that certificate is used to establish the session key for data transmission, which can only be 40-bit or 128-bit encryption.

5. The next page of the wizard is where you define information about your organization, including name, unit, and common name (typically the domain name of the server). Fill in the information and then click Next.

6. You are asked to identify your geographic location by country, state/province, and city/locale. Do this and click Next.

7. Next, identify yourself by name, email address, and phone number. Click Next.

8. The last page of the wizard informs you that your request file will be stored in the file name you specified in Step 3. Click Finish to complete the request generation.

9. You'll see animation while the request is generated. When the process is completed, click OK.

Figure 5.7 The contents of a sample key request file.

The key request file is a plain text file that contains a section of encrypted information that only the CA will be able to decipher (see Figure 5.7). This file is sent to the CA via predefined means, such as email, FTP, or snail mail. Once your identity is verified and your certificate is granted, you'll receive your certificate via email, FTP, or snail mail.

Once you receive the certificate, you must install it. This process is as follows:

1. Launch the Key Manager.

2. Select the named key item below the WWW service when you have received a certificate from a CA.

3. Select Install Key Certificate from the Key menu.

4. Use the Browse window to locate and select the certificate file; then click Open.

5. You'll be prompted for the password used to create the original key request file. Type in the password and then click OK.

6. If Step 5 was successful, the Server Bindings dialog box appears. Through this dialog box, you can define which IP addresses and port numbers on this server can use this certificate for SSL communications. After defining at least one IP address, click OK.

7. This returns you to the main Key Manager window. By selecting the newly installed key certificate, you can obtain information about the

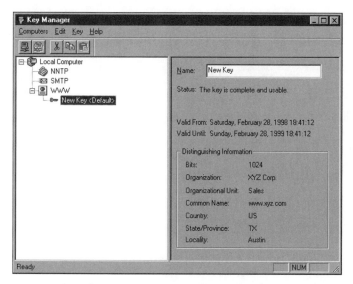

Figure 5.8   The Key Manager with a certificate installed.

certificate, such as validity dates, bit length, and identification informa-tion (see Figure 5.8).

Once a key certificate is installed, you can set the Web server to use SSL exclu-sively or only as needed. Several configuration settings are now available that can be made to manage how SSL is used by IIS. The first is made on the Web Site tab of the Properties dialog box of the Web server, listed in MMC.

 You can define the SSL port for secure communications. The default is 443. If you change this, users will need to add the port address to their URLs, for example, **www.domain.com:812/**.

The rest of the options are accessed on the Directory Security tab, but the button previously labeled Key Manager now reads Edit. Clicking the Edit button reveals a new dialog box, enabled by the presence of a certificate or an incomplete key request, called Secure Communications (see Figure 5.9). In this dialog box, you can force all communications for this site to use SSL by selecting Require Secure Channel when accessing this resource. By clicking the Encryption Settings button, you can choose to require 128-bit encryption (available only if the 128-bit Windows NT Service Pack has been applied). By requiring 128-bit encryption, you limit your audience to mostly domestic North American users with modern browsers. Remember that only Internet Explorer and Netscape Navigator versions 3 and higher support 128-bit encryption.

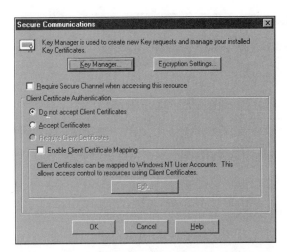

Figure 5.9   The Secure Communications dialog box.

When a browser attempts to access resources from a secure server, but does not request a secure channel when required (https://) or does not support the required level of encryption (128-bit), the error message "HTTP/1.1 403 Access Forbidden (Secure Channel Required)" is sent to the browser.

IIS 4.0 supports SSL 3, SSL 2, and PCT 1. PCT, or Private Communication Technology, is an encryption technology similar to SSL. Through these secure communication protocols, IIS is able to offer the widest range of compatibility with client browsers.

Client SSL Features

Once your IIS 4-hosted Web site has a certificate installed, you can select to require client certificates before granting access to resources. Client certificates give you greater access control over your resources by forcing clients to properly identify themselves with a respected or trusted CA. Without a valid client certificate, all secure resources are restricted from use. SSL Client Authentication (SSLCA) is another, more secure authentication scheme (added to the existing set of three—anonymous, basic/clear text, and Microsoft Challenge/Response). However, with SSLCA, the identity of the client is verified.

SSL client certificates are enabled in the Secure Communications dialog box. It's accessed by clicking the Edit button on the Directory Security tab of the Web Site Properties dialog box. The default setting does not accept client certificates. The next option is to accept client certificates if available and when necessary. Forcing a client to have a certificate can only be enabled when Require Secure Channel when accessing this resource is selected for the entire site (that is, no insecure communications).

The purpose of client certificates is twofold: to verify the identity of the client and to associate that client with a user account hosted by the system. When client certificate mapping is enabled, you can map client certificates to specific NT user accounts. Therefore, each time a client accesses an IIS 4-hosted resource, access is granted based on the access permissions of the user account associated with the validated certificate. Mapping can be a one-to-one relationship or multiple certificates to a single user account. One-to-many mapping can be performed using wildcards to match any field stored in a certificate.

SSL And Certificate Server

Included on the Option Pack for integration with IIS is the Microsoft Certificate Server. This application is used to organize, issue, renew, and revoke private certificates without relying on a third-party external CA. The role of Certificate Server is to receive Public Key Cryptography Standards (PKCS) #10 certificate requests and to issue X.509 certificates in PKCS #7 format. Certificate Server gives you the ability to be your own CA, which gives you a wider range of control over certificates and what they can be used for.

Certificate Server is designed to support Web applications that rely on SSL-based secure communication and authentication. In addition to SSL, Certificate Server also supports other certificate-based applications, including Secure/Multipurpose Internet Mail Extensions (S/MIME) and Secure Electronic Extensions (SET), plus Microsoft Authenticated digital signatures.

Certificate Server is installed through the Option Pack Setup program's custom setup. During the setup, you'll be prompted for several items, including the following:

➤ **Configuration Data Storage Location** A shared folder used by the Certificate Server to store certificates and configuration files.

➤ **Database Location** The location of the server's database. By default, this is Winnt\System32\CertLog.

➤ **Log Location** The location to store the server's log files. By default, this is Winnt\System32\CertLog.

➤ **Select CSP And Hashing (Advanced)** The Cryptographic Service Provider (CSP) and the hash algorithm used by the CSP. The default CSP is Microsoft Base Cryptographic Provider (MBCP) and the default hash algorithm is MD5.

➤ **Use Existing Keys (Advanced)** If existing keys are present, this selection retains those keys for use with Certificate Server.

➤ **Erase All Previous Configuration Information (Advanced)** Performs a fresh installation with new configurations. Deselect to retain existing settings.

➤ **Make This Installation The Default (Advanced)** On a network with multiple instances of Certificate Server, this option sets the current installation as the default.

➤ **Select Certificate Authority Hierarchy (Advanced)** Hierarchies are not supported in Certificate Server 1. However, you can select this server to be a root CA or a nonroot CA.

➤ **Identifying Information** You must provide details about this installation, such as the name of the CA, the organization name, the department or unit, as well as the city, state, country, and a comment.

Once these items are defined, the server is installed. A public/private key pair is generated to be used as the self-signed root or site certificate for this installation. This key is written to the shared certificate folder, and the server is added to the list of CAs.

Certificate Server is installed as a Windows NT service that is launched automatically under the system account each time the system is booted. This is the preferred and default method of launching the application, but it can be set to manual and be set to launch under a different security level, if desired, through the Services applet.

Certificate Server is primarily managed through Web-based administration tools. Several command-line tools can be used in cases of restoring the system or performing operations more easily accomplished through the Web interface. The Web utilities are accessed by requesting the default URL: **http:// localhost/CertSvr/**. The Web interface gives you quick access to the Log utility, the Queue utility, Enrollment Tools, and online documentation.

The Certificate Log Administration utility is used to manage active certificates and the CRL (see Figure 5.10). Each known certificate is displayed in the default List view. Individual certificates can be inspected more closely in the Form view by clicking a certificate's number or by using the Form View button and its arrows to select the certificate. In Form view, you can revoke a certificate by clicking the Revoke button followed by the Requery button.

The Certificate Server Queue Administration utility is used to manage requests. Each action requested or performed by the Certificate Server is listed here. As in the Log utility, the Form view offers a more detailed look at individual items. In Form view, you can define a filter to reduce the number of displayed items in the List view (see Figure 5.11).

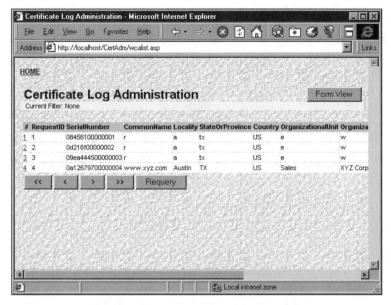

Figure 5.10 The Certificate Log Administration utility.

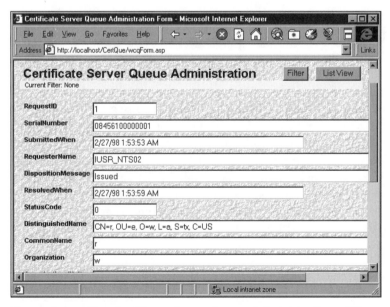

Figure 5.11 The Certificate Server Queue Administration utility.

The Certificate Enrollment Tools perform three functions: install CA certificates, process certificate requests, and request client authentication certificates. Installing CA certificates adds a CA's certificate to the Web browser being used. This configures the browser to automatically support and accept secure communications from all Web sites using certificates issued by that CA. Processing a certificate request is where the contents of a key request file (as created by the Key Manager) can be sent via a Web form to obtain a certificate for your server. Requesting a client authentication certificate allows you to obtain a client certificate to prove your identity.

The current version of Certificate Server is set to issue all certificate requests, by default. This is obviously a security problem. The evaluation of requests and the issuing of new certificates are governed through the use of policies. Policies are installed by an administrator; they instruct the Certificate Server to accept, deny, or delay a request based on the contents of the request.

CryptoAPI

In an effort to move the underlying details of cryptography away from application developers, Microsoft has developed the CryptoAPI. This application programming interface (API) allows programmers to create applications that can use or even rely upon cryptography without requiring knowledge of the encryption system. The CryptoAPI separates applications from encryption, thus enabling an application without modification to use different types or new technologies of encryption. The ability to change the strength and type of encryption used by an application is provided by the Cryptographic Service Provider (CSP) interface. This component is supported by the Certificate Server and allows alternate CSPs to be used for certificate management. Certificate Server supports CryptoAPI 2.

Practice Questions

Question 1

Which technology is used most often to establish secure communications over networks where data interception is possible?

○ a. CRC

○ b. Encryption

○ c. TCP/IP

○ d. DHCP

Answer b is correct. Encryption is the technology used to establish secure communications over insecure networks. CRC is a technology used to verify the integrity of transmitted data; it's not associated with security. Therefore, answer a is incorrect. TCP/IP is a network protocol. Secure communications can occur over it (hence, the "trick"), but TCP/IP does not directly provide for security. Therefore, answer c is incorrect. DHCP is a technology used to dynamically configure clients. Therefore, answer d is incorrect.

Question 2

Which of the following are typical concepts or terms associated with encryption? [Check all correct answers]

❑ a. Public keys

❑ b. Identify verification

❑ c. Certificates

❑ d. Digital signatures

Answers a, b, c, and d are all correct. All of these items are associated with encryption.

Question 3

A digital signature performs two functions—it indicates the identity of the sender, as well as encrypts the signed message.

○ a. True

○ b. False

Answer b is correct. This statement is false. A digital signature is only used to indicate the identity of the sender; it's not used to encrypt data.

Question 4

What is a certificate's primary purpose?

○ a. Encrypting data

○ b. Advertising

○ c. Identifying a sender or a client

○ d. Proving the value of online products and services

Answer c is correct. A certificate is used primarily to identify a sender or a client. Certificates are not used to encrypt data. Therefore, answer a is incorrect. Certificates are not a form of advertisement. Therefore, answer b is incorrect. Certificates are not used to prove the value or worth of products and services found online; rather, they are only used to prove the identity of the owner of the site distributing such items. Therefore, answer d is incorrect.

Question 5

What is a certificate authority (CA)?

○ a. The single worldwide distribution point for client identities

○ b. An Internet standards organization, similar to IETF and IEEE, that sets the requirements for certificates

○ c. A division of the National Security Council (NSC) with the sole purpose of cracking down on computer fraud

○ d. A third-party organization that is trusted to verify the identity of servers and individuals

Answer d is correct. A certificate authority (CA) is a third-party organization that is trusted to verify the identity of servers and individuals. A CA is not a single worldwide distribution point for client identities. This type of entity does not currently exist. Therefore, answer a is incorrect. A CA is not an Internet standards organization similar to IETF and IEEE that sets the requirements for certificates. Therefore, answer b is incorrect. A CA is not part of the NSC. Therefore, answer c is incorrect.

Question 6

If you secure a Web site called www.domain.com using SSL encryption, how must you change the URL to access the secured pages?

○ a. **http://www.domain.com/ssl/**

○ b. **https://www.domain.com**

○ c. **httpssl://www.domain.com**

○ d. **shttp://www.domain.com**

Answer b is correct. The correct syntax of a URL for a Web site that uses SSL encryption is https://www.domain.com. None of the other answers correctly identify the structure of an SSL-encrypted URL. Therefore, answers a, c, and d are incorrect.

Question 7

Creating a key certificate request is an integral step of what process?

○ a. Installing IIS 4

○ b. Configuring a Web server to offer SSL-based secure communications

○ c. As a client, purchasing a product with a credit card over a secure link

○ d. Applying Service Pack 3 to Windows NT Server

Answer b is correct. Creating a key certificate request is an integral part of configuring a Web server to offer SSL-based secure communications. Installing IIS and applying Service Pack 3 do not require a key request. Therefore, answers a and d are incorrect. As a client, purchasing a product with a credit card over a secure link does not require a key request to be generated, but it does rely on the Web server to have already installed a certificate. Therefore, answer c is incorrect.

Question 8

What is the maximum strength of data encryption that can be used by IIS 4 when communicating with clients outside of North America?

○ a. 40

○ b. 128

○ c. 512

○ d. 1,024

Answer a is correct. The strongest encryption that can be used across North America's borders is 40-bit encryption. One hundred twenty eight-bit encryption can only be used within North America. Therefore, answer b is incorrect. Five hundred twelve and 1,024 bits are encryption strengths for certificates that are used for identity verification, not data encryption. Therefore, answers c and d are incorrect.

Question 9

Which of the following components must be installed before IIS can require 128-bit data encryption?

○ a. An InterNIC-assigned domain name

○ b. Microsoft Transaction Server

○ c. Service Pack 3 (domestic version)

○ d. Microsoft Certificate Server

Answer c is correct. A domestic version of Service Pack 3 is the component required for 128-bit data encryption. IIS does not need a true Internet domain name assigned by the InterNIC, Microsoft Transaction Server, or Microsoft Certificate Server to use 128-bit encryption. Therefore, answers a, b, and d are incorrect.

Question 10

> If you change the default SSL port from 443 to 1013, what is the syntax of the
> URL used to access the site?
>
> ○ a. **http://www.domain.com/1013/**
>
> ○ b. **shttp:/www.domain.com:1013/**
>
> ○ c. **https://www.domain.com/**
>
> ○ d. **https://www.domain.com:1013/**

Answer d is correct. The only correct URL for accessing an SSL-secured site
with a nonstandard port is **https://www.domain.com:1013/**. All the other selections are invalid. Therefore, answers a, b, and c are incorrect.

Need To Know More?

 Howell, Nelson, and Ben Forta, Special Editor: *Using Microsoft Internet Information Server 4.* Que Publishing, Indianapolis, IN, 1997. ISBN: 0-7897-1263-6. This book contains excellent information on using SSL with IIS (Chapter 21); however, it lacks coverage of Certificate Server.

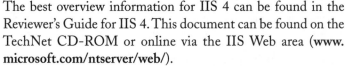 The best overview information for IIS 4 can be found in the Reviewer's Guide for IIS 4. This document can be found on the TechNet CD-ROM or online via the IIS Web area (**www. microsoft.com/ntserver/web/**).

 A useful white paper from Microsoft is the "Internet Information Server Security Overview." This white paper is available from the IIS Web area (**www.microsoft.com/ntserver/web/**).

Virtual Directories And Virtual Servers

6

Terms you'll need to understand:
√ Virtual directory and site

√ Access permissions

√ Physical path

Techniques you'll need to master:
√ Creating and configuring virtual directories

√ Creating and configuring virtual servers

In this chapter, we show you how to configure virtual servers and virtual directories. However, we'll begin with some IIS basics that are necessary to understand before making use of additional IIS features.

Home Directory

An IIS directory is a location on an IIS server where you store Web files such as HTML (Hypertext Markup Language) pages and images. To understand the concept of virtual directories in an IIS environment, you must understand the concept of an IIS home directory. When you install IIS, the installation program creates a home directory for the WWW (the default is C:\InetPub\ Wwwroot) and FTP services (the default is C:\InetPub\Ftproot). By default, IIS routes the user connecting to your Web site to the WWW service's home directory.

For an intranet, the Web site's home directory is mapped to the site's server name. For example, if the server name is your_edge, you can reach the Web site's home directory by typing "**http://your_edge**" in your browser's URL text box.

For the Internet, the Web site's home directory is mapped to the site's domain name. For example, if the domain name is **www.yourcompany.com** and the Web site's default home page is in C:\InetPub\Wwwroot, you can reach the Web site's home page by typing "**www.yourcompany.com**" in your browser's URL text box.

WWW Service: Home Directory

To start the Microsoft Management Console, click Start|Programs|Windows NT Option Pack|Microsoft Internet Information Server|Internet Service Manager. Windows NT, in turn, starts the Microsoft Management Console1, as shown in Figure 6.1.

After MMC is launched, right-click on the site to be configured and select Properties. By using the Properties|Home Directory tab, you can change your site's home directory or the home directory's characteristics (see Figure 6.2). At IIS installation time, the installation program creates a default home directory: Wwwroot (the default path is C:\InetPub\Wwwroot).

You can change the home directory's location to one of the following:

➤ A directory located on the local computer (default)

➤ A directory (share) located on another computer

➤ A URL

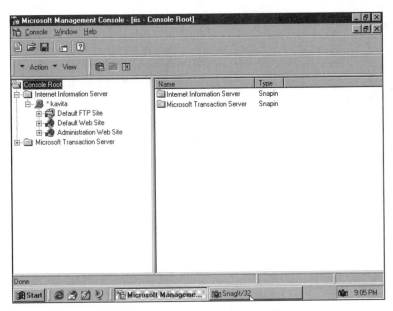

Figure 6.1   The Microsoft Management Console.

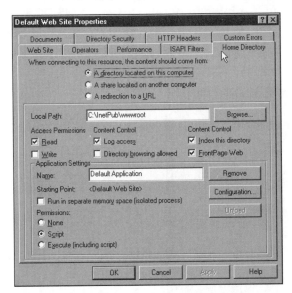

Figure 6.2   The Default Web Site Properties page's Home Directory tab.

For a local directory, specify the full path in the Local Path text box. For a network share, specify the Universal Naming Convention (UNC) and the name of the share (for example, \\Iis\Htmlfiles). For a redirection to a URL, specify the entire URL of the server to which you want to direct requests.

FTP Service: Home Directory

To change your site's home directory or the home directory's characteristics, use the Home Directory tab (see Figure 6.3). When you install IIS, the installation program creates a default home directory, Ftproot (the default path is C:\InetPub\Ftproot).

A user connecting to the home directory can see the context coming from one of the following:

➤ A directory located on this computer (default)

➤ A share located on another computer

In the Local Path text box, specify the root directory for the FTP service (the default is C:\InetPub\Ftproot). For a network share, specify the UNC with the name of the share.

In addition, you can choose the directory listing style—Unix or MS-DOS.

 The Unix directory listing style is recommended because many non-Windows client machines are not able to view an MS-DOS directory listing.

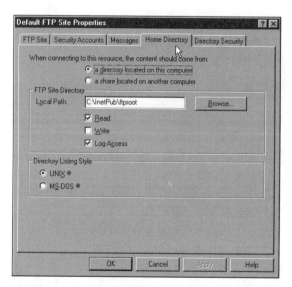

Figure 6.3 The Default FTP Site Properties page's Home Directory tab.

Virtual Directory

A virtual directory is a subdirectory of a URL that is mapped to a path that might not be in the home directory of the IIS server. The following sections outline the steps to create and delete virtual directories on your WWW and FTP server.

 The IIS 4 exam might contain simulations asking you to create a virtual directory. The simulation will present you with the MMC, and you must follow the steps below. Once you create the virtual directory, close the MMC using the FilelClose command.

Creating And Deleting A Virtual WWW Directory

To create a virtual WWW directory, follow these steps:

1. Click StartlProgramslWindows NT Option PacklMicrosoft Internet Information ServerlInternet Service Manager. Windows NT, in turn, starts the Microsoft Management Console.

2. Click Default Web Site, click Action, and then select NewlVirtual Directory. Microsoft Management Console, in turn, displays the New Virtual Directory Wizard (shown in Figure 6.4).

3. In the text box, type an alias for the virtual directory you want IIS to create. An *alias* is a short name for the directory that is easy to use and remember. To proceed, click Next.

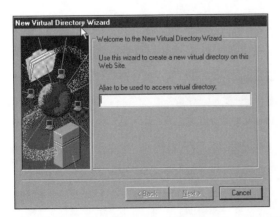

Figure 6.4   Creating a virtual Web directory with the New Virtual Directory Wizard.

4. The wizard, in turn, prompts you to display the physical path of the directory containing the content you want to publish, as shown in Figure 6.5. To specify the path, click Browse. To proceed, click Next.

5. The wizard, in turn, prompts you to choose the access permissions you want to set for the virtual directory, as shown in Figure 6.6.

6. Now choose one or more of the following options:

➤ **Allow Read Access (default)** A user connecting to the Web site has only Read access to the files in this virtual directory. The user does not have Script, Execute, and Write access to these files.

➤ **Allow Script Access (default)** A user can access scripts, such as Active Server Pages, in the virtual directory.

➤ **Allow Execute Access (Includes Script Access)** A user connecting to the Web site has both Script and Execute access to the files in

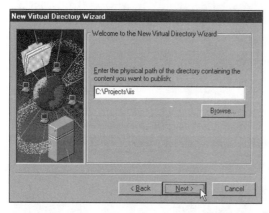

Figure 6.5   Specifying the virtual Web directory's physical path.

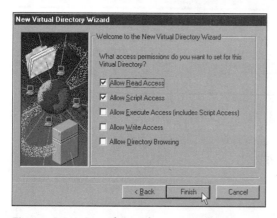

Figure 6.6   Specifying the access permissions for the virtual directory.

this virtual directory. That is, the user can execute the files in this virtual directory.

➤ **Allow Write Access** A user connecting to the Web site can write to the files in this virtual directory.

➤ **Allow Directory Browsing** A user connecting to the Web site can browse the files in this virtual directory.

Depending on your application requirements, click the appropriate options. To proceed, click Finish. The wizard, in turn, creates the virtual directory, as shown in Figure 6.7.

7. IIS denotes the virtual Web directory with a folder and a little globe at the bottom-right corner of the folder. Notice that IIS shows the directory's physical path mapped to the virtual directory.

To delete a virtual WWW directory, the process is pretty simple: Right-click the virtual directory name and select Delete from the pop-up menu.

Creating And Deleting A Virtual FTP Directory

To create a virtual FTP directory, follow these steps:

1. Click Start|Programs|Windows NT Option Pack|Microsoft Internet Information Server|Internet Service Manager. Windows NT, in turn, starts the Microsoft Management Console 1.

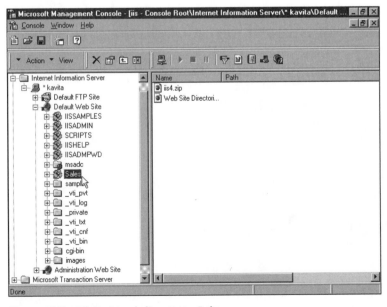

Figure 6.7   The virtual directory: Sales.

2. Click Default FTP Site, click Action, and then select New|Virtual Directory. Microsoft Management Console, in turn, displays the New Virtual Directory Wizard.

3. In the text box, type an alias for the virtual directory you want IIS to create. To proceed, click Next.

4. The wizard, in turn, prompts you to display the physical path of the directory containing the content you want to publish. To specify the path, click Browse. To proceed, click Next.

5. The wizard, in turn, prompts you to choose the access permissions you want to set for the virtual directory, as shown in Figure 6.8.

6. Now, choose one or both of the following options:

   ➤ **Allow Read Access (default)** A user connecting to the FTP site has only Read and Download access to the files in this virtual directory. The user can neither write to these files nor upload any files to this directory.

   ➤ **Allow Write Access** A user connecting to the FTP site has Write access to the files in this virtual directory. In addition, the user can upload files to this directory.

   Depending on your application requirements, click the appropriate options. To proceed, click Finish.

7. The wizard, in turn, creates the virtual directory, as shown in Figure 6.9.

8. IIS denotes the virtual FTP directory with a folder and a little globe at the bottom-right corner of the folder. Notice that IIS shows the directory's physical path mapped to the virtual directory.

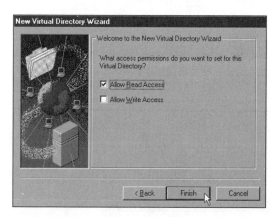

Figure 6.8 Specifying the access permissions for the virtual FTP directory.

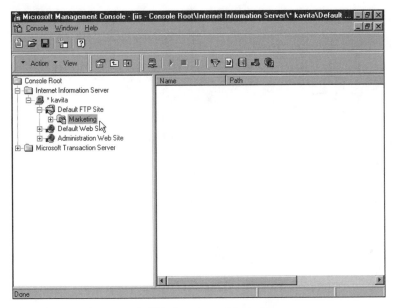

Figure 6.9   The virtual FTP directory: Marketing.

To delete a virtual FTP directory, right-click the virtual directory name and select Delete from the pop-up menu.

Virtual Directory Administration

Right-click the virtual directory and then select Properties from the pop-up menu. The Microsoft Management Console, in turn, displays the Sales Properties dialog box, as shown in Figure 6.10. Notice that the same tabs and configurable parameters are available for a virtual directory and a local directory.

At this point, you can configure two items: Virtual Directory and Directory Security. To learn more about configuring a directory's properties, refer to Chapter 4.

Virtual Server

You can host several Web and FTP sites on the same IIS server. At the time of installation, the IIS installation program creates a default Web and FTP site; you can create additional Web and FTP sites. Each such additional site is known as a *virtual server*.

It is important that you understand how to create a virtual site from MMC. Once you create a virtual site, be sure to start the service. Then, close MMC using the File|Close command.

Figure 6.10 Configuring the virtual directory's properties.

Creating And Deleting A Virtual Web Server

To create a virtual Web server, follow these steps:

1. Click Start|Programs|Windows NT Option Pack|Microsoft Internet Information Server|Internet Service Manager. Windows NT, in turn, starts the Microsoft Management Console.

2. Click Default Web Site, click Action, and then select New|Virtual Site. Microsoft Management Console, in turn, displays the New Web Site Wizard, as shown in Figure 6.11.

Figure 6.11 Creating a virtual Web site with the New Web Site Wizard.

3. In the text box, type a name for the virtual Web site you want IIS to create. This name is simply used to help identify it in the MMC. To proceed, click Next.

4. The wizard, in turn, prompts you to specify the IP address and TCP/IP port, as shown in Figure 6.12. If you are using multiple IP addresses, select the alternate address from the list. If you want to use the same IP address but different ports, define an alternate port. If you want to use host headers so multiple sites are hosted by the same IP address and port, select All Unassigned and 80. To proceed, click Next.

5. The wizard, in turn, prompts you to specify the path for the new Web site's home directory, as shown in Figure 6.13. Note that, by default, anonymous access is allowed to this Web site. To proceed, click Next.

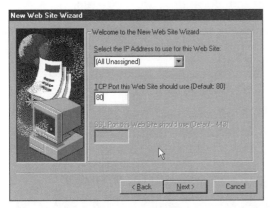

Figure 6.12   Specifying the IP address and TCP port.

Figure 6.13   Specifying the path for the new site's home directory.

6. The wizard, in turn, prompts you to choose the access permissions you want to set for the virtual Web site.

Now choose one or more of the following options:

➤ **Allow Read Access (default)** A user connecting to the Web site has only Read access to the directories and files in this virtual Web site.

➤ **Allow Script Access (default)** A user can access scripts, such as Active Server Pages, in the virtual site.

➤ **Allow Execute Access (Includes Script Access)** A user connecting to the Web site has the ability to interact with scripts and applications in this virtual Web site.

➤ **Allow Write Access** A user connecting to the Web site has Write access to the directories and files in this virtual Web site.

➤ **Allow Directory Browsing** A user connecting to the Web site can browse the directories in this virtual Web site.

7. Depending on your application requirements, click the appropriate options. To proceed, click Finish. The wizard, in turn, creates the virtual Web site, as shown in Figure 6.14.

8. To enable host headers, open the Web Site Properties for the site that is to use a host header name. Be sure All Unassigned is selected as the IP

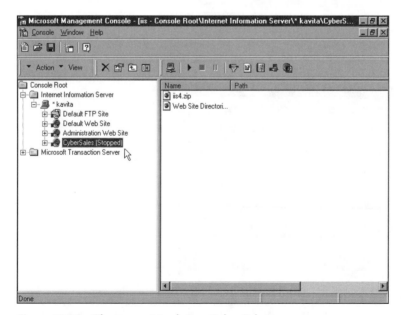

Figure 6.14 The new virtual site: CyberSales.

Address, and then click Advanced. Select the identity from Multiple Identities For This Web Site and click Edit. Type in a host header name (this can be a domain name or a NetBIOS [Network Basic Input/ Output System] name). You can add additional host headers for this site by clicking the Add button. Once a host header is defined, it must be registered with the correct name resolution server (DNS for domain name and WINS for NetBIOS name host headers).

 Notice that the virtual Web site's default state is Stopped. To start this server, right-click on the Web server and then select Start from the pop-up menu, or click the Start button from the toolbar.

To delete a virtual Web server, right-click on the server name and select Delete from the pop-up menu.

Creating And Deleting A Virtual FTP Server

To create a virtual FTP server:

1. Click Start|Programs|Windows NT Option Pack|Microsoft Internet Information Server|Internet Service Manager. Windows NT, in turn, starts the Microsoft Management Console.

2. Click Default FTP Site, click Action, and then select New|Virtual Site. Microsoft Management Console, in turn, displays the New Virtual Site Wizard, as shown in Figure 6.15.

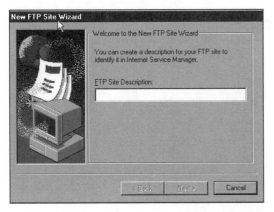

Figure 6.15   Creating a virtual FTP site with the New FTP Site Wizard.

3. In the text box, type a name for the virtual FTP site you want IIS to create. This name is simply used to help identify it in MMC. To proceed, click Next.

4. The wizard, in turn, prompts you to specify the IP address and TCP/IP port. To host more than one FTP site on IIS, each site must have its own IP address or port number. IIS simulates the environment for the users to think each site corresponding to its IP address is hosted on a separate IIS server. To proceed with the wizard, click Next.

5. The wizard, in turn, prompts you to specify the path for the new FTP site's home directory. To proceed, click Next.

6. The wizard prompts you to choose the access permissions you want to set for the virtual FTP site, as shown in Figure 6.16.

7. Now, choose one or both of the following options:

➤ **Allow Read Access (default)** A user connecting to the FTP site has only Read and Download access to the files in this virtual site. The user can neither write nor upload any files to this site.

➤ **Allow Write Access** A user connecting to the FTP site has Write access to the files in this virtual site. In addition, the user can upload files to this site.

8. Depending on your application requirements, click the appropriate options. To proceed, click Finish. The wizard, in turn, creates the virtual FTP server, as shown in Figure 6.17. Notice that the virtual FTP server's default state is Stopped. To start this server, right-click the FTP server and then select Start from the pop-up menu.

Figure 6.16 Specifying the access permissions for the virtual FTP site.

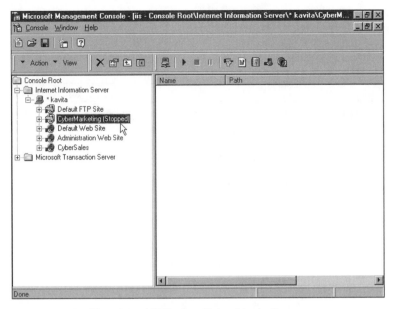

Figure 6.17   The virtual FTP site: CyberMarketing.

To delete a virtual FTP server, right-click the server name and select Delete from the pop-up menu.

Virtual Server Administration

To administer a virtual server, right-click the virtual server and then select Properties from the pop-up menu. The Microsoft Management Console, in turn, displays the Properties dialog box. Notice that the same tabs and configurable parameters are available for a virtual server and a local server.

Practice Questions

Question 1

> You are the Webmaster in an organization. You have set the default document for your Web site to INDEX.ASP. However, whenever a user tries reaching your Web site, he gets the error message "Directory listing not allowed." Which of the following could be causing this problem?
>
> ○ a. INDEX.ASP needs to be added to the Default Documents list.
>
> ○ b. You cannot use an ASP page as your Web site's default page.
>
> ○ c. Execute rights need to be allowed on the directory where the DEFAULT.ASP page physically resides on your Web server.
>
> ○ d. The directory listing style needs to be set to Unix.

Answer a is correct. It doesn't matter if you use an HTML or ASP page as your Web server's default page as long as the page is in the Default Documents list. Therefore, answer b is incorrect. By default, script rights are enabled on the directory; execute rights are not required to run Active Server Pages. Therefore, answer c is incorrect. Setting the directory listing style to MS-DOS or Unix is not relevant. Therefore, answer d is incorrect.

Question 2

> You have two virtual Web servers for two departments in your company. The first Web site, **http://mainoffice.com**, has a GLOBAL.ASP file that stores the session variables. The user must log in with this site before moving to the second Web site, **http://dept-b.com**. You've been using this Web application for more than six months on IIS 3 and it has been working fine. Now, you port your application to IIS 4 and you find that the application does not work. What is the reason?
>
> ○ a. IIS 4 did not install properly. You must reinstall it.
>
> ○ b. You must install Active Server Pages on IIS 4 before you can get any ASP application to work with IIS 4.
>
> ○ c. IIS 4 provides an individual application scope for each application. You must have separate GLOBAL.ASP files for each Web site.
>
> ○ d. Active Server Pages must be ported for IIS 4.

Answer c is correct. One of the main differences between IIS 3 and IIS 4 is the application scope. In IIS 3, the application's scope covers the entire server; therein lies the "trick." That is, if you had a couple of Web sites running under IIS 3, both would share the same application scope. In IIS 4, you can have more than one application within each Web site and several application scopes on the entire server. There's no need to reinstall IIS 4. By default, the IIS installation program installs ASP when you install IIS 4. Porting ASP to IIS 4 is invalid because IIS 4 already supports ASP. Therefore, answers a, b, and d are incorrect.

Question 3

Which of the following do you need before creating a virtual directory?

○ a. A physical path

○ b. Read and Write permissions

○ c. Gopher

○ d. An IP address

Answer a is correct. When creating the virtual directory, you need to provide the directory's physical path. If you do not grant the Read and Write permissions for the directory, the client browser may not be able to browse the virtual directory; however, you can grant these permissions at a later stage. IIS 4 does not support Gopher. Also, you need an IP address for a virtual server, not for a virtual directory. Therefore, answers b, c, and d are incorrect.

Question 4

Unless you use host headers for each virtual server you create on IIS, you must have a unique IP address or a unique port number.

○ a. True

○ b. False

Answer a is correct. This is a true statement. You can host more than one Web site on IIS; however, each site must have its own IP address or port number for the users connecting to that site. Through the use of host headers, IIS simulates the environment for the users to think each site corresponding to its IP address is hosted on a separate IIS server. Therefore, answer b is incorrect.

Question 5

For an intranet, if the server name is "marketing", which of the following URLs would you type in the browser's URL text box to reach the Web site's home directory?

○ a. **http://localhost/marketing**

○ b. **http://marketing**

○ c. **http://www.iis.com/marketing**

○ d. None of the above

Answer b is correct. For an intranet, the Web site's home directory is mapped to the server name. **http://marketing** represents a direct mapping between the Web site's home directory and the server name. None of the other options represents this direct mapping. Therefore, answers a, c, and d are incorrect.

Question 6

You must manually start a virtual Web or FTP server.

○ a. True

○ b. False

Answer a is correct. This is a true statement. When you first create a virtual Web or FTP server, the server's default state is Stopped. Therefore, answer b is incorrect.

Question 7

You must manually start a virtual Web or FTP directory.

○ a. True

○ b. False

Answer b is correct. This is a false statement. A virtual directory is a part of an existing WWW or FTP service. Only services, not directories, need to be started. Therefore, answer a is incorrect.

Question 8

> You are the administrator of a Web site whose home directory is f:\inetpub\website. You have files that you would like to make available from this Web site, but they reside in the c:\otherfiles directory. Which of the following actions could you take to add these files to your Web site? [Check all correct answers]
>
> ❑ a. Change the home directory for the default Web site to c:\otherfiles.
>
> ❑ b. Add a virtual directory for d:\webpub
>
> ❑ c. Create a virtual server and assign it the home directory of d:\webpub
>
> ❑ d. Move all of the files and associated subdirectories from the c:\otherfiles directory to an "otherfiles" directory in the f:\inetpub\website directory.

Answers a, b, c, and d are correct. Changing the home directory to c:\otherfiles would be an efficient solution as long as there are no files currently being accessed from the existing home directory (f:\inetpub\website). Therefore, answer a is correct. Adding a virtual directory for d:\webpub is probably the best solution, because users can simply access the existing home directory as usual, and in the URL, the new directory will seem as if it is simply a subdirectory in that home directory. Therefore, answer b is correct. As long as you are using host headers or are willing to use a different IP address or port number for the new Web site, creating a virtual server would work as well. Therefore, answer c is correct. Moving the necessary files from the c:\otherfiles directory to a subdirectory in the Web site is a simple solution, and would generally provide the requested access to these files. Therefore, answer d is correct.

Question 9

> When creating a virtual FTP server, which of the following sets of access permissions can you grant?
>
> ○ a. Read, Write, Script
>
> ○ b. Read, Write, Script, Execute
>
> ○ c. Read, Write
>
> ○ d. Read, Write, Script, Execute, Directory Browsing

Answer c is correct. You can only read (download) and write (upload) files to an FTP server. The other options are not applicable to an FTP server. This is because an FTP server's primary function is to enable file download and upload. Therefore, answers a, b, and d are incorrect.

Need To Know More?

 Stewart, James Michael, and Ramesh Chandak: *MCSE Exam Prep IIS 4*. Certification Insider Press, Scottsdale, AZ, 1998. ISBN: 1-57610-267-X. Chapter 8 provides detailed coverage of creating virtual servers and directories.

 The 15 Seconds Web site has additional information on creating and using virtual directories at its site **www.15seconds.com/ Issue/970828.htm**. This article also discusses associated topics, such as creating, implementing, and accessing Web sites and applications from virtual directories and subdirectories.

Active Content

Terms you'll need to understand:

- √ Active Platform, Client, and Server
- √ ActiveX
- √ Server-side scripting
- √ Active Server Pages (ASP), Active Objects, and Active Components
- √ ASP scripts
- √ Common Gateway Interface (CGI)
- √ Internet Server Application Programming Interface (ISAPI)
- √ Server Side Includes (SSIs)
- √ Microsoft Script Debugger
- √ Open Database Connectivity (OBDC)
- √ Server extension
- √ Internet Database Connector (IDC)
- √ HTML Extension Template file (HTX)

Techniques you'll need to master:

- √ Programming with CGI
- √ Understanding when to use CGI programs
- √ Understanding when to use ISAPI filters
- √ Understanding when to use SSIs
- √ Designing ASP applications
- √ Debugging ASP applications

In this chapter, we explore ActiveX technology and offer a thorough examination of Active Server Pages (ASP), CGI applications, ISAPI applications, and Server Side Includes (SSIs). Finally, we discuss the steps involved in creating and maintaining an active Web application.

The Active Platform

The Microsoft Active Platform is the foundation for designing and developing Internet and intranet business solutions by using Microsoft tools and technologies. A three-tier client/server model, the Active Platform is an extensible component-based architecture. The biggest advantages of using the Active Platform are its ease of use and reduced learning curve. To design both the client and server components of your application, you can use the same set of tools with which you are already familiar. For a developer, this reduces your learning curve, thus helping you deliver business solutions quickly and efficiently. The Active Platform includes the following three core components:

➤ Active Client (or Desktop)

➤ ActiveX

➤ Active Server

Active Client

Internet Explorer is a good example of an Active Client. Internet Explorer includes built-in support for ActiveX technology and supports client-side scripting. That is, you can write Active scripts that execute on the client side by using scripting languages such as JScript, VBScript, and JavaScript. The scripts interact with HTML, Java applets, ActiveX controls, and so on, delivering information to the browser. The browser, in turn, displays the information to the end user.

ActiveX

ActiveX is not a programming language. In fact, ActiveX represents a suite of technologies you can use to deliver business solutions over the Internet and an intranet. ActiveX technology includes developing and integrating ActiveX controls, writing ActiveX scripts, and so on.

ActiveX Controls

ActiveX controls are stripped-down versions of OLE controls with their size and speed optimized for use over the Internet. Both ActiveX and OLE are based on the Microsoft COM technology. The basic premise of COM is that two objects can interact and communicate with each other over a network of heterogeneous systems, irrespective of the language and platform of their origin, as long as they are written to conform to the COM specification.

ActiveX Scripting

Microsoft develops and supports two scripting languages: JScript and VBScript. JScript is Microsoft's open implementation of JavaScript (Netscape's scripting language). Whereas JScript follows the C-style convention for writing scripts, VBScript is a subset of Microsoft's most popular programming language—Visual Basic. Either of these scripting languages can be used to manipulate ActiveX controls.

Active Server

IIS is an Active Server. An Active Server supports server-side scripting, better known as Active Server Pages (ASPs). Check out the Microsoft Web site and you'll notice the Microsoft server delivering client-side HTML by using Active Server Pages. Whereas an HTML file has the extension .HTML, an Active Server Page has the extension .ASP. To view ASP in action, visit the Microsoft Web site at **www.microsoft.com/default.asp**.

An ASP script executes on the server, taking advantage of the server's processing power and delivering client-side HTML. Just as you can use scripting languages such as VBScript and JScript with reusable objects such as ActiveX controls and Java applets, you can use the same scripting languages with the same objects in conjunction with the five core server objects and Active Server Components to build ASP scripts. You'll learn more about the five core server objects and Active Server Components in the section titled "Prepackaged Active Server Components" later in this chapter.

CGI

You may have seen Web pages on the Internet with guestbooks and various other forms. The most popular technology used for these forms has been CGI (Common Gateway Interface) programs, which are usually written in a programming language called Perl (Practical Extraction and Report Language).

 For a Perl script to execute on an IIS server, a Perl interpreter must be installed.

However, with the advent of Active technology, ASPs, ActiveX controls, and ISAPI filters are quickly displacing the use of CGI programs. One advantage of using the Active Platform instead of CGI scripts is the ease of use in creating ASP scripts. To create ASP scripts, you can use the same set of tools and programming or scripting languages with which you're already familiar. For example, if you're familiar with creating client-side HTML by using HTML, JScript, ActiveX controls, Java applets, and so on, you can create ASP scripts by using the same set of tools and technologies. In addition, ASP embeds well within regular HTML. Another advantage of using ASP over CGI is that you can use an Active Server Component to keep the HTTP connection alive with the database server. This helps improve your Web application's overall performance.

 A CGI application requires Execute permissions both at the Web server level and in its NTFS permissions.

ISAPI Filters

An ISAPI (Internet Server Application Programming Interface) filter is a DLL (dynamic link library) that a server calls when there are certain HTTP requests. For example, an ISAPI filter could be created and loaded. A Web page could then request authentication information from a user and use the ISAPI filter to authenticate the user.

To add an ISAPI filter to a Web site, open the Internet Service Manager via MMC (you could use the HTMLA as well). Right-click on the Web site, and choose Properties. Click on the ISAPI Filters tab, and click Add. MMC, in turn, displays the Filter Properties dialog box. Specify the filter's name in the Filter Name text box. In addition, specify the path and filename of the ISAPI filter in the Executable text box.

 Finally, verify that the directory the ISAPI filter is in includes Script access in IIS and NTFS Execute permissions. Also note that when new users are granted access to run the ISAPI application, the Web service must be stopped and restarted to reinitialize the ISAPI application.

Active Server Pages

Active Server Pages (ASPs) are Web pages that can contain both HTML and script commands. They are made possible by the ISAPI filter called ASP.DLL. The main difference between an ASP script (.asp file) and an HTML page (.html or .htm) is that an ASP script executes on the server, whereas an HTML file executes on the client.

The following code is a sample Active Server Page. Notice the code between the pair of **<%** and **%>** tags. This is how you define ASP code. The first pair of **<%** and **%>** tags defines an ASP subroutine (**HelloASP**). Also, notice how the **HelloASP** subroutine uses the Response object's **write** method. The second pair of **<%** and **%>** tags calls the **HelloASP** subroutine. Notice also how these ASP routines are enclosed within the pair of HTML tags (**<HTML>...</HTML>**):

```
<HTML>
<HEAD>
<TITLE>
Welcome to the IIS Exam Cram
</TITLE>
</HEAD>
<BODY>
<%                '=== ASP begins
Sub HelloASP()
   Dim ASPGreeting

   ASPGreeting = "Hello ASP"
   Response.write ASPGreeting
End Sub
%>                '=== ASP ends
<% Call HelloASP %>        '=== Calling the ASP subroutine
</BODY>
</HTML>
```

Active Server Objects

The following are the five core server objects that constitute the core functionality of ASP. These server objects contain methods and properties that you can configure to meet your application's requirements:

➤ **Application** To manage your Web application's information, use the Application object.

➤ **Request** To retrieve information from the browser for processing at the server, use the Request object.

➤ **Response** To transmit information from the server to the browser, use the Response object.

➤ **Server** To administer and manage your Web server, use the Server object.

➤ **Session** To manage and track individual user sessions in your Web application, use the Session object.

Listing 7.1 is an example of an ASP script that uses three of the five server objects—Session, Response, and Request—to process the information. The script uses the Request object to retrieve and store information from the client form into the Session object's variables. The Session object's variables in this example are **User_ID** and **Officer**. The variable **User_ID** stores the ID of the user logging into the system. The variable **Officer** stores the user type (for example, Officer, Manager, Administrator, and so on).

Next, the script checks whether the variable **User_ID** is empty. If this variable is empty, it redirects the user to the HTML file **NOACCESS.HTM** by using the Response object's **Redirect** method. If this variable is not empty, check the **Officer** variable's value. If the variable's value is Y, it displays the HTML file **OFFICER.HTM** by using the Response object's **Redirect** method. Otherwise, it displays the HTML file **MANAGER.HTM**.

 The **RUNAT=SERVER** option indicates that the script executes on the server.

Listing 7.1   An example of an ASP script.

```
<% @LANGUAGE="VBSCRIPT" RUNAT=SERVER %>
<% Session("User_ID") = Request.Form("User_Id") %>
<% Session("Officer") = Request.Form("user_type") %>
<%
If IsEmpty(Session("User_Id")) Then
    Response.Redirect "noaccess.htm"
Else
    If Session("Officer") = "Y" Then
        Response.Redirect "officer.htm"
    Else
        Response.Redirect "manager.htm"
    End If
End If
%>
```

Prepackaged Active Server Components

IIS also comes with a number of predefined Active Server Components. You can use these components to build your ASP applications quickly and efficiently. Some of the components are described in the following subsections.

Active Data Object (ADO)

The ADO is probably the most important and popular ASP component. By using the ADO, you can build data-driven dynamic Web applications. You can use the ADO to connect your Web site to back-end relational database management systems such as Microsoft Access, Microsoft SQL Server, Sybase SQL Server, and Oracle. When you use the ADO in an ASP, the script communicates the SQL request that the browser sent to the ADO. The ADO, in turn, communicates the query to the database. The database processes the query and returns the result to the browser via the ADO and ASP.

Content Rotator

The Web is not only today's medium of information, but also the future's. The widespread dissemination of information and the amount of traffic on the Web only makes it logical for businesses to flock to the Web to advertise their products and services. IIS comes with an Active Server Component called the Content Rotator. This component—as well as its properties, methods, and events—makes it very easy for you to handle and dynamically display advertisement banners or dynamic content in your Web site.

Browser Capabilities

Even though Internet Explorer's market share has increased over the past few years, there are a number of clients using Netscape Navigator. Although both browsers support the same basic set of technologies, a number of differences exist between the two browsers. For example, Netscape Navigator does not include built-in support for ActiveX controls and Microsoft ActiveX technology, in general. As a result, if a client using Netscape Navigator visits an ActiveX-enabled Web site, the client cannot really take advantage of the capabilities and features ActiveX technology offers. In some cases, this can even render a Web site useless. To resolve this type of problem, IIS comes with an Active Server Component called the Browser Capabilities component. By using this component, you can detect the type of browser the client is using. In addition, you can determine the browser's capabilities through an INI file and accordingly render HTML that the browser is capable of handling. For example, if the client browser does not support frames and tables, you can generate a simple HTML page that does not use the <FRAME>...</FRAME> and <TABLE>...</TABLE> tags.

Content Linking

Every site needs a navigation scheme. The Content Linking component makes it easy for you to design and develop a navigation scheme for your Web site so that users can access the information they need, with ease.

Page Counter

You may have noticed Web sites that display a page counter at the bottom of a site's home page. The page counter indicates the traffic the site generated since its inception. The Page Counter component helps you do exactly this. With this component, you can determine the amount of interest your site generates.

Permission Checker Component

To determine whether a user has access permission to a given file on the server, use the Permission Checker component. In addition to using the prepackaged components, you can write your own Active Server Components. To write your own Active Server Component, you can use any of the programming tools you're familiar with, including Visual Basic, Visual C++, and Visual InterDev.

Microsoft Script Debugger

When you install IIS, you can choose to install the Microsoft Script Debugger. You can use the Microsoft Script Debugger to debug your application scripts. Note, however, that the Microsoft Script Debugger works only with Internet Explorer; the debugger does not work with Netscape Navigator.

The debugger offers the following useful features:

➤ **Breakpoints** You can set breakpoints in your scripts. At the breakpoint, you can evaluate expressions or examine a variable's value.

➤ **Code Coloring** The debugger uses color codes to display the script. Color codes make it easy for you to read, understand, and differentiate the code.

➤ **Immediate Expression Evaluation** In the Immediate window, you can evaluate new code or an expression in the call stack's context.

➤ **Integrated Call Stack** The debugger combines the VBScript and JScript call stacks into a single, seamless, integrated call stack. The Call Stack window displays the active procedure call.

➤ **Scripting Language Independent** You can use the debugger to debug scripts that may include both scripting languages (JScript and VBScript).

➤ **Stepping Through Code** You can use the debugger to step into, over, and out of the procedures in a script. In addition, you can step from a VBScript procedure to a JScript procedure, and vice versa.

Server Side Includes

Server Side Includes (SSIs) are components of a Web page. They provide common elements to multiple pages. For example, a large Web site may include a section on all of its pages that includes a logo or a slogan. If the slogan changes and the company takes advantage of SSIs, it can simply make the change to the one SSI file rather than to every page on the Web site.

To add an SSI to a Web page, simply include a reference to the file with the following syntax:

```
<!-- #include virtual="/pathname/filename.ssi"-->
```

Open Database Connectivity

Open Database Connectivity (ODBC) is the industry standard for connecting your application to relational databases. The Internet Database Connector (IDC) that comes with IIS lets you connect IIS to 32-bit relational databases, including Microsoft SQL Server, Microsoft Access, Microsoft FoxPro, Sybase SQL Server, and dBASE. The IDC is a server extension—in fact, it's an ISAPI DLL (HTTPODBC.DLL). It's also a communication layer between IIS and the database. By using the IDC, you can build dynamic data-driven Web sites. Here's how the IDC mechanism works:

1. The browser issues a SQL request.

2. IIS routes the request to the IDC.

3. The IDC, in turn, routes the request to the database.

4. The database processes the request and returns the results to the browser via the IDC and IIS.

 The IDC file contains the SQL query the client browser wants the database server to execute.

Creating An IDC Application

To create an IDC application, perform the following steps:

1. Create the logical model of the database. To create the logical model, you can use tools such as LogicWorks ERWin/SQL.

2. Generate the physical model from the logical model. You can do so with tools such as ERWin/SQL.

3. Create the ODBC datasource that works with the database.

4. Create the IDC file. In addition to the SQL query, the IDC file includes user name, password, and DSN (Data Source Name) to connect to the database by using ODBC. The following is an example of an IDC file that uses the **INSERT** statement:

```
Datasource: StatusReport
Template: statinsrt.htx
SQLStatement: INSERT INTO STATREPORT(ApplicationName,
ApplicationVersion, StatusNature, StatusDescription,
ReportedBy) + VALUES('%ApplicationName%',
'%ApplicationVersion%', '%StatusNature%',
'%StatusDescription%', '%ReportedBy%')
```

STATINSRT.HTX is the template page that the IDC uses to display the results of executing the SQL query. The values from the form replace the variables within the %...% signs. Place the IDC file in the \Scripts directory on the server.

5. Create the Web form that the user will use to input the data. To create the form, you can use any Web development tools, such as Microsoft FrontPage. Use the following form action line of code to specify the IDC file and the associated action (that is, **POST**):

```
<form action="/Scripts/statinsrt.idc" method="POST">
```

6. Build the template page (.HTX) that the IDC uses to display the results of executing the SQL query. The HTX file includes information for formatting the data as HTML. The following is an example of an .HTX file:

```
<HTML>
<HEAD>
<TITLE>Status Report</TITLE>
</HEAD>

<BODY BGCOLOR="#FFFFFF" text="#008000">
<H1>Status Report</H1>

<HR>

<P>
Thank You, %ReportedBy%, for the status report.
</P>

</HR>

</BODY>
</HTML>
```

Practice Questions

Question 1

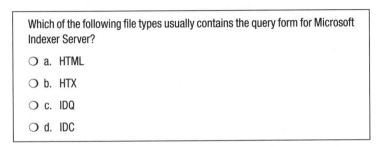

Which of the following file types usually contains the query form for Microsoft Indexer Server?

○ a. HTML

○ b. HTX

○ c. IDQ

○ d. IDC

Answer a is correct. And HTML document usually contains the Microsoft Index Server query form. An HTX file is an HTML extension file that is used to format a query's results. Therefore, answer b is incorrect. An IDQ file is a file with parameters that are used to define the scope and restrictions of a query. Therefore, answer c is incorrect. An IDC file is used to connect to a database. Therefore, answer d is incorrect.

Question 2

You are the administrator of a Web site that has 300 pages with similar elements. Which technology should you use to change these elements quickly if necessary?

○ a. SSI

○ b. ASP

○ c. CGI

○ d. SSL

Answer a is correct. A Server Side Include (SSI) provides a quick and easy way to make changes to common elements. Although an ASP can include a SSI, it is not the most appropriate answer in this case—and the trick to this question. Therefore, answer b is incorrect. CGI is a type of application used to create forms and other dynamic applications. Therefore, answer c is incorrect. SSL (Secure Socket Layer) is a type of encryption. Therefore, answer d is incorrect.

Question 3

> Which of the following sequences shows the order in which a Web-based database application works?
>
> ○ a. HTML file → IDC file → HTX file → database
>
> ○ b. HTML file → HTX file → database → IDC file
>
> ○ c. HTML file → IDC file → database → HTX file
>
> ○ d. IDC file → HTX file → database → HTML file

Answer c is correct. Typically, a user first enters a query via an HTML document. The HTML page will reference an IDC file, which will access the database via ODBC. Finally, the results are displayed via an HTX file. Because this order is not included in any of the other sequences mentioned, answers a, b, and d are incorrect.

Question 4

> You would like to design an HTML form that accepts data from the user, processes the data on IIS, and returns results to the browser. Choose the IIS extensions for this type of implementation. [Check all correct answers]
>
> ❏ a. JScript
>
> ❏ b. VBScript
>
> ❏ c. CGI
>
> ❏ d. ASP

The correct answers to this question are a, b, c, and d. Both JScript and VBScript are scripting languages you can use with ASP. ASP is an alternative to CGI, which is the standard Web mechanism for transmitting data between the client and server.

Question 5

> JavaScript is Microsoft's open implementation of JScript.
>
> ○ a. True
>
> ○ b. False

The correct answer to this question is b, False. It's the other way around. JScript is Microsoft's open implementation of JavaScript. Therefore, answer a is incorrect.

Question 6

> You can use the Microsoft Script Debugger with Netscape Navigator.
>
> ○ a. True
>
> ○ b. False

The correct answer to this question is b, False. Microsoft Script Debugger works only with Internet Explorer. Therefore, answer a is incorrect.

Question 7

> Which of the following components renders HTML based on the client browser?
>
> ○ a. Browser Capabilities component
>
> ○ b. Active Data Object
>
> ○ c. Permission Checker component
>
> ○ d. Page Counter component

The correct answer to this question is a. By using the Browser Capabilities component, you can detect the type of client browser and accordingly render HTML. None of the other three components has anything to do with detecting the type of client browser. Therefore, answers b, c, and d are incorrect.

Question 8

Which one of the following lines of code should you add to the first line in the following script so that the script runs on the server?

```
<SCRIPT LANGUAGE=VBScript>
<!--
Option Explicit

Dim validCreditCardNumber
Sub Submit_OnClick
    validCreditCardNumber = True
    Call CheckCreditCardNumber(CreditCardNumber
        Field.Value,
      "Please enter your credit card number.")
    If validCreditCardNumber then
        MsgBox "Thank you for your order"
    End if
End Sub
</SCRIPT>
```

○ a. **RUNAT=SERVER**

○ b. **EXECUTEAT=SERVER**

○ c. **PARSEAT=SERVER**

○ d. None of the above

The correct answer to this question is a. **RUNAT=SERVER** is the keyword. The others are not. Therefore, answers b, c, and d are incorrect.

Question 9

Which of the following browsers can be used with the Microsoft Script Debugger? [Check all correct answers]

❏ a. IE 4.01

❏ b. IE 5

❏ c. Netscape Navigator

Answers a and b are correct. Only Internet Explorer (IE) can be used with the Script Debugger. The Script Debugger is not compatible with Netscape Navigator. Therefore, answer c is incorrect.

Question 10

> Which of the following objects handles session management for an ASP server?
>
> ○ a. Application
>
> ○ b. Server
>
> ○ c. Session
>
> ○ d. Request
>
> ○ e. Response

The correct answer to this question is c. To store and track session variables and their values, use the Session object. To manage the Web application, use the Application object. To manage the Web server, use the Server object. To request information from the browser, use the Request object. To return information to the browser, use the Response object. For these reasons, answers a, b, d, and e are incorrect.

Question 11

> Netscape Navigator is an Active Client.
>
> ○ a. True
>
> ○ b. False

The correct answer to this question is b, False. Netscape Navigator does not include built-in support for Microsoft ActiveX technology. Therefore, answer a is incorrect.

Need To Know More?

 Hiller, Scot and Daniel Mezick: *Programming Active Server Pages*. Microsoft Press, Redmond, WA, 1997. ISBN: 1-57231-700-0. This book is a tutorial and guide for creating dynamic Web pages. The book shows how to use all the relevant tools and necessary Microsoft technologies required to build state-of-the-art Web sites. Sections are included that introduce IIS, Personal Web Server as a development tool, and ODBC basics for connecting to databases.

 Johnson, Scot, et al.: *Using Active Server Pages, Special Edition*. Que Publishing, Indianapolis, IN, 1997. ISBN: 0-78971-389-6. This authoritative guide is your all-in-one guide to creating dynamic Web sites for both business and personal use. Jam-packed with timesaving advice and hands-on techniques, this tutorial and reference is your complete resource for using Active Server Pages to their fullest potential.

 Walther, Stephen: *Active Server Pages 2 Unleashed*. Sams Publishing, Indianapolis, IN, 1999. ISBN: 0-67231-613-7. This book is one of the few advanced-level books for Active Server developers. It gives you an in-depth examination of creating commercial-quality dynamic Web sites. This book assumes a knowledge of at least one language and Web site administration, and it builds on that knowledge to enhance your ability to provide dynamic pages for the World Wide Web. The CD-ROM contains the author's source code as well as third-party tools.

 Microsoft TechNet. January, 1998. The technical notes for Microsoft Active Server Pages provide insight into its design and implementation. Also, perform a search using the following key words: "virtual directory," "virtual site," "access permissions," "ActiveX," "server-side scripting," and "ASP scripts."

 The Microsoft Web site at **www.microsoft.com/ntserver/web/deployment/planguide/WebAppDev.asp** provides a wealth of information regarding ASP, including white papers, FAQs, tips, tricks, and lots more.

Managing
And Tuning IIS

Terms you'll need to understand:

√ Microsoft Management Console (MMC)

√ Snap-in

√ Scope pane

√ Results pane

√ Rebar

√ Internet Service Manager—MMC snap-in

√ Internet Service Manager (ISM)—HTML, HTMLA

√ **http://localhost:port/iisadmin/**

√ Windows Scripting Host (WSH)

√ Metabase

√ Bandwidth throttling

√ HTTP keep-alives

Techniques you'll need to master:

√ Understanding MMC

√ Examining the available IIS administrative tools for local and remote management

√ Understanding WSH

√ Understanding the Metabase

√ Identifying Performance Monitor objects for IIS activities

√ Tuning IIS performance, bandwidth, traffic, connections, HTTP keep-alives, pipeline size, and hardware

In this chapter, we'll discuss the administration tools used to manage IIS. Actual use of these tools is detailed in other chapters, where topic-, purpose-, and command-specific items are discussed. This chapter concludes with tips on performance monitoring and tuning IIS.

The Microsoft Management Console

The most obvious change or improvement to IIS 4 is the introduction of the Microsoft Management Console (MMC), which is shown in Figure 8.1. MMC is a Windows-based tool that offers total management of all services and applications within a single utility. MMC is also Active Desktop-capable and will eventually be used to access management and control aspects of the entire Windows NT system. In fact, Windows 2000's control mechanisms center on snap-ins for MMC.

MMC itself offers no management capabilities, but instead offers a common environment where components called snap-ins reside. Snap-ins are product- or service-specific COM or DCOM object management utilities. When IIS 4 is installed, MMC is installed with the Internet Information Server snap-in. This snap-in gives you access to all the configuration and administration functions associated with IIS, which were accessed through the Internet Service Manager in previous versions of IIS.

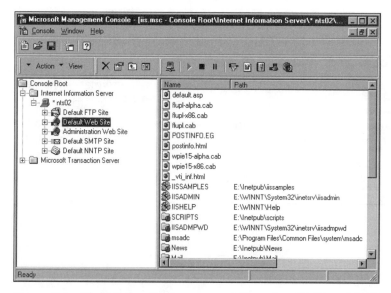

Figure 8.1   The Microsoft Management Console with IIS and MTS snap-ins.

If you have only IIS installed on your Windows NT Server system, you have only the IIS snap-in (and possibly the Transaction Server snap-in if it was selected for installation). Therefore, you don't have many configuration options for MMC. However, the MMC utility itself was designed to be a customizable interface. Most of the customization features center on adding and removing snap-ins to create a set of commonly used tools. Once MMC is configured, the state of the utility can be saved in a settings file with an .MSC extension. An MMC console configuration is stored using the Console|Save Console As command. An MSC file can be loaded back into MMC with the Console|Open command.

Snap-ins are added to MMC using the Console|Add/Remove Snap-In command from the menu bar. This reveals the Snap-In Manager, where installed snap-ins can be removed or new snap-ins added. The extent of control of MMC is only to create new windows (where MSC layouts are displayed) and to add or remove snap-ins. All other functions are provided for through the snap-in itself, and those functions are dependent on the service, application, or protocol the snap-in is intended to administer. Thus, MMC offers a standardized administrative tool interface that is easy to use.

An MMC console is divided into two panes (refer to Figure 8.1). The left pane, known as the scope pane, displays the namespace tree where all items, called nodes, to be managed are listed. Each node is an object that can be managed through MMC by means of an installed snap-in. The right pane, known as the results pane, displays the contents of the selected node. Most objects are managed by selecting Properties from a pop-up menu. MMC also has three command bars: the top bar is a typical menu bar, the middle bar is a typical button bar, and the bottom bar is a new bar known as the rebar. The rebar lists node- and object-specific commands. Each time a new object is selected, the command selections in the rebar change.

IIS Administrative Tools

Earlier versions of IIS were managed through the Internet Service Manager (ISM) or through an HTML interface. In IIS 4 the HTML interface still exists, but the previous standalone utility of the ISM has been transformed into an MMC snap-in. Also, with the help of the Windows Scripting Host (WSH), some administration features are available from the command line. These three methods are discussed in the following sections.

Internet Service Manager—MMC Snap-In

The Internet Service Manager MMC (ISM-MMC) snap-in is the primary means by which IIS is configured locally. ISM-MMC is accessed through the

Start menu (Start|Programs|Windows NT 4 Option Pack|Microsoft Internet Information Server|Internet Service Manager). This brings up the MMC with the default MSC file (or the previously saved MSC file if it has already been accessed) for IIS.

The ISM snap-in gives access to all computers hosting IIS services within the local network. As shown in Figure 8.1, the sample installation exists only on a single server named "nts02," where all the FTP, Web, SMTP, and NNTP sites are hosted.

The IIS snap-in also modifies the rebar to offer quick access to five standard Windows NT administration tools, which are commonly used in relation to IIS. These are the Key Manager, User Manager For Domains, Server Manager, Event Viewer, and Performance Monitor. These five tools are accessed using the five buttons located at the far right on the rebar.

 If you need to administer IIS 4 remotely and there is a firewall between you and the IIS server, the firewall must allow RPC (Remote Procedure Call) traffic through to the server. IIS listens to this port for remote administration requests.

Internet Service Manager (ISM)—HTML

The HTML Administration (HTMLA) feature gives administrators remote access to the IIS server as a whole or to limited portions of IIS, such as a single hosted Web site (see Figure 8.2). The ISM HTML allows management to be performed from any Internet/intranet-accessible client. Through the remote Administration interface, you can perform most of the same functions you can through the locally accessed ISM snap-in. These include managing logging, adjusting performance, altering server properties (including stopping and re-starting individual sites), creating new virtual directories, managing access properties, altering security, and customizing HTTP headers and error messages. Basically, the only functions that can't be managed remotely with HTMLA are certificate mapping and starting and stopping the services.

HTMLA can be accessed locally through the URL **http://localhost:port/ iisadmin/**. However, there are a few important items to take note of in regard to this URL. By default, HTMLA is accessible only on the same server that hosts IIS itself. In fact, you must use either "localhost" or "127.0.0.1" to access the Administration site. Using the correct IP address for the site won't grant access. This means that HTMLA cannot be accessed for remote administration until you enable this feature specifically. HTMLA is configured this way to provide the highest possible level of security around administrative access.

Figure 8.2   The Internet Service Manager HTML viewed through Internet Explorer 4.

Remote access can be enabled by HTMLA in the same way as granting or restricting access to any other Web site—on the Directory Security tab of the Properties dialog box of the Administrative Web site, using the ISM snap-in of MMC. The following are the steps required to grant access to HTMLA:

1. Launch MMC with the ISM snap-in (Start|Programs|Windows NT 4 Option Pack|Microsoft Internet Information Server|Internet Service Manager).

2. Scroll down in the scope pane to reveal the Administration Web Site node, and then select the Administration Web site.

3. Select Properties from the Action pull-down menu of the rebar.

4. Select the Directory Security tab.

5. Click the Edit button under the IP Address And Domain Name Restrictions area.

6. Notice that on the IP Address And Domain Name Restrictions dialog box, all access is denied except for 127.0.0.1 (localhost). To enable access to HTMLA from other workstations or clients, either add an exception or change the default action to Grant Access.

If you change the default action to Grant Access, you should go to the \Winnt\System32\Inetsrv\Iisadmin folder and change its user/group NTFS access permissions. This is the default installation location of the Web-based administration tools. By default, this directory is set to grant Full Control to Administrators and Change to Everyone. To minimize security risks, you may want to give Change Access only to Administrators.

Another important item to note about the iisadmin folder is the use of a port address. When IIS is installed, a random port is selected and used to gain access to the Web-based administration tools. To determine which port is selected or to change the port to your own preference, go to the Web Site tab on the Administration Web site's Properties dialog box. The TCP Port field under Web Site Identification is where this value is set.

So, if you enable remote access and determine the access port, the URL could be this: www.mydomain.com:2831/iisadmin.

 To administer IIS through a firewall using HTMLA, remember that you must open the Administration Web Site port number on the firewall.

Windows Scripting Host

The Windows Scripting Host (WSH) is a language-independent, shell-based host that adds a wide range of scripting capabilities to Windows NT. WSH is installed as part of the Option Pack when IIS 4 is installed.

The version of WSH included in the Option Pack adds scripting support for VBScript and JScript, as well as maintaining compatibility with MS-DOS command scripts. WSH is based on the ActiveX scripting engine, which may encourage third-party vendors to develop add-in engines for other common Web/Internet scripting languages, such as Perl, TCL, REXX, and Python.

WSH can be used directly on the Windows desktop (WSCRIPT.EXE) or via a command console (CSCRIPT.EXE). Therefore, scripts can be executed without need of embedding them in an HTML document. This greatly expands the versatility of Windows NT-hosted Web activity by enabling both local and remote execution of scripts.

The most significant benefit from WSH for IIS administrators is the ability to write administration scripts that can be launched locally or remotely. For example, if you need to convert several Web sites to use a .COM rather than an

.ORG extension, a script can be written and run to do this conversion on all of your sites at once.

IIS Metabase

Due to the nature of the services hosted by IIS, the Registry does not serve as an efficient storage device for most of the configuration parameters used by IIS. Instead, a high-speed, memory-resident, hierarchical system known as the Metabase is used. The Metabase is not a replacement for the Registry; in fact, it does not contain or duplicate Registry information. The Metabase holds only data that is key to IIS administration. Here are some examples:

➤ FTP and Web site properties

➤ Logging properties

➤ FTP and HTTP service-specific properties

➤ Directory and virtual directory configurations

➤ File properties

➤ Filter configurations

➤ SSL properties

➤ MIME mappings

The Metabase is stored in the \Winnt\System32\Inetsrv directory. Each change is recorded in the METABASE.BIN file, but IIS uses the version stored in active memory. When the configuration information for a server is backed up through the MMC (using the Action|Backup/Restore Configuration command), the backup files are stored in \Winnt\System32\inetsrv\MetaBack as MD0 files. These files can only be altered using the standard IIS administration tools or edited directly using the Metabase Editor (metaedit.exe) that is included with the Windows NT Server Resource Kit.

Monitoring IIS Performance

The activity of IIS and its hosted services can be monitored through two tools native to Windows NT—namely Performance Monitor and the Event Viewer.

This book assumes you already have working knowledge of these tools. If not, please refer to *MCSE NT Server 4 Exam Cram* (1-57610-190-8) or *MCSE NT Workstation 4 Exam Cram* (1-57610-193-2), both published by Certification Insider Press.

IIS installs many objects and counters that can be monitored with the Performance Monitor. Here's a list of the objects added by IIS:

➤ **Internet Information Services Global** This object is used to measure performance for IIS as a whole, including request activity, bandwidth, cache activity, and object access.

➤ **Web Service** This object is used to measure Web service as a whole or Web site-specific performance, including request activity, bandwidth, throughput, CGI requests and activity, errors, connections, and users.

➤ **FTP Service** This object is used to measure FTP service as a whole or FTP site-specific performance, including request activity, throughput, connections, users, and logon activity.

➤ **Active Server Pages** This object is used to measure overall ASP performance, including errors, requests, sessions, transactions, and caching.

Other Option Pack services or IIS add-on applications add objects to Performance Monitor to broaden the scope of available monitoring points. These include the following:

➤ **Index Server** Content Index, Content Index Filter, HTTP Content Index objects

➤ **NNTP Service** NNTP Command and NTTP Server objects

➤ **SMTP Service** SMTP Server object

The Event Viewer is where many IIS events are logged with Windows NT (a separate and distinct issue from IIS's own internal logging; see Chapter 10). You should check the system and application logs for IIS-related events. This includes service starts and stops, errors encountered on bootup, and the normal reporting of successful completion of administrative tasks.

Performance Tuning IIS

If your IIS-hosted site is not providing the performance you expect initially, you can tweak the performance of IIS through several built-in features. IIS is configured by default to adequately handle most standard sites, but fine-tuning Microsoft's defaults can often result in significant improvements. In the next few sections, we'll take a look at each of the IIS performance-tuning options available.

Restricting Bandwidth

By default, IIS attempts to use all the available bandwidth made available to the server for network or Internet connections. You may find that allowing IIS to allocate bandwidth use as it sees fit can cause non-IIS services to function poorly or to stifle one Web site in favor of another.

Bandwidth throttling can be enabled on a server (computer) level or on a service (site) level. Server- or computer-level throttling is configured on the Properties dialog box of that computer (see Figure 8.3). This dialog is accessed through MMC by selecting the computer/server in the scope pane and then selecting the Action|Properties command. Marking the Enable Bandwidth Throttling option limits the total bandwidth used by all IIS sites to the kilobytes per second defined in the associated field. The default value is 1,024.

Individual service or site throttling is enabled on the Performance tab of the Properties dialog box of each site (see Figure 8.4). Once again, marking the Enable Bandwidth Throttling option limits the total bandwidth used by all IIS sites to the kilobytes per second defined in the associated field. However, defining a value for bandwidth throttling for a specific Web site overrides any setting made at the server/computer level for that site. The server/computer throttling setting will still apply to all other sites.

Traffic Estimation

By estimating the traffic you expect within a standard 24-hour period, you can set the memory management preferences to match. Here are your options:

➤ Fewer than 10,000

➤ Fewer than 100,000

➤ More than 100,000

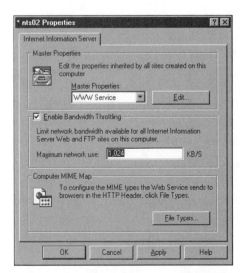

Figure 8.3   The Properties dialog box of the server or computer.

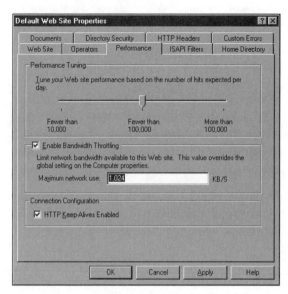

Figure 8.4   A Web site's Properties dialog box with the Performance tab selected.

These are broad settings for low-, moderate-, and high-traffic sites. This is enabled on a site-by-site basis on the Performance tab of a Web site's Properties dialog box (refer to Figure 8.4). This setting actually alters the way the server manages memory. If you set this slide bar to the selection that matches the closest to the reality of your traffic, your users will experience the highest level of performance.

Connection Management

By default, each Web site hosted by IIS can accept an unlimited number of simultaneous connections, whereas FTP sites are set to a limit of 100,000 connections. However, both these settings are unrealistic. Just compare that to the new record set by the RS/6000 IBM Unix mainframe machine that hosted the Nagano Games Official Web site. It had 103,429 hits in a single minute. If that's the record for the latest high-end mainframe, any Intel or Alpha machine you deploy IIS on won't be able to even get close.

Resource processing is divided among all of IIS's connections. If your site is flooded with resource requests, your server will be so tied up establishing communication pathways that it will never get around to sending the requested resource. However, limiting connections may produce numerous "Server Too Busy" errors. It's important to find a balance and limit the number of connections appropriately.

To limit the number of connections, right-click on the Web or FTP site and choose Properties. Choose the FTP site tab, choose the Limited To option, and type the number of connections, as appropriate, in the Connections field (see Figure 8.5).

You can also define the connection timeout parameter on this tab. This determines how long a connection is kept alive by IIS before it's terminated. For both Web and FTP, the default is 900 seconds (15 minutes). For FTP sites, a more reasonable value of 120 seconds (2 minutes) may improve performance by removing inactive users. For Web sites, a setting of 300 seconds (5 minutes) gives visitors time to read a lengthy document before making their next selection before their session is terminated. Remember, if fewer connections are being managed by IIS at any given moment, the performance of the server for all other sites and active connections is improved.

HTTP Keep-Alives

It has become a standard feature of modern browsers to request that the Web server keep a communication connection open across multiple requests. This request is known as an HTTP keep-alive. Keep-alives improve server performance by removing the overhead of tearing down and rebuilding connections between requests from the same browser. This means that a single document containing multiple items, such as graphics, can be sent over fewer connections instead of each over a separate connection. Keep-alives are enabled by default, which is the best performance setting for this item.

Figure 8.5   The Default FTP Site Properties dialog box with the FTP Site tab selected.

To disable HTTP keep-alives, right-click on the Web site and choose Properties. Choose the Performance tab, then uncheck the HTTP Keep-Alives Enabled option (refer to Figure 8.4).

Selecting A Pipeline

Your choice for the network connection to your intranet or the Internet can directly determine how much data you can transmit and how many simultaneous users you can support. By making an assumption that the average document or item on a Web site is 24K, you can see how large a connection you'll need based on the number of items transferred per second, as shown in Table 8.1. (Note that Table 8.1 reflects the calculation assuming four bits of overhead are required for each eight bits of data.)

The values in Table 8.1 are calculated using the following formula:

```
SPEED/(OBJECT*1.5)
```

where 1.5 represents the 12 bytes required to transmit 8 bytes of data (1MB=1024KB).

You can also make this decision depending on the number of simultaneous users you can support (as shown in Table 8.2). By selecting to deliver each document within 5 seconds, with an average document consisting of four 24K components plus overhead, you must deliver 144K in 5 seconds—about 29Kbps.

A final useful calculation for determining required bandwidth is the possible hits per day per connection type (as shown in Table 8.3). This value is determined by dividing the available bandwidth by 12 (8 bits data and 4 bits overhead), multiplying by seconds in a day (86,400), and then dividing by the average component size (24K).

Table 8.1	Connection types and the objects transmitted per second.
Connection Type	**Objects Transmitted Per Second**
28.8 to 56K modem	.8 to 1.6
56K Frame Relay	1.6
ISDN (64KB or 128KB)	1.8 or 3.6
T1 (1.54MB)	43.8
T3 (44.736MB)	1272.5
10MB Ethernet	284.4
100MB Ethernet	2844.4

Table 8.2 Connection types and the number of simultaneous users.

Connection Type	Simultaneous Users
28.8 to 56K modem	1 to 2
56K Frame Relay	2
ISDN (64KB or 128KB)	4 to 5
T1 (1.54MB)	52
T3 (44.736MB)	1,688
10MB Ethernet	353
100MB Ethernet	3,531

Table 8.3 Connection types and the number of hits per day.

Connection Type	Hits Per Day
28.8 to 56K modem	8,600 to 16,722
56K Frame Relay	16,722
ISDN (64KB or 128KB)	38,222
T1 (1.54MB)	470,897
T3 (44.736MB)	13,760,000
10MB Ethernet	3,057,777
100MB Ethernet	30,577,777

Hardware Bottlenecks

In addition to tuning IIS itself, you may also need to improve Windows NT Server's performance. IIS can only operate at its best if Windows NT gives it a reliable and responsive foundation. There are four main areas where Windows NT's performance is crucial—storage devices, CPU, memory, and network.

Storage device or hard drive bottlenecks occur when the physical drive and/or the drive's controller are unable to process the number of requests or the volume of reads and writes demanded. Typically, a slow or below-par storage system will also be accompanied by low CPU and network activity. Through the Performance Monitor, check the PhysicalDisk object's % Disk Time counter. If this consistently reads over 60 percent, you should improve your storage subsystem. Another useful counter is the Current Disk Queue Length. If this consistently reads 2 or greater (per drive), your storage system is too slow. You should consider adding additional drives and using Windows NT's software

RAID (Redundant Array of Inexpensive Disks) for disk striping or purchase a hardware RAID solution. However, you should inspect the memory before making a storage system change because you may have a memory bottleneck instead.

CPU bottlenecks occur when requests devour all available processing cycles. Typically, a CPU bottleneck is accompanied by low network utilization and low disk usage. If the Processor object's % Processor Time is consistently over 85 percent, you should consider improving the system's CPU. Another related counter is the System object's Processor Queue Length. If this consistently reads one more than the total number of CPUs, the CPU is a bottleneck. This can be remedied by replacing the current CPU with a faster chip or by adding additional CPUs.

Memory bottlenecks occur when there's too little physical RAM, which forces the system to rely more upon the pagefile. Because the pagefile is stored on a hard drive, it operates at 10 to 1,000 times slower than physical RAM. By comparing the Memory objects' Page Faults/sec counter to the Page Inputs/ sec counter, you can determine if your system needs more physical RAM. Page Faults/sec indicates the number of times per second a requested memory page is not immediately available and must be moved from another section of physical RAM or the pagefile. Page Inputs/sec indicates how many page faults must be read from disk. If the Page Inputs counter is consistently more than 20 percent of Page Faults, you may be adding significant strain on your disk subsystem. This would indicate a need for more physical RAM.

Network bottlenecks occur when the network adapter card itself cannot handle the level of traffic or when the network media is saturated with other traffic. IIS can easily flood a 10MB Ethernet card and a network with traffic on a moderately active site. You can determine the network load by inspecting the Network Segment object's % Network Utilization counter. If this consistently reads 85 percent or more, you should consider improving the speed of your network from 10MB to 100MB or adding additional network interfaces to this server. If your network card's driver adds the Network Interface to Performance Monitor, you should inspect each interface's % Utilization and Queue Length counters. If these counters read consistently more than 85 percent or one more than the total number of network interface cards (NICs), respectively, your network interface card is the bottleneck.

Practice Questions

Question 1

> Which of the following interfaces or utilities can be used to administer IIS? [Check all correct answers]
>
> ❑ a. Internet Service Manager MMC snap-in
>
> ❑ b. Internet Service Manager applet in the Control Panel
>
> ❑ c. Internet Service Manager Administrative wizard
>
> ❑ d. Internet Service Manager HTML via a Web browser

Answers a and d are correct. IIS can be administered through an MMC snap-in and HTMLA. Some IIS features are also available through a command prompt. IIS does not have an applet or an Administrative wizard. Therefore, answers b and c are incorrect.

Question 2

> The IIS MMC snap-in alters the rebar menu to grant you quick one-button access to which standard Windows NT Server utilities? [Check all correct answers]
>
> ❑ a. Performance Monitor
>
> ❑ b. Server Manager
>
> ❑ c. Registry Editor
>
> ❑ d. Event Viewer
>
> ❑ e. User Manager For Domains
>
> ❑ f. Network Monitor

Answers a, b, d, and e are correct. The IIS snap-in modifies the MMC rebar to give single-button access to Performance Monitor, Server Manager, Event Viewer, and User Manager For Domains. The Registry Editor and Network Monitor are not accessed via the MMC IIS snap-in rebar. Therefore, answers c and f are incorrect.

Question 3

> To administer your IIS server using the MMC through a firewall, what port needs to be open on the firewall?
>
> ○ a. 80
>
> ○ b. 21
>
> ○ c. The randomly generated port for HTMLA
>
> ○ d. The RPC port

Answer d is correct. You must configure your firewall to allow traffic on the RPC port used by IIS. Port 80 is the port used by the Web server itself and port 21 is the port used by the FTP server, both of which are not actually necessary when administering IIS using the MMC. Therefore, answers a and b are incorrect. The randomly generated port for the Administration Web site would have to be opened if you were going to administer your site using HTMLA. However, because you will be administering the IIS server using the MMC instead, this port number is not necessary.

Question 4

> The Action and View pull-down command lists that are customized by each snap-in are found on or in which standard MMC component or area?
>
> ○ a. The scope pane
>
> ○ b. Nodes
>
> ○ c. The rebar
>
> ○ d. The results pane

Answer c is correct. The rebar hosts the Action and View command lists. The scope pane, nodes, and results pane are components of MMC, but do not host these lists. Therefore, answers a, b, and d are incorrect.

Question 5

> If you need to make modifications to the certificate key mappings for a Web site, which administration utility can you use?
>
> ○ a. Internet Service Manager snap-in
>
> ○ b. Server Manager
>
> ○ c. Internet Service Manager HTML
>
> ○ d. Certificate Server

Answer a is correct. Only the locally accessible ISM snap-in can be used to manage certificate mappings. The Server Manager is not involved with certificate management. Therefore, answer b is incorrect. ISM HTML does not have the ability to manage certificate mappings. Therefore, answer c is incorrect. The Certificate Server is only used to issue certificates if you want to be a certificate authority—it is not used to map certificates to Web sites. Therefore, answer d is incorrect.

Question 6

> Immediately after installing IIS, you determine that the TCP port for the Administration Web site is 1234. You already know that the IP address of the site is 172.16.1.1. Which of the following URLs and access locations can be used to administer IIS?
>
> ○ a. Remote Web browser: **http://172.16.1.1:1234/iisadmin/**
>
> ○ b. Local Web browser: **http://172.16.1.1:1234/iisadmin/**
>
> ○ c. Local Web browser: **http://localhost/iisadmin/**
>
> ○ d. Local Web browser: **http://127.0.0.1:1234/iisadmin/**

Answer d is correct. Only Local Web browser: **http://127.0.0.1:1234/iisadmin/** will function without making other modifications to IIS's security. However, Local Web browser: **http://localhost:1234/iisadmin/** is another method, which is not listed as a possible solution. Remote Web browser: **http://172.16.1.1:1234/iisadmin/** will not function because access is limited to local access only, by default. Therefore, answer a is incorrect. Local Web browser: **http://172.16.1.1:1234/iisadmin/** will not function because the default security settings will only work with localhost or 127.0.0.1, not the IP address of the server. Therefore, answer b is incorrect. Local Web browser: **http://localhost/iisadmin/** will not function because the port is not included. Therefore, answer c is incorrect.

Question 7

> Where are the files that comprise the HTML Administration tools for remotely managing IIS stored by default?
>
> ○ a. \Inetpub\Iisadmin
>
> ○ b. \Winnt\System32\Inetsrv\Iisadmin
>
> ○ c. \Program Files\Inetput\Admin
>
> ○ d. \Inetpub\Adminroot

Answer b is correct. The IIS HTML Administration tool files are stored in \Winnt\System32\Inetsrv\Iisadmin, by default. The other listed folders are incorrect. Therefore, answers a, c, and d are incorrect.

Question 8

> If you need to monitor the throughput of a specific Web site, which Performance Monitor counter added by IIS should you select counters from?
>
> ○ a. Internet Information Services Global
>
> ○ b. Web Service
>
> ○ c. FTP Service
>
> ○ d. Active Server Pages

Answer b is correct. You should use the Web Service object because it enables you to select the instance of a single site. The IIS Global object does not have granular focus on sites. Therefore, answer a is incorrect. The FTP Service object is not for Web sites. Therefore, answer c is incorrect. The ASP object is not related to a specific site's throughput, but rather the overall performance of scripting. Therefore, answer d is incorrect.

Question 9

IIS is used to host four Web sites, named SITE1, SITE2, SITE3, and SITE4. You enable bandwidth throttling for the server/computer and set it to 4,096KB. SITE3 and SITE4 are the most popular sites hosted by your installation of IIS. You want to grant each of them twice the bandwidth of the other sites. Which modification should you perform?

○ a. Set server/computer-level bandwidth throttling to 8,192KB.

○ b. Set service/site-level bandwidth throttling to 2,046KB for SITE1 and SITE2.

○ c. Set service/site-level bandwidth throttling to 8,192KB for SITE3 and SITE4.

○ d. This cannot be done with IIS 4.

Answer c is correct. The correct modification is to set service/site-level bandwidth throttling to 8,192KB for SITE3 and SITE4. This will grant twice the bandwidth granted to SITE1 and SITE2 for both SITE3 and SITE4. Setting server/computer-level bandwidth throttling to 8,192KB will not specifically grant twice the bandwidth to SITE3 and SITE4; instead, it will just double the total bandwidth shared by all four sites. Therefore, answer a is incorrect. Setting service/site-level bandwidth throttling to 2,046KB for SITE1 and SITE2 will not double the available bandwidth to SITE3 and SITE4 but will only force SITE3 and SITE4 to compete for the 4,096KB server/computer throttle limit. Therefore, answer b is incorrect. Throttling by site and by computer is possible with IIS. Therefore, answer d is incorrect.

Question 10

Which of the following setting changes will improve the performance of a high-volume Web site?

○ a. Disable HTTP keep-alives

○ b. Set Web timeouts to 1,800 seconds

○ c. Set Performance Tuning to fewer than 10,000

○ d. Connect a T3 to IIS

Answer d is correct. Using a T3 line will improve the site's performance by allowing more hits per day, more simultaneous users, and more objects transmitted per second. Disabling keep-alives, increasing Web timeouts, and setting Performance Tuning to fewer than 10,000 will only degrade the performance of IIS. Therefore, answers a, b, and c are incorrect.

Need To Know More?

 Howell, Nelson, and Ben Forta: *Using Microsoft Internet Information Server 4, Special Edition*. Que Publishing, Indianapolis, IN, 1997. ISBN: 0-7897-1263-6. This book discusses at length MMC (Chapter 13), performance tuning (Chapters 15 and 16), and using Performance Monitor (Chapters 15 and 16).

 The best overview information for Internet Information Server 4 can be found in the Reviewer's Guide for IIS 4. This document can be found on the TechNet CD-ROM or online via the IIS Web area (**www.microsoft.com/ntserver/web/**).

 IIS's own online documentation, accessed through Start|Programs| Windows NT 4 Option Pack|Product Documentation, contains extensive detail on the subjects of IIS management, performance monitoring, and IIS tuning.

Indexing Web Sites With Index Server

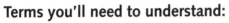

Terms you'll need to understand:

√ Index Server

√ Unicode

√ CATALOG.WCI

√ Corpus

√ Content filters

√ Word breaker

√ Normalizer

√ Noise word and noise word list (NOISE.ENU)

√ Index

√ Word list

√ Shadow index, persistent index

√ Catalog

√ Master index

√ .HTM (HTML) form document

√ .IDQ (Internet Data Query) file

√ .HTX (HTML Extension) template file

√ Merge

√ .IDA (Internet Data Administration) file

Techniques you'll need to master:

√ Learning the basic installation and configuration requirements

√ Understanding the indexing process

√ Understanding the parts and process of queries

√ Administering and maintaining Index Server

√ Maintaining security with Index Server

In this chapter, we'll discuss Index Server's content indexing and searching application. Index Server is designed to operate pretty much automatically without requiring administration after its initial configuration. This chapter will familiarize you with Index Server.

Index Server: Explored And Explained

As the sheer size and volume of information on the Internet, an intranet, or even on a single Web site grows, it becomes increasingly difficult to locate items of relevance. In response to this problem, Microsoft has developed Index Server, a solid indexing and content-searching application. Index Server, currently in its version 2 release, is an add-on product for IIS.

Using Index Server 2, you can index and search the full text and properties of documents hosted by your Web and FTP sites. In fact, Index Server 2 can index and search any document or file on any accessible drive in the UNC namespace of a Windows NT Server system hosting IIS or PWS (Peer Web Services on Windows NT Workstation or Personal Web Server on Windows 95 and 98). Out of the box, Index Server 2 supports full content indexing of the following file types:

➤ Text files (.TXT)

➤ HTML 3 and later documents (.HTM, .HTML)

➤ Microsoft Word 95 and Word 97 documents (.DOC)

➤ Microsoft Excel 95 and Excel 97 documents (.XLS)

➤ Microsoft PowerPoint 95 and PowerPoint 97 documents (.PPT)

All other file and document types are indexed by their file properties. You can add support for other Microsoft or third-party documents and file types, such as Adobe PDF or WordPerfect documents, by installing content filters. All OLE linked documents and elements within a document are indexed as well. For example, an Excel chart contained in a Word document is indexed and searchable.

Index Server 2 includes native support for indexing and querying in several languages, including Dutch, French, German, Italian, Japanese, Spanish, Swedish, U.K. English, and U.S. English. Index Server's multilingual support also applies to documents that contain several languages; Index Server maintains indexes in Unicode, and all queries are converted to Unicode before they are processed.

Index Server was designed with zero maintenance in mind; once it's installed and its query pages are configured, no further administration is required. Index Server automatically maintains its indexes, and all changes and additions to Web sites, FTP sites, and network/local directories monitored by Index Server are automatically incorporated into the master index.

Users interact with Index Server through the use of Web-based forms that help construct a query to be processed against the index of all monitored documents. Index Server comes with sample query forms to help you get up and running quickly. These forms can be used as templates in constructing your own query forms.

Understanding The Terminology

To understand how Index Server works, you need to become familiar with the Index Server concepts and terms described in the following list:

➤ **Corpus** The collection of all documents that Index Server is configured to monitor and index.

➤ **Content filters** The file format-specific add-ons that enable Index Server to index contents of non-Microsoft documents.

➤ **Word breaker** A software tool that takes the stream of characters emitted by a content filter and breaks it into words based on known language-dependent syntax and structure rules.

➤ **Normalizer** A software tool that standardizes words produced by a word breaker. Standardization includes removing capitalization, plurality, and punctuation. In addition, the normalizer identifies and removes noise words from the index.

➤ **Noise word list** A noise word is a language-specific word that Index Server ignores when creating the index. "The," "a," "of," and "you" are common English noise words. Index Server maintains a customizable list of noise words that can be used to fine-tune data stored in the index. The list of noise words is stored in \Winnt\System32\NOISE.ENU.

 Typically, it's a good idea to add your company name and other widely used words on your Web site to the noise word list.

➤ **Index** The database of all remaining words extracted from the corpus after it has been handled by the content filters, word breakers, normalizers, and noise word filters. Index Server uses two types of indexes. The first is a word list, which is the list of non-noise words and relevant properties extracted from a document. This list exists only in memory, so all word lists are lost if the server loses power; however, the next time Index Server is active, the word lists will be rebuilt. The second is a persistent index or shadow index, which is the combination of one or more word lists located on a file stored on the hard drive. The process of moving word lists into shadow indexes is known as a shadow merge. Because they are stored on the hard disk, shadow indexes can survive a power loss or a system reboot.

➤ **Catalog** Index Server moves all word lists into shadow indexes, and all shadow indexes into the catalog, or master index. The catalog is stored on the hard drive and used when a client queries the information.

Running Index Server

Index Server is installed through the Option Pack installation wizard; you select the languages for which to install support as a subcomponent of Index Server. During the installation process, you'll be prompted for the location in which to store the catalog directory. Because the CATALOG.WCI file created by Index Server in the catalog directory can be as large as 40 percent of the corpus (all indexed documents), you need to point the installation wizard to a location with significant free space.

 During installation, the following items are added:

➤ Sample query documents and script files are copied to \InetPub\Iissamples (**http://localhost/iissamples/**).

➤ Administration files are copied to \Winnt\System32\Inetsrv\Iisadmin\Isadmin (**http://localhost/iisadmin/isadmin/**).

➤ Documentation is copied to \Winnt\Help\Ix (**http://localhost/iishelp/ix**).

Once the installation is complete, Index Server starts indexing all the local and virtual default IIS directories. Index Server remains active in memory until the Content Index service is stopped or the machine is powered down. Index Server can continue to update indexes even when all IIS-hosted sites are stopped.

 Unlike with IIS 3, Index Server is launched when IIS is launched.

Each Web site hosted by Index Server can be configured so that it has its own unique master index; however, queries cannot span multiple indexes. If you divide your hosted Web sites into multiple Index Server master indexes, you limit the user's ability to search multiple Web sites with a single query.

The Index Server's indexing process allows the application to operate without an administrator. The indexing process begins when a new file is added to the corpus or an existing file is changed and these systems are recognized by the Content Index service scanning process. The Content Index service, or CISVC.EXE, scans the known corpus at a regular interval that's defined by the HKEY_LOCAL_MACHINE\SYSTEM\CurrentControlSet\Control\ ContentIndex\ForceNetPathScanInterval Registry entry. The default value for this interval is 120 seconds.

Index Server performs a full scan the first time it scans a directory. After that, a full scan is necessary only if a catastrophic failure damages the master index; only an incremental scan is necessary to index new or changed items. An administrator can force a full scan through the Index Server MMC snap-in or the HTML Administration tool.

Index Server Queries

A query or search is performed by means of a Web form. A form submits a query to Index Server using Structured Query Language (SQL). Index Server can use simple standard HTML forms or complex ASP or SQL forms. Here are some important points concerning the Index Server query language:

➤ It supports Boolean operators: **AND, OR,** and **NOT.**

➤ It supports the proximity operator: **NEAR.**

➤ It is case-insensitive.

➤ It supports wildcards: *frag**.

➤ It supports stem roots: *stem***.

➤ It ignores punctuation.

➤ It ignores noise words except those in phrases enclosed with double quotes.

➤ It supports free-text queries (phrases preceded by $).

➤ It supports properties searches (property operator value; for example, size < 1024).

Query controls can be entered manually or included as part of the Web form to simplify user interaction. The actual resolution of a query involves three files—form, IDQ, and HTX. The form can be a standard HTML file (.HTM, .HTML) or an ASP file (.ASP). The IDQ (Internet Data Query) file specifies how the query is to be processed. The HTX (HTML Extension) file is used to format query results for presentation back to the user.

HTML Form

As mentioned earlier, the HTML form functions as the interface for initiating queries, and it can be simple or complex. Several examples of HTML forms are included with Index Server. These forms are stored in \InetPub\Iissamples\ Issamples\. You can also design your own forms. Here are the key elements in a form:

```
<FORM ACTION="query.idq" METHOD="GET">
<INPUT TYPE="TEXT" NAME="CiRestriction" SIZE="60"
MAXLENGTH="100"  VALUE=" ">
<INPUT TYPE="SUBMIT" VALUE="Execute Query">
<INPUT TYPE="RESET" VALUE="Clear">
</FORM>
```

This form simply offers a field in which a query string can be typed. It also offers a Submit button that executes the query. Further details about constructing forms and SQL queries can be found in Index Server's online documentation.

The IDQ File

An Internet Data Query (IDQ) file defines a query's parameters, including the scope of the search (which portions of the corpus are to be searched), the restrictions of the search (format type, file properties, and so on), and how hits are displayed back to the user (number of records per page, highlighting hits, and so on). A basic IDQ file may contain the following data:

```
[Query]
CiCatalog=d:\
CiColumns=filename,size,rank,characterization,vpath,DocTitle,write
CiRestriction=%CiRestriction%
CiMaxRecordsInResultSet=150
CiMaxRecordsPerPage=10
CiScope=/
CiFlags=DEEP
CiTemplate=/iisamples/issamples/query.htx
CiSort=rank[d]
CiForceUseCi=true
```

The following items contained in an IDQ file each have a specific function, as described in the list:

➤ **[Query]** Identifies the following items as query restrictions.

➤ **CiCatalog=d:** Defines which master index to use.

➤ **CiColumns=filename,size,rank,characterization,vpath, DocTitle, write** Determines what types of information are returned for each document hit.

➤ **CiRestriction=%CiRestriction%** A variable placeholder for the query string from the HTML form.

➤ **CiMaxRecordsInResultSet=150** Sets the maximum number of returned results.

➤ **CiMaxRecordsPerPage=10** Sets the maximum number of returned results per page.

➤ **CiScope=/** Sets the level or virtual directory within the corpus to restrict the query.

➤ **CiFlags=DEEP** Sets the query to search all subfolders of the scope.

➤ **CiTemplate=/iisamples/issamples/query.htx** Defines the template file to use to format the results.

➤ **CiSort=rank[d]** Sets the results sort method (descending in this case).

The HTX File

An HTML Extension (HTX) file is used to format query results into HTML to be displayed in the user's Web browser. An HTX file defines the layout of each result record, the navigation among multiple returned pages, and the footer of the result's documents. The following code is a header definition from an HTX file:

```
<%if CiMatchedRecordCount eq 0%>
<H4>No documents matched the query "<%CiRestrictionHTML%>".</H4>
<%else%>
<H4>Documents <%CiFirstRecordNumber%> to <%CiLastRecordNumber%> of
<%if CiMatchedRecordCount eq CiMaxRecordsInResultSet%> the first
<%endif%>
<%CiMatchedRecordCount%> matching the query
<%CiRestrictionHTML%>".</H4>
<%endif%>
```

If the search phrase "network segment" is used, this code could return:

```
Documents 1 to 10 of the first 150 matching the query "network
segment".
```

Administering An Index

Index Server administration takes place through either the Index Server MMC snap-in or the HTML Administration interface.

The MMC snap-in (see Figure 9.1) offers you basic status information about each defined corpus. The status items include the size of the master index, the number of documents in the corpus, the number of memory-resident word lists, and the number of persistent indexes. Selecting the Directories item under a catalog allows you to view the virtual roots that comprise a particular corpus. Selecting the Properties item under a catalog allows you to view the indexed properties and which of these properties is stored in cache.

You can add new catalogs by selecting Index Server On Local Machine in the left pane and then issuing the command Action|New|Catalog. You'll be prompted for a name and a location in which to store the catalog. To associate the new catalog with a specific virtual server, you must create a Registry value for it under HKEY_LOCAL_MACHINE\CurrentControlSet\ContentIndex.

 To reduce the number of false hits in a query, divide the sets of virtual servers into separate catalogs. Keep in mind, though, that the ability to query the entire corpus at once would be lost because users can query only one catalog at a time.

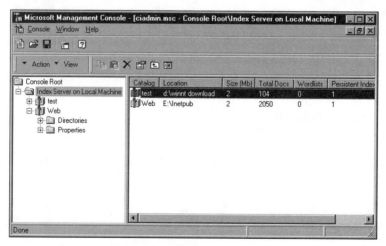

Figure 9.1   MMC with the Index Server snap-in.

You can add directories to control the scope of a corpus, with an option to include or exclude the added directory from the indexing process. New directories are added by selecting the Directories item below a catalog and then issuing the command Action|New|Directory. You'll be prompted for the path, an alias, a user account and password (if required) for access, and you'll be asked whether to include or exclude the directory from the corpus.

You can modify the global generation properties for all catalogs by selecting Index Server On Local Machine and issuing the command Action|Properties. The global generation options allow you to decide whether to filter files with unknown extensions, whether to generate characterizations (abstracts and summaries), and to establish the maximum size of the summaries in characters. These settings are also available on a catalog level; any changes made on the Generation tab of a catalog's Properties dialog override the global settings.

A catalog's Properties dialog is accessed by selecting a catalog and then issuing the Action|Properties command, and it also offers a Web tab that enables you to turn off automatic indexing of virtual roots based on a virtual server and to determine whether to track NNTP messages.

If you make a change to Index Server—such as changing the characterization or adding or removing a filter—you can force a rescan of the corpus on a per-directory basis. First, select Directories below a catalog and then select one of the listed directories from the right pane. Issue the Action|Rescan command and then choose Yes for a full rescan (choosing No results in an incremental rescan).

 You can force a merge of all word lists to shadow indexes to the master index on a per-catalog basis. Select the catalog and then issue the Action|Merge command from the rebar tools of the MMC. You can also decrease the MaxIndexes value within the Registry to reduce the maximum number of persistent connections.

The HTML Administration interface is mainly to be used as a remote status monitor and to force merges, and it offers a slightly different set of administration features. As shown in Figure 9.2, this interface offers four main controls or selections:

➤ Index Statistics

➤ Unfiltered Documents

➤ Virtual Root Data

➤ Merge Index

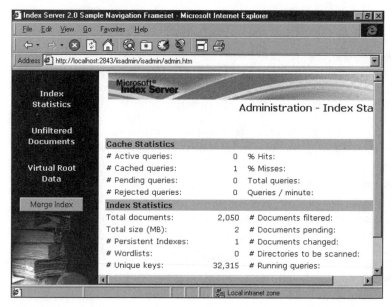

Figure 9.2 The HTML Administration interface for Index Server.

Index Statistics displays cache and index statistics, as well as the status of the indexing process. Unfiltered Documents lists information about unfiltered documents. Virtual Root Data allows you to set the type of scan to perform on a per-directory basis. Once changes to the scan type are submitted, the Merge Index button will instruct Index Server to rescan based on the settings made on the Virtual Root Data page.

Index Server Security

When Index Server is first installed, the location of the initial catalog is securely set up; Index Server defines the Access Control List (ACL) on the catalog directory and defines its contents so that access is restricted to the system and administrators. This prevents users from accessing the catalog directly or attempting to decipher a catalog's contents. If additional catalogs are created elsewhere on the system, be sure that the correct ACLs are defined for the catalogs. Because Index Server runs as a service, additional catalog directories should be set so the system and administrators have Full Control access.

Index Server's filtering process retains the ACLs in the index. When a user performs a query, his or her access credentials are checked against the ACLs stored for each document. If a user does not have proper permissions, Index Server will not return that document as an item in the query results. Users with valid accounts, other than anonymous, should properly authenticate with their user name and password before issuing queries.

There are three possible situations under which a particular document will not be returned as an item in the results of a query:

➤ The user failed to authenticate before issuing a query.

➤ The user does not have at least Read access to the document.

➤ The document is outside the corpus of the catalog used in the query.

If authentication is required to gain access to most documents on your particular system, incorporate authentication into your query form by adding a name and password field. These data items can be used during the query process to authenticate a user when the query is submitted.

Index Server Performance Monitoring

You can monitor the performance of Index Server via one of two methods. You can use the Windows NT Performance Monitor utility to watch counters from the Content Index objects, or you can use an IDA script and an HTX template. The Index Statistics selection of the HTML Administration tool uses the IDA and HTX method. The Performance Monitor method gives you real-time information and a graphical display. The IDA method updates only when refreshed and allows remote monitoring.

Practice Questions

Question 1

You want to create a new Index Server catalog for a Web site. The corpus of the Web site is 500MB. How much space will be required by the catalog?

○ a. 100MB

○ b. 200MB

○ c. 500MB

○ d. 800MB

Answer b is correct. The index catalog is typically 40 percent of the corpus, so 200MB is required in this scenario. Therefore, answers a, c, and d are incorrect.

Question 2

How many Index Server catalogs can be selected for searching from a single query?

○ a. 1

○ b. 2

○ c. 10

○ d. Unlimited

Answer a is correct. Only a single catalog can be searched per query. Therefore, answers b, c, and d are incorrect.

Question 3

Which do you use to monitor the performance of Index Server? [Check all correct answers]

❏ a. Index Server MMC snap-in

❏ b. Performance Monitor

❏ c. Server Manager

❏ d. Use an IDA script

Answers b and d are correct. You can monitor Index Server's performance via the Performance Monitor or an IDA script. The Index Server MMC snap-in is not used to monitor Index Server's performance, but instead it is used to manage indexed directories and indexes. Therefore, answer a is incorrect. Server Manager is not used in any way with Index Server. Therefore, answer c is incorrect.

Question 4

What Index Server file type is used to format the results from a query?

○ a. HTM

○ b. IDQ

○ c. HTX

○ d. ENU

Answer c is correct. An HTX is an HTML template extension file that is used to format a query's results. An HTM is an HTML document that usually contains the query form. Therefore, answer a is incorrect. An IDQ is a parameters file used to define the scope and restrictions of a query. Therefore, answer b is incorrect. An ENU is the extension of the noise word list file. Therefore, answer d is incorrect.

Question 5

Which of the following Index Server indexes are stored only in memory?

○ a.   Word lists

○ b.   Persistent index

○ c.   Shadow index

○ d.   Master index

Answer a is correct. Only word lists are stored only in memory. Both persistent and master indexes are stored on a hard drive. Persistent indexes are also known as shadow indexes. Therefore, answers b, c, and d are incorrect.

Question 6

> The Index Server service is started only when a query is issued by a user.
>
> ○ a. True
>
> ○ b. False

Answer b is correct. This statement is false. Index Server is launched when IIS 4 is launched. Therefore, answer a is incorrect.

Question 7

> A user performs a query using an Index Server query form on the office's intranet. The results from his query fail to list the SALES1997.DOC file, which he knows contains the words "April" and "1997". What could be the reason for this? [Check all correct answers]
>
> ❑ a. The user was not authenticated.
>
> ❑ b. The user does not have Read access to the file.
>
> ❑ c. Another user was accessing the document at the time the query was performed.
>
> ❑ d. The file is not included in the corpus.

Answers a, b, and d are correct. The nonappearance of a known file in a results list can be the result of a user not being authenticated, a user not having at least Read access, or the file not being part of the corpus. Because a query is performed against an index and not the original file, it is not affected by the use status of the document. Therefore, answer c is incorrect.

Question 8

> Which of the following words are most likely to appear in the Acme company's NOISE.ENU file by default? [Check all correct answers]
>
> ❑ a. and
>
> ❑ b. 1999
>
> ❑ c. Acme
>
> ❑ d. of

Answers a and d are correct. The words "and" and "of" are most likely to appear in the NOISE.ENU file. Although the words "1999" and "Acme" are typical words that should be added to a noise word list for a company called Acme, they are not likely to appear in the NOISE.ENU file by default. Therefore, answers b and c are incorrect.

Question 9

Your public Web server also hosts a private data area. You have configured Index Server to index every document stored on the server in both the Web root and the data directory. All the files in the data directory are set so that only internal users have Read access. If an external user performs a search using a word that exists in one or more files from both the Web root and the data directory, how will items from the data directory appear in the results lists?

- ○ a. They will appear without hyperlinks.
- ○ b. They will appear with authentication fields to gain access.
- ○ c. They will appear just as any item from the Web root.
- ○ d. They will not appear, and the external user will be unaware of their presence.

Answer d is correct. Items from an ACL restricted directory will not appear in the results list for a user without proper access privileges. That user will be unaware of the existence of those documents because Index Server will not even show the file name of restricted items to nonauthorized users. Because Index Server will not display restricted items to unauthorized users in any way, answers a, b, and c are incorrect. Even when items are included in the index files used by a search to which the current user does not have valid access, these items are not displayed in the results, which makes this a trick question.

Question 10

How many shadow indexes and master indexes can exist within a single Index Server catalog?

○ a. One shadow index; sixteen master indexes

○ b. Sixteen shadow indexes; four master indexes

○ c. Unlimited shadow indexes; one master index

○ d. Four shadow indexes; unlimited master indexes

Answer c is correct. Only one master index can exist within a single catalog, whereas an unlimited number of shadow indexes can exist. Therefore, answers a, b, and d are incorrect.

Need To Know More?

 Howell, Nelson, and Ben Forta: *Using Microsoft Internet Informa-tion Server 4, Special Edition*. Que Publishing, Indianapolis, IN, 1997. ISBN: 0-7897-1263-6. Chapter 12 discusses Index Server.

 The best overview information for Index Server 2 can be found in the "Reviewer's Guide for IIS 4." This document can be found on the TechNet CD-ROM or online via the IIS Web area at **www.microsoft.com/ntserver/web/**.

 The IIS online documentation, accessed through Start|Programs| Windows NT 4 Option Pack|Product Documentation, contains extensive detail on Index Server.

Web Site Management And Analysis

- -

Terms you'll need to understand:

√ Content Analyzer

√ Web maps (tree and cyberbolic views)

√ Robot, spider, Robot protocol

√ Site Server Express

√ Report Writer

√ Usage Import

√ W3C extended log file format

√ Cookie

√ Hits, requests, visits, users, organizations

√ Inference algorithm

Techniques you'll need to master:

√ Using Content Analyzer to examine the structure of a Web site

√ Using spiders to test links

√ Automating log imports, database filters, and reports with Usage Import

√ Creating Web site reports with Report Writer

√ Filtering and importing log files

√ Organizing data on site structure with quick searches and site summary reports

√ Setting log parameters on IIS

Web sites are becoming increasingly complex. To examine Web site performance, a hit count is not enough. With the right tools, it's possible to maintain a Web site, as well as to collect profiles of Web site users. Microsoft developed the Site Server suites (Site Server Express, Site Server, and Site Server Commerce Edition) to address this need.

Microsoft makes it relatively easy to install Site Server Express with IIS 4, both of which are included in the Windows NT 4 Option Pack 3. Although Site Server Express is the least functional member of the Site Server series, it's still a marvelous tool for identifying everything on a Web site, from bottlenecks to user habits.

Site Server Express includes three major tools: Content Analyzer, Usage Import, and Report Writer. Content Analyzer maps and tests the integrity of the Web site. Usage Import brings Web site logs into a database, which can then be refined by Report Writer into any number of formats. The calculation, filtering, and report generation functions of Usage Import and Report Writer can be set up and run on a preset schedule.

Content Analyzer: Explored And Explained

Site Server Express Content Analyzer is used to visualize what is and is not working on a Web site. It eases the burden of managing a large number of pages, resources, and links. Its tree structure and cyberbolic views are customized ways to visualize site structure. Its preformatted reports highlight various problems, from broken Web links to pages big enough to annoy typical modem users.

Web Maps

A Web site is more than just a series of linked Web pages. The other objects in a Web page, such as images and Java applets, require more memory and download time than a text-only Web page. Content Analyzer organizes these components in two ways—the tree and cyberbolic views. The level of detail can be customized through the View|Display Options menu.

Content Analyzer begins with a visual representation of a Web site. At a minimum, each view shows Web pages and their links. Other significant objects can be added through the View|Display Options menu. General properties of each object are then available through the Object Properties option of the View menu.

Tree View

As shown in Figure 10.1, the tree view was designed to look like the directory pane of Windows NT Explorer. Starting at the home page, every object that is a part of the home page is directly linked one level below it. Each page with links is like a directory that contains subdirectories and files in Windows NT Explorer.

There are four different control icons associated with each page—the plus, minus, question, and robot icons. The plus and minus icons work the same way as they do in Explorer: If a plus sign is next to a Web page, you can click it and view more detail about that page. Conversely, the minus icon condenses the view. The question icon indicates a page for which the Content Analyzer has not yet explored the links.

The robot icon is shown next to pages in which the Robot protocol is active. Generally, the Robot protocol stops the Content Analyzer Explore Site and Verify Links tools from checking links on or beyond that page. Details of these two commands are included in the subsection on tools.

The difference between robots and the Robot protocol can be confusing. It's important to remember that the Robot protocol stops robots. A robot, also called a *spider*, is an automated tool used to explore links. In the General tab of the Mapping Options dialog box, the Content Analyzer default is set to Honor Robot Protocol, which prevents robots from checking the page. The Explore Site and Verify Links tools of Site Server both use spiders.

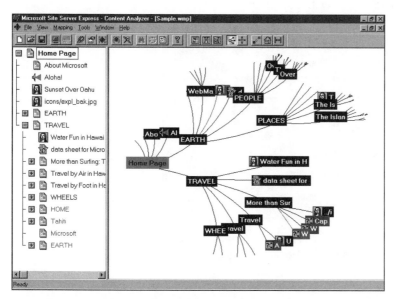

Figure 10.1   A sample Web map: tree and cyberbolic views.

The tree view also has object icons. They are rather self-explanatory. For example, the page icon represents a page in a Web site, the Mona Lisa picture represents an image, and the speaker icon represents an audio file.

Cyberbolic View

The cyberbolic view shows a graphical flowchart of the Web site. At first glance, it looks like a mix between a spider web and an overgrown bush. The power of the cyberbolic view is in how it shows the demands on each part of the Web site. Large numbers of links can represent potential bottlenecks, and a small number of links can represent objects that may be difficult for a user to find.

Maneuvering around a cyberbolic view of a Web site is as easy as moving a mouse. As with program taskbars, a cursor over an icon shows the full name of the object. A left click focuses the view on the links closest to that object in the Web site. A left-click and drag on the object changes perspectives relative to other objects linked to that page.

Functions

Content Analyzer may be customized through the Program Options menu (see Figure 10.2). The default browser is set in the General tab. Proxies that contain the structure of the Web site are specified or bypassed in the Proxy tab. The Cyberbolic tab adjusts how this view moves in response to mouse commands. In the Passwords tab area, domain and user IDs are set to allow Content Analyzer to search through restricted areas of a site. (The Helpers tab is not active in Site Server Express.)

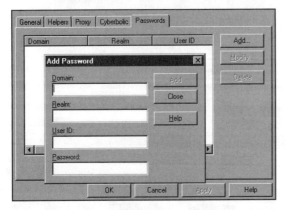

Figure 10.2   Content Analyzer program options: setup for password-protected areas.

Tools

Content Analyzer includes several important tools to help you search through a Web site to verify objects, Uniform Resource Locators (URLs), and links as far as you can go within or outside a site:

➤ **Mapping Options** Sets the defaults for searches by the Content Analyzer spider through the site and through links to other sites. Search engines use spiders to glean content from new areas of the Internet.

➤ **Site Statistics** Creates a quick visual count of what the spider has found, inside and outside a Web site. Site Statistics counts include relevant objects such as pages, links, images, Web maps, gateways, Internet services, Java applets, application calls, and audio, video, and text files.

➤ **Mapping|Explore Site Command** Sends the spider to get URLs through as many pages and/or levels as set for that particular search. A spider does not connect to a link any faster than you do; therefore, calling too many Web pages via the Internet may create performance problems. When this command is complete, unverifiable links are highlighted in red in both the tree and cyberbolic views.

➤ **Mapping|Verify Links Command** Checks the status of all links (or just the broken links) internal and/or external to the site. When the checking process is complete, all unverifiable links turn red in both the tree and cyberbolic views.

Site Summary Reports

The Site Summary report is a big picture snapshot of the Web site that takes data from wherever the Content Analyzer spider has searched. Components include statistics on the major Web site objects, collected into an easy-to-read HTML-formatted file. A sample Site Summary report is shown in Figure 10.3.

Quick Search

Content Analyzer includes a number of quick search tools. These searches go one step further than the summary report. They specify everything needed to get to the Web page with the problem. The different searches (listed in Table 10.1) include some of the key criteria needed to determine if a Web site is working properly.

A more comprehensive analysis of the Web site requires the tools and filters included with Usage Import and Report Writer.

Object Statistics			Status Summary			Map Statistics	
Type	Count	Size		Objects	Links	Map Date	Mar 21 11:16 1998
Pages	62	47325	Onsite	62	177	Levels	7
Images	26	711579	OK	2	25	Avg Links/Page	3
Gateways	0	N/A	Not Found (404)	0	0		
Internet	0	N/A	Other Errors	61	153	**Server Summary**	
Java	0	0	Unverified	0	0	Domain:	site-analyst.backoffice.microsoft.com
Applications	3	55299				Server Version:	Microsoft-IIS/4.0
Audio	3	595320	Offsite	34	34	HTTP Version:	1.1
Video	0	0	OK	0	0		
Text	0	0	Not Found (404)	0	0		
WebMaps	5	529712	Other Errors	34	34		
Other Media	0	0	Unverified	0	0		
Totals	99	1939235	Totals	99	214		

Microsoft SiteServer Express — Content Analyzer

Figure 10.3 The Site Server Express site summary report.

Table 10.1 Content Analyzer quick search tools.	
Quick Search	**Searches For**
Home Site Object	Objects in the same domain as the home page.
Images Without ALT	Images without the HTML **<ALT>** label. Not usable by text browsers.
Load Size Over 32KB	Web pages (including inline images, and so on) with more than 32KB of data.
Non-Home Site Objects	Pages and resources on a different domain than the site's home page.
Not Found Objects (404)	Pages and resources that could not be found (also known as "HTTP 404 file not found" error).
Unavailable Objects	Pages and resources that could not be reached, including all searches that return "HTTP 404 file not found," "server down (502)," and "object is password-protected (401)" errors.
Unverified Objects	Pages and resources for which links have been found, but where the Content Analyzer has not searched.

Usage Import And Report Writer: Explored And Explained

When boiled down to their essence, Usage Import and Report Writer are a series of filters and algorithms. Usage Import reads in log files from Internet servers, such as IIS 4, into a relational database. Report Writer uses a series of filters to provide statistics on everything from browser profiles to a geographical distribution of users. All these tasks can be set to extrapolate and filter logs and databases, as well as create reports on a regular basis.

Log Files

In MMC, log files are set up in the Web Site tab of the Properties dialog box for each IIS Web site. Among the available choices for logging, the emerging standard is the World Wide Web Consortium (W3C) extended logging format. Table 10.2 describes the categories that Usage Import uses.

For a log file to be compatible with Site Server Express, Open Database Connectivity (ODBC) 2.5 or higher must be installed on the Windows NT Server.

The W3C extended logging format can collect considerable detail on every hit to a Web site. Several of these options (shown in Figure 10.4) work well with Site Server Express. With this much potential data, the performance penalty

Table 10.2	Usage import database categories.	
Database	**Description**	**W3C Extended Category Logging Property**
Internet address	To and from Internet address (IP address or host name)	Client IP Address
Time stamp	Date and time of server response	Date, Time
File name	File name or URL sent to the client IP address	URO Query, URI Stem
User name	User name used to log in to a site requiring registration	User Name
Size	Size of response in bytes	Bytes Sent
User agent	Browser name, version, security level	User Agent
Referrer	The page (URL) from where the user linked to your site	Referrer
Cookie	User ID code allows tracking through multiple visits	Cookie
HTTP code	The HTTP code (200, 304, or 302) for a request	Http Status
Site type	The type of Internet site (Web, Gopher, FTP)	Protocol Version
Server IP	The IP address of the individual server performing the logging	Server IP

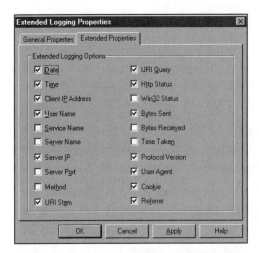

Figure 10.4   IIS 4 W3C extended log file format: Extended Properties.

from collecting every detail in an IIS log file could be serious. It's important to keep the data requirements for each hit to a minimum.

In the following section, we examine how Usage Import brings log data into a database. As shown in Table 10.2, there are a number of important categories. Each of these categories can be associated with W3C Extended Properties logging fields. Most of these associations are fairly straightforward.

Importing Log Files

Log files can be imported from different Web sites. Each IIS Web site is associated with a server. The Usage Import Server Manager tool allows proper identification of all log files. In Server Manager, each log file source is associated with a server and site. If logs are being imported from more than one server, their IP addresses are also used. Sites are uniquely identified through their URL. All logs require the applicable server default pages (usually DEFAULT.HTM and DEFAULT.ASP).

Note: The Usage Import Server Manager tool is not the Windows NT 4 Administrative Server Manager.

Some of the larger Web sites have mirror sites in different time zones. When importing logs from different physical locations of the same site, it's important to synchronize these logs to one time zone. This is done by establishing a server's time zone through the hosting facility settings of the server's properties.

The Usage Import Log File Manager coordinates the different log files that make up the Usage Import database. Normally, IIS log files are created on a regular (daily or weekly) basis. With the Scheduling tool, these log files can be imported and processed automatically on a regular schedule.

Inference Algorithms

Usage Import uses *inference algorithms* to extrapolate some basic properties. Essentially, an inference algorithm is a statistical correction factor for situations, such as hits, that are not recorded due to proxy server caching. Usage Import applies inference algorithms to five categories of data:

➤ **Hits** Any line in a log file is a hit. Every request for content creates a hit. For example, a request to a page with five pictures creates six total hits. Even search errors such as the "HTTP 404 file not found" errors are recorded as hits. The inference algorithms adjust hit counts. For example, the inference algorithm makes sure that one page does not look more popular just because it has twice the number of pictures.

➤ **Requests** Any hit that successfully retrieves content is a request. However, some requests never get logged. Browsers, gateways, and proxy servers have caches that send the data to the user without the Web site ever getting the request. The inference algorithms provide correction factors that more accurately reflect the popularity of the page.

➤ **Visits** Because TCP/IP uses discrete packets, it's not possible to calibrate the start and stop of a visit with the start and stop of data transfer. To determine the duration of a visit, the inference algorithm sorts requests based on IP address, user name, user agent (browser type), cookie data, and a preset "timeout" period (default is 30 minutes).

➤ **Users** Within a TCP/IP packet, the one way to uniquely identify the user is through the source IP address. However, the way TCP/IP is set up, there are not enough IP addresses to uniquely identify all users. Cookies were developed to address this problem. A cookie is a marker downloaded to a PC that identifies a specific user to a Web site. However, with the use of proxy servers, gateways (firewalls), and anti-cookie software, not all cookies make it to user PCs.

➤ **Organizations** Loosely, an organization is any group that connects its users to the Internet (for example, **microsoft.com**). By definition, IP addresses have four octets of binary digits. If the IP address cannot be resolved to an organization name, the first three octets of the IP address are designated as the organization.

Filters

It may be useful to apply a few more filters in the log file import process. In the Usage Import process, filtering is a balancing act between quality of the information and server performance. The following is a brief description of the Usage Import Options tabs (see Figure 10.5):

➤ **Import** Although database indexes can slow the import, they take time to reconstruct for larger log files. Excluding spiders eliminates hits from the spiders shown under the Spider List tab.

➤ **Default Directories** Logs are imported from this directory.

➤ **Spider List** The list of spiders that won't have their hits counted.

➤ **IP Resolution** Includes caching and timeout options to optimize IP-to-host name resolution. Caches generally include the most common host name addresses.

➤ **IP Servers** Specifies domain and proxy servers best able to manage host name (DNS) and Whois query resolution.

➤ **Log File Overlaps and Log File Rotation** Log files are generally made for a set time period (for example, noon to 11:59 A.M.). These settings address what to do with data from visits that overlap multiple logs.

There are three special filters: HTML Title, IP Address Resolution, and Whois Organization lookups. Because these are resource-intensive operations, use these filters only if and when necessary. Briefly, their functions are as follows:

Figure 10.5 Usage Import Options menu: sample list of spiders.

➤ **HTML Title Lookup** Pulls the words associated with the HTML <TITLE> tag on each page.

➤ **IP Address Resolution** Looks for host names associated with IP addresses.

 Be careful! For Site Server, IP address resolution is essentially the same as a reverse DNS lookup. In some TCP/IP books, IP address resolution is the Address Resolution Protocol (ARP). IP address resolution in Usage Import has nothing to do with ARP.

➤ **Whois organization lookups** Identifies organizations associated with host names after IP address resolution.

Usage Import collects log data from a number of servers and time periods into a single database. In general, the size of a daily log file from a business Web site is anywhere from 150K to 1GB (for the most heavily used commercial sites). Databases are usually a collection of logs from a number of days. It generally pays to compact the database on a regular basis.

Reports

Site Server Express Report Writer is a versatile way to mine information from the Usage Import database. With the right types of logs from IIS 4, reports can be generated on anything from how users navigate through your site to identifying the sites from where they came.

Report Writer is essentially another series of filters, but this time on the database assembled in the Usage Import utility. When Report Writer is opened, the user is given a series of prompts and options, similar to a program setup wizard. Before we get into an actual report, here are the main steps:

1. When Report Writer is opened, the first step is to select the desired report, either from a preset list (see Table 10.3) or from previously customized report filters. If there's more than one database (for example, if there are multiple Web sites), Report Writer adds this step to allow a choice on the database(s) to be used.

2. The next step is to filter the database(s) for the desired time period (see Figure 10.6). Include/exclude filters can be added for the database. Some care is required; for example, it would not be a good idea to filter a database to use only information from March 23, 1998, and then to exclude all information from the week of March 22, 1998.

Note: For more information on Boolean filters, see Chapter 10 of MCSE NT Server 4 in the Enterprise Exam Cram *(ISBN 1-57610-191-6), also published by Certification Insider Press.*

Table 10.3	Preformatted reports.
Report Type	**Description**
Executive Summary	Top-level activity report. Requires Usage Import IP filters.
Bandwidth Report	Byte transfer loafing averages and peaks. Key for network planning.
Browser/OS	Shows browser/operating system market share. Can be used to customize Web sites.
Geography	Correlates users by city, U.S. state/Canadian province, and country. Useful not only for market customization, but also may show the need for a mirror site. Requires IP filters.
Hits	Shows server hits on an hourly, daily, and weekly basis.
Organization	This report identifies the domain origins of your Web site visitors. Requires Usage Import IP resolution and Whois queries.
Path	Summarizes how users navigate through the Web site. Helps highlight changes that can optimize Web site structure. Requires HTML **\<TITLE\>** lookups.
Referrer	Statistics on sites where users are coming from. Helps evaluate effectiveness of ads. Requires referrer data and IP resolution in server log files.
Request	Popularity of different Web site documents. Requires HTML **\<TITLE\>** lookups.
User	Trends for user visits and frequency. Requires user registration or cookie data.
Visits Detail	Visits on an hourly, daily, and weekly basis.

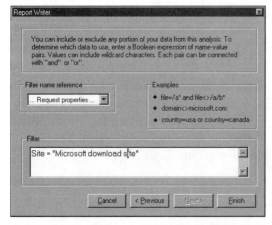

Figure 10.6 Example of Boolean expression database filtering.

3. Output properties (usually in the Row Dimensions) can be changed in the Report Request Detail. For example, one default property in the Geography report is to show the top 15 user origin cities in the U.S. Double-clicking the "cities" block allows you to adjust the number of cities listed. In a similar fashion, the appearance properties of the report can also be changed; fonts can be added, cell sizes can be changed, and colors can be revised.

4. When adjustments are complete, the Create Report Document command of the File menu allows you to choose output file formats. The default format is HTML. If MS Word and Excel are installed, reports can also be formatted for these programs.

5. Once everything is ready, you are not prompted. The command to generate the report is File|Create Report Document. To save what was customized, the command is File|Save Report Definition.

Practice Questions

Question 1

Which views are available in the Display Options menu in the Site Server Express Content Analyzer? [Check all correct answers]

❑ a. Orthogonal

❑ b. Tree

❑ c. Cyberbolic

❑ d. Visual

❑ e. Web

Answers b and c are correct. The tree and cyberbolic views are the two views available in Site Server Express Content Analyzer. The other answers are not options in Content Analyzer. Therefore, answers a, d, and e are incorrect.

Question 2

As one of several Webmasters for the growing company Web site, you have been asked to publish a Web map. For security reasons, the sales manager has asked you to exclude information from the internal sales servers. The password-protected entry page to the sales server is several levels below the Web site home page. The Honor Robot Protocol box in the General tab of the Mapping Options dialog is not checked. In your Content Analyzer Web map, you see a robot icon at the firewall to the sales server. What do you do to protect the sales server from searches?

○ a. The Robot protocol is bad news in a secure area. If you see the Robot protocol icon where the Web site links to the secured part of the sales server, you need to do whatever is necessary to get rid of this robot; otherwise, the rest of the world will have easy access to your company's confidential sales information.

○ b. When you explore the site, limit the levels explored so that the Content Analyzer spider can't get to the secured area of the sales server.

○ c. Create a separate secure Web site for the sales server. Delete all links from your Web site to the secure area.

○ d. The Robot protocol icon is okay, but you need to make sure that the Honor Robot Protocol checkbox in the General tab of the Mapping Options dialog is checked.

○ e. If you see the Robot protocol icon, it's too late. The secure part of your site has already been penetrated by someone else's spider.

Answer d is correct. The Robot protocol, when honored, actually acts as a firewall to the automated Content Analyzer and search engine spiders. This can be confusing, because spiders are actually sometimes known as robots, and the Robot protocol actually stops robots. Therefore, answers a and e are incorrect. Although limiting the levels searched may prevent getting to the secured area entry page, it would also prevent searching through other areas of the site that could also be important. Therefore, answer b is incorrect. Even though it's technically possible to create a separate Web site for the secure sales area, anyone creating a Web page on the main site can create links to the secure area. Without the Robot protocol, the sales area is not as secure as it could be. Therefore, answer c is incorrect.

Question 3

As a busy Webmaster, you would like to automate the process of creating regular reports on the popularity of your Web site. However, you're concerned about the performance of your severely underpowered server. You've already set up the W3C extended log to take the data you need. Which of the following actions can you add to the Scheduler that won't compromise performance on your server?

○ a. Look up HTML titles.

○ b. Resolve IP addresses.

○ c. Perform Whois organization queries.

○ d. All of the above. This is all good information for reports to management.

○ e. None of the above. Each of these actions is performance-intensive on the server.

Answer e is correct. HTML title lookup, IP address resolution, and Whois organization queries are all resource-intensive operations and should be avoided whenever possible when performance is an issue. However, if you can find a time of day when demand on this server is low, it's certainly possible to schedule these operations for specific times. It would be helpful to find out when these times are through the appropriate report. However, you don't know what these times are right now. Therefore, answers a, b, c, and d are incorrect.

Question 4

Your manager has asked you for a quick "big picture" review of the Web site. He has heard complaints that there are a number of links at various places in the Web site that "just lead out into space." You are confident that this is not so, but need data to back you up. Which type of report do you need?

○ a. Report Writer Context Detail report

○ b. Report Writer Comprehensive Analysis

○ c. Quick search for broken links and unavailable objects

○ d. Content Analyzer Site Summary report

○ e. Report Writer Cookie report

Answer d is correct. The Content Analyzer Site Summary report will give you and your manager a quick big picture view on the status of your Web site, including the required data. A quick search for broken links and unavailable objects will give you quick, detailed information on links that are no longer working and pages and other objects that are no longer available. Because these searches provide heavy detail on each problem link and object, they are not appropriate for an overview of the site. Therefore, answer c is incorrect. Because we're looking for data on specific pages and links on the Web site, Report Writer is not necessary. Besides, the Report Writer options given in answers a, b, and e do not exist, making those answers incorrect.

Question 5

As the Webmaster of the growing company Web site, you're getting a number of complaints from users: pages are too slow to load, text browsers just can't search through your site, and a number of links just end up in space.

You've already used the Verify Links tool. Which type of data can you get on these issues without having to go through the time and trouble of a Usage Import of a log file? [Check all correct answers]

- ❑ a. Perform a quick search for all images without HTML **<ALT>** tags.
- ❑ b. Do a quick search for all pages above 32KB.
- ❑ c. Create a Site Summary report.
- ❑ d. Check the links and HTML tags on each page one by one. There's no other way to be sure what is and isn't working.

Answers a, b, and c are correct. Not everyone has a browser that shows images. When a text-based browser gets to an image without an HTML <ALT> tag, it stops the browser. For test purposes, all pages with more than 32KB are too slow to load for all modem users. A Site Summary report is a useful overview of the status of key quick search items on the Web site. Because you've already used the Verify Links tool, broken links will be reported. It isn't necessary to go into a Web page to check all the links. Therefore, answer d is incorrect.

Question 6

Log files in IIS 4 are set up by Web site. To use the IIS 4 log files, a number of parameters have to be set in Usage Import to match what has been set in the properties of each Web site. Which of the following do these settings include? [Check all correct answers]

❑ a. Default home page

❑ b. Time zone

❑ c. Spider list

❑ d. HTML **<ALT>** tags

❑ e. Domain

Answers a and e are correct. Without the default home page and server domain, Usage Import cannot identify the right database for the site. The time zone is set in Usage Import to make sure that log data from different servers of a Web site, such as a mirror "site" in a different part of the world, is synchronized. By definition, you want times in a site to match their local time zones. Therefore, answer b is incorrect. Spider lists and images without HTML <ALT> tags are not part of the setup for IIS logging. Therefore, answers c and d are not correct.

Question 7

Your supervisor has just read an article that mentioned the power of inference algorithms. She asks you to explain to her what an inference algorithm is and what it has to do with measuring the performance of the Web server. Which of the following would be an accurate description?

- ○ a. An inference algorithm is a program that uses fuzzy logic to perform tasks such as HTML title lookups and IP address resolution. Because it simplifies the lookup of things such as DNS files, it improves performance of these otherwise high-intensity tasks.

- ○ b. An inference algorithm is a set of calculations that improves logging speed in IIS. Without it, ODBC logging would be a process that would overcome all but the fastest processors with at least 64MB of memory.

- ○ c. An inference algorithm works like a statistical correction factor for things such as request data in an ODBC-compliant log file. Without it, Web pages with 100 thumbnail images would appear to be many times more popular than they really are.

- ○ d. An inference algorithm works like a set of statistical correction factors for things such as IP address resolution and database caching. Without it, database references to cached data would not be possible.

- ○ e. An inference algorithm is a set of calculations that improves the speed of Site Server Express Report Writer.

Answer c is correct. Without inference algorithms, a Web page with 100 thumbnail images would get 101 hits each time a user links to it. This would make the page seem much more popular than a text-only page that gets only one hit for each time a user links to it. Inference algorithms correct for this discrepancy. However, they address only the data related to hits, requests, visits, users, and organizations. Although IP address resolution is loosely related to organizations, database caching is not an inference algorithm function. Therefore, answer d is incorrect. None of the other answers are related to the function of inference algorithms. Therefore, answers a, b, and e are incorrect.

Question 8

> Before setting up Site Server Express to import log files from IIS 4, which of the following conditions are required?
>
> ○ a. Install Internet Explorer 4 or higher on your server.
>
> ○ b. Make sure ODBC 2.5 or higher is installed. Enable ODBC logging from each Web site.
>
> ○ c. Set the default directory for the ARP cache.
>
> ○ d. Set up the Scheduler to import log files directly from the IIS 4 generated log file.

Answer b is correct. ODBC 2.5 or higher is a prerequisite for IIS to work with Site Server Express. Although Internet Explorer 4 is a requirement for installing Site Server Express, you can set a different default browser in the Content Analyzer Program Options dialog's General tab. Therefore, answer a is incorrect. Although IP address resolution in TCP/IP refers to ARP, it does not apply here. Besides, IP address resolution as a Usage Import filter is completely different from ARP. Therefore, answer d is incorrect. Although the Scheduler can import log files from IIS 4, its use is not required. Therefore, answer d is incorrect.

Question 9

> You are running a Web site for a winery in the state of Washington. There's a steady stream of users from all over the country who go to your Web site to purchase wines and to get advice on winemaking. You're looking to customize the site to provide the best possible experience for your users. You're even considering the use of a mirror site in Delaware if you can show sufficient demand from the East Coast. Which of the following preformatted Report Writer reports could help you meet this need? [Check all correct answers]
>
> ❑ a. IP Server
>
> ❑ b. Geography
>
> ❑ c. Browser and Operating System
>
> ❑ d. Referrer
>
> ❑ e. Path

Answers b, c, and e are correct. A Geography report will help you determine the distribution of where your users are coming from. Knowing the browser of most of your users will help determine the type of add-ons that are more important for your site (for example, ActiveX for MSIE or Java for Netscape). The Path report shows how your users are navigating through the site, and therefore helps determine whether you need to change the locations and sizes of some pages, images, and other objects to make navigation easier. There is no IP Server report. Therefore, answer a is incorrect. The Referrer report provides data on where users are coming from, meaning which ISP they are using. Although this can provide useful data on where your advertising is working best on the Web, this does not address the user's experience once he or she has reached your site. Therefore, answer d is incorrect.

Need To Know More?

It's unfortunate that the *Microsoft IIS 4 Resource Kit* barely addresses Site Server Express. The best sources of information for Site Server Express are the user guides included with each SSE program. However, be cautious: Several areas in the Site Server Express user guides seem to apply to the more functional Site Server versions.

 Amirfaiz, Farhad: *Official Microsoft Site Server 2 Enterprise Edition Toolkit,* Microsoft Press, Redmond, WA, 1998. ISBN: 1-57231-622-5. Source for full capabilities of the most scalable version of Site Server.

 Muller, John Paul and Tom Sheldon: *The Complete Reference, Microsoft Internet Information Server 4,* Osborne/McGraw-Hill, Berkeley, CA, 1998. ISBN: 0-07882-457-5. See Chapter 16 for a brief overview of IIS 4 logging, as well as Site Server Express Usage Import and Report Writer.

SMTP And NNTP Services

Terms you'll need to understand:

√ Simple Mail Transfer Protocol (SMTP)

√ Masquerade domain

√ Smart hosts

√ Email messages

√ Network News Transfer Protocol (NNTP)

√ Newsgroups

√ UA (user agent)

Techniques you'll need to master:

√ Installing and configuring the SMTP service

√ Installing and configuring the NNTP service

√ Using the SMTP and NNTP services

Along with IIS, the Windows NT Option Pack includes several optional services, including mail and news services. In this chapter, we'll discuss the value of adding these servers to a multifunctional Web server.

IIS Components

As discussed in Chapter 2, IIS 4 is distributed as part of the Windows NT Option Pack. The Option Pack contains seven distinct software components or applications that can be installed as an integrated whole to provide a wide range of Internet hosting and management capabilities. In the following sections, we'll take a look at two of the additional IIS components that ship as part of the Option Pack—the SMTP service and the NNTP service.

SMTP Service: Explored And Explained

Prior to IIS 4 and its add-on Simple Mail Transfer Protocol (SMTP) service, hosted Web sites relied on third-party email systems to manage all email communications. Now, with the integrated SMTP service, hosted Web sites can easily integrate email as an additional means of communicating with site visitors. However, this SMTP service does not include a POP3 server; therefore, it cannot deliver messages to POP3 user agents (UAs, also known as standard email client utilities). However, it can accept messages from UAs that use SMTP.

The SMTP service allows Web applications to send and receive email messages. In addition, Web server events can trigger email notification to administrators. The SMTP service gives the Web server an email message box in which error messages, user feedback, or undelivered messages can be deposited for manual administrator processing.

The IIS SMTP service is a relay agent for email messages. Messages originating from IIS, sent to IIS by a UA, or routed from another SMTP server can be deposited in a local drop box or forwarded on to other SMTP servers. The SMTP service is installed as an optional component through the Option Pack setup routine. The only configuration option defined during installation is the location of the Mailroot directory. This directory is where all the messages handled by the SMTP service are stored and processed. The default location for this directory is within the InetPub directory (C:\InetPub\Mailroot).

Installing the SMTP service requires the use of NTFS on the Web server.

The Mailroot directory is a top-level root directory for the SMTP service that is the parent of several other directories where the actual storage, processing, and operations of the mail service take place. Following is a list of the Mailroot child directories:

➤ **Badmail** All undeliverable messages that cannot be returned to the sender are saved in this directory with a .BAD extension.

➤ **Drop** All the messages for the domains hosted by IIS are placed in this directory.

➤ **Pickup** Any outgoing messages copied into this directory as a text file are automatically processed.

➤ **Queue** All active messages in the process of being delivered are held in this directory.

➤ **SortTemp** Temporary files are stored in this directory.

The Queue directory is the starting place for all email messages that are to be processed by the SMTP service. All messages that IIS receives from a UA or an SMTP server are placed into the Queue directory. The SMTP service then inspects the header of the message. If the header is invalid, the SMTP service attempts to return the message to the sender. If this fails, the message is moved into the Badmail directory. If the header is valid, the SMTP service determines whether the destination is local (a domain hosted by IIS) or remote. If it's local, the message is placed in the Drop directory. If it's remote, the SMTP service attempts to forward the message on to the remote destination.

The SMTP service is managed primarily through the same MMC snap-in as IIS (Start|Programs|Windows NT 4 Option Pack|Microsoft Internet Information Server|Internet Service Manager). Notice that the node below the IIS computer is named Default SMTP Site. Below this node are Domains and Current Sessions. The Domains entry lists the default domain and all aliased domains for which the SMTP service can receive email. Through a listed domain's Properties menu, you can alter its remote routing, relaying, and security settings. Current Sessions lists the current active connections to the SMTP service.

You can also manage the SMTP service through its HTML interface. It's accessed via the URL **http://localhost:port/mail/Smtp/Admin/Default.htm**. This interface offers you the same controls and information as the MMC snap-in.

Configuration of the SMTP service is handled through the Properties dialog box. This is accessed by selecting the Default SMTP Site node and then issuing the Action|Properties command. Here are the options on the SMTP Site tab of this dialog box (see Figure 11.1):

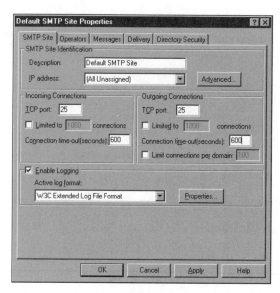

Figure 11.1 The Default SMTP Site tab of the SMTP Site Properties dialog box.

➤ **Description** A name for the site that easily identifies it to an administrator.

➤ **IP Address** The IP address of the SMTP site.

➤ **Incoming and Outgoing Connection Parameters** TCP port (the default is 25), limitation on simultaneous connections (the default is No Limit), and connection timeout (the default is 600 seconds). For outgoing messages, you can also limit the number of connections per domain (the default is No Limit).

➤ **Enable Logging** Records SMTP activity in NCSA, ODBC, or W3C extended format.

The Operators tab (shown in Figure 11.2) is where the operators of the SMTP site are defined. It is a simple, standard, add-user-to-list interface.

The Messages tab (shown in Figure 11.3) is where message parameters are defined:

➤ Size limitations for a single message (default 2048K) and a single session (default 10240K)

➤ Maximum number of outbound messages per connection (default 20)

➤ Maximum number of recipients per message (default 100)

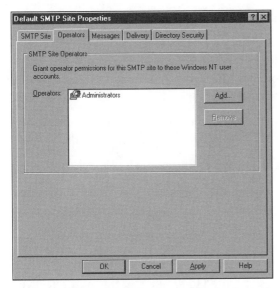

Figure 11.2   The Operators tab of the Default SMTP Site Properties
                   dialog box.

➤ Email a copy of the nondelivery report to a user

➤ The directory in which to store undeliverable messages (also known as
  Badmail)

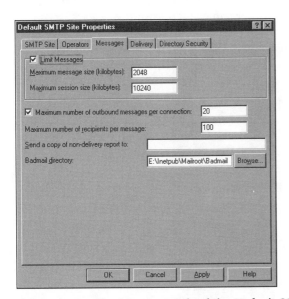

Figure 11.3   The Messages tab of the Default SMTP Site Properties
                   dialog box.

The Delivery tab (shown in Figure 11.4) is where the delivery parameters are defined:

➤ **Maximum Retries and Retry Interval (Minutes)** The number of retries (default 48) and the amount of time between retries (default 60 minutes) for both local and remote queues.

➤ **Maximum Hop Count** Maximum number of hops a message can take before reaching another SMTP server and being labeled as nondeliverable.

➤ **Masquerade Domain** The domain to list the email as being sent from.

➤ **Fully Qualified Domain Name** The FQDN for this SMTP server used for message origin identification.

➤ **Smart Host** Sends all outgoing messages to this designated SMTP server.

 Smart hosts are usually used to ensure that the most effective or most secure route is used.

➤ **Perform Reverse DNS Lookup On Incoming Messages** Performs a reverse DNS lookup on incoming messages to verify their origin.

➤ **Outbound Security** Provides a remote SMTP server with access credentials in the form of a user name and password via clear text or

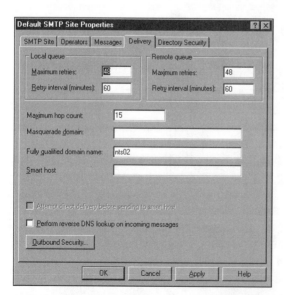

Figure 11.4 The Delivery tab of the Default SMTP Site Properties dialog box.

Windows NT Challenge/Response; also, you can turn on Transport Layer Security (TLS) to encrypt messages.

The Directory Security tab is where security for the SMTP service is defined:

➤ **Authentication Methods** The standard control of allowing anonymous access, Basic Authentication, or Windows NT Challenge/Response to verify users before allowing them to use the SMTP service.

➤ **Secure Communications** The standard control for installing and using certificates; includes access to the Key Manager.

➤ **IP Address And Domain Name Restrictions** The standard control for granting or denying access to groups, subnets, or individual computers.

➤ **Relay Restrictions** A control similar to IP Address And Domain Name Restrictions, where groups, subnets, or individual computers are allowed or restricted from being allowed to relay email messages through this SMTP server (by default, this privilege is restricted).

NNTP Service: Explored And Explained

Newsgroups are another method to promote communication on a Web server. IIS 4 includes an Network News Transfer Protocol (NNTP) service that can be used to host these discussion forums. A news client, such as Microsoft Outlook Express, can connect to the NNTP service and read or post articles to newsgroups.

The NNTP service is installed as an optional component through the Custom Setup option of the IIS setup routine. The setup routine creates an Nntpfile directory under the InetPub directory (C:\InetPub\Nntpfile). This directory stores all the messages handled by the NNTP service.

 Distributing newsgroup files on multiple disk drives may improve performance and provide more storage space. Using virtual directories enables you to add multiple locations for a single NNTP service.

The NNTP service can be managed through the IIS MMC snap-in or via a Web interface; both tools offer the same controls. The IIS MMC snap-in is accessed by selecting Start|Programs|Windows NT 4 Option Pack|Microsoft Internet Information Server|Internet Service Manager. Notice that the node below the IIS computer is named Default NNTP Site. Below this node are the Expiration Policies, Directories, and Current Sessions options. The Expiration Policies option includes rules that define when one or more discussion groups' messages will be automatically deleted. An expiration policy can be based on age in days or size in megabytes. The Directories option is used to spread the storage of discussion group messages across multiple servers. By default, all files are stored in the \InetPub\Nntpfile directory. The Current Sessions option displays the currently active discussion group users.

To access the HTML administration interface for the NNTP service, use a URL with the following construction: **http://localhost:port/news/Admin/ Default.htm**.

Configuration and management of the NNTP service is handled through the service's Properties dialog box. This is accessed by selecting the Default NNTP Site node and then issuing the Action|Properties command. The News Site tab (shown in Figure 11.5) is where the following general properties about the NNTP service are set:

➤ Site description, path header, IP address, TCP port (default 119), and SSL port (if secure communications is enabled; default 563)

➤ Number of simultaneous connections (default 5,000) and timeout (600 seconds)

➤ Logging, which records NNTP activity in IIS, NCSA, ODBC, or W3C extended format

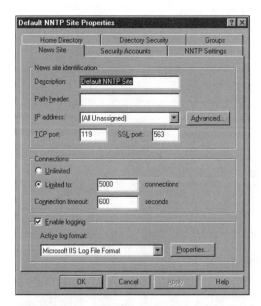

Figure 11.5   The News Site tab of the Default NNTP Site Properties dialog box.

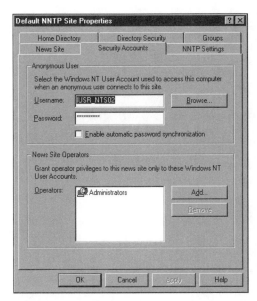

Figure 11.6   The Security Accounts tab of the Default NNTP Site Properties dialog box.

The Security Accounts tab (shown in Figure 11.6) is where the Windows NT user account for anonymous access is defined, as well as where the accounts with Administrative access are defined. Both of these settings use the standard Add User dialog boxes, accessed by clicking the Add button.

The NNTP Settings tab (shown in Figure 11.7) is where NNTP-specific settings are defined:

➤ Enable or disable client posting, with post and connection size limitations

➤ Allow other servers to pull articles from this server

➤ Enable control message processing

➤ Define an SMTP server where all moderated group messages are mailed

➤ Define the aliasing default moderator domain name

➤ Define the administrator's email account

The Home Directory tab (shown in Figure 11.8) is where the location for message storage is configured:

➤ Define the default storage path locally or to a network share

➤ Restrict posting, restrict visibility, log access, and index new content

➤ Enable SSL-secured transactions

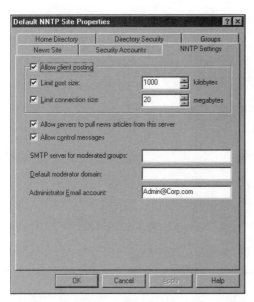

Figure 11.7 The Default NNTP Settings tab of the NNTP Site Properties dialog box.

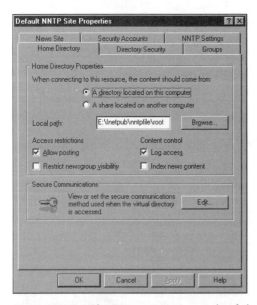

Figure 11.8 The Home Directory tab of the NNTP Site Properties dialog box.

The Directory Security tab is where the authentication methods and IP address and domain name restrictions are defined. These are the standard control interfaces, as seen throughout IIS.

Newsgroups are created and configured using the Groups tab (see in Figure 11.9). To create a newsgroup, click the Create New Newsgroup button. A Newsgroup Properties dialog box prompts you for a name and description and asks you to specify whether the group is read-only and if it's moderated (by the default moderator or by a specified user). You can alter an existing newsgroup's settings by selecting it in the display list and clicking Edit. This brings up the same Newsgroup Properties dialog box used for new groups. Similarly, you can delete a newsgroup, by selecting it and clicking the Delete button.

The NNTP service otherwise functions automatically. You can simply point a UA, such as Outlook Express, at the news server (typically by providing the IP address, FQDN, or NetBIOS name). You can then subscribe to a newsgroup and read or post messages as you would with any other Internet NNTP server.

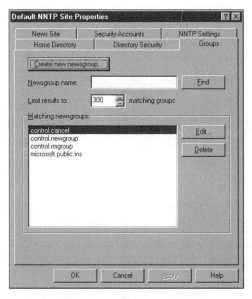

Figure 11.9 The Groups tab of the NNTP Site Properties dialog box.

Practice Questions

Question 1

> Your domain name is currently set to one of your subsidiaries, but you want all of your email messages coming from your IIS server to seem as if they are coming from your corporate domain name. Which SMTP service setting should you use to define this parameter?
>
> O a. Alias Domain
>
> O b. Smart Host
>
> O c. Masquerade Domain
>
> O d. Badmail

Answer C is correct. The Masquerade Domain setting is used to define an alias domain for the SMTP service. There is no setting called Alias Domain, making answer a incorrect. A smart host is a designated SMTP server through which to route outgoing messages. Changing this parameter would not affect the origin's domain name. Therefore, answer b is incorrect. Badmail is a term used for undeliverable messages that cannot be returned to the sender. Therefore, answer d is incorrect.

Question 2

> Under the SMTP service of IIS, what happens to email messages that cannot be delivered to their intended recipient? [Check all correct answers]
>
> ❏ a. They are sent to a default remote SMTP server.
>
> ❏ b. They are returned to the sender.
>
> ❏ c. They are stored in the local queue.
>
> ❏ d. They are deposited in the Badmail directory.

Answers b and d are correct. First, undeliverable email is returned to the sender. If it can't be returned, it's placed in the Badmail directory. Undeliverable email is not sent to a remote SMTP server, nor is it stored in the local queue. Therefore, answers a and c are incorrect.

Question 3

Which of the following measures are used to secure the SMTP service of IIS?
[Check all correct answers]

❑ a. SSL identity verification

❑ b. Windows NT Challenge/Response authentication

❑ c. Reverse DNS lookup

❑ d. IP address and domain name restrictions

Answers a, b, c, and d are correct. The SMTP service can be secured using any of these methods.

Question 4

Which directory can serve as a deposit box for email messages so that when they're copied or placed in that directory, they are automatically processed by the SMTP service?

○ a. Drop

○ b. Pickup

○ c. Queue

○ d. SortTemp

Answer b is correct. The Pickup directory serves as an inbox for email messages to be copied. All files in this directory are automatically processed by the SMTP service. The Drop directory is where all messages directed at the domains hosted by this SMTP service are stored. Therefore, answer a is incorrect. Queue is the folder used by the SMTP service that holds all active messages in the process of being delivered. Therefore, answer c is incorrect. SortTemp is just a storage folder for temporary files. Therefore, answer d is incorrect.

Question 5

> By default, email with a remote recipient is automatically forwarded or re-layed on to other SMTP servers, no matter where the message originated.
>
> ○ a. True
>
> ○ b. False

Answer b is correct. The SMTP service is configured so that no message relay-ing to remote SMTP servers occurs. This prevents malicious users from spamming (sending lots of unsolicited, anonymous, untraceable email).

Question 6

> The IIS SMTP service can host multiple user mailboxes, so clients with POP3-compliant user agents (email client software) can retrieve messages.
>
> ○ a. True
>
> ○ b. False

Answer b is correct. This statement is false. The IIS SMTP service does not in-clude POP3 support or the ability to host multiple mailboxes. All mail sent to the SMTP service for the domains hosted by this service is deposited in the Drop folder and must be read with a text editor or a UA that can import text email messages.

Question 7

> The NNTP service of IIS supports which of the following functions or fea-tures? [Check all correct answers]
>
> ❑ a. Hosting of multiple discussion groups
>
> ❑ b. Access to standard Usenet newsfeeds
>
> ❑ c. Moderated groups
>
> ❑ d. SSL-secured transmissions

Answers a, c, and d are correct. The IIS NNTP service supports multiple discussion groups, moderated groups, and SSL. The IIS NNTP service is unable to access Usenet newsfeeds. It's restricted to host discussion groups within a single server. Therefore, answer b is incorrect.

Question 8

> The IIS SMTP and NNTP services can be administered and managed through which utilities or interfaces? [Check all correct answers]
>
> ❑ a. Server Manager
>
> ❑ b. The IIS MMC snap-in
>
> ❑ c. Network Monitor
>
> ❑ d. An HTML interface

Answers b and d are correct. The IIS SMTP and NNTP services can be administered through the IIS MMC snap-in or through separate HTML interfaces. Server Manager and Network Monitor are not used to administer these services. Therefore, answers a and c are incorrect.

Question 9

> The IIS NNTP service allows the storage of a discussion group's files on a network share in addition to the local IIS host computer.
>
> ○ a. True
>
> ○ b. False

Answer a is correct. Group files can be stored on network shares instead of the local computer to distribute the file storage requirements for large discussion groups across multiple systems in the network.

Need To Know More?

 Howell, Nelson, and Ben Forta: *Using Microsoft Internet Information Server 4, Special Edition.* Que Publishing, Indianapolis, IN, 1997. ISBN: 0-7897-1263-6. This book discusses the SMTP service in Chapter 7 and the NNTP service in Chapter 8.

 IIS's own online documentation, accessed through Start|Programs|Windows NT 4 Option Pack|Product Documentation, contains extensive detail on the SMTP and NNTP services.

Troubleshooting IIS

. . . .

Terms you'll need to understand:

√ Configuration errors

√ HTTP errors

√ ODBC errors

√ Dependency errors

√ DNS

√ WINS

√ HOSTS file

√ LMHOSTS file

Techniques you'll need to master:

√ Knowing how to perform systematic troubleshooting

√ Understanding common IIS configuration errors

√ Understanding common HTTP and ODBC errors

√ Knowing how to resolve installation problems

√ Understanding how Windows NT system and networking errors can affect IIS

√ Knowing how to resolve name resolution problems

Troubleshooting is a very important aspect of any type of software installation, and Internet Information Server (IIS) 4 is certainly no exception. In this chapter, we'll discuss various aspects of troubleshooting the installation, configuration, and operation of IIS 4.

General Troubleshooting

Your ability to adapt your knowledge and experience to problems that arise with IIS is a skill that is often innate rather than learned. However, systematic or structured troubleshooting is a reliable method of locating and resolving problems—even if you're not naturally inclined toward technical resolution. A systematic approach to troubleshooting is a philosophy or generalized, step-by-step "how-to" system to aid you in eliminating issues that prevent productive use of your computer system. Here are the general steps of this process:

1. Investigate the symptoms.

2. Review previous logs of resolutions.

3. Isolate, identify, and define the problem.

4. Hypothesize resolutions.

5. Test these hypotheses individually.

6. Maintain a log of the resolution process.

Taking the time to understand what is going on and why will often lead you directly to the solution. In addition to intimate knowledge about the setup and configuration of your own system, it's often important to have other documentation and resources available. One such resource that is invaluable to anyone administrating a Microsoft product—especially IIS—is the TechNet CD-ROM. This product is a collection of manuals, resource kits, training materials, technical notes, technical resolution messages, and more, in electronic text format. All this data is combined into a single interface that allows keyword searches across all or part of the text—this single feature makes the TechNet CD-ROM the most valuable resource Microsoft has ever produced. TechNet is a yearly subscription service with a monthly issue/update for about $300 per user. To request a trial issue, more information, or ordering details, go to **www.microsoft.com/technet/**.

You'll need to have a solid understanding of the product, its normal functions, and what can go wrong with it. Know how to use troubleshooting logic and your own knowledge of the product to resolve an issue.

The remainder of this chapter highlights specific problems that you should be aware of and accustomed to resolving. This information is not exhaustive. Your own hands-on experience with the product in an operating (if not production) environment is indispensable. You will benefit by your ability to quickly recognize possible viable solutions from actions that either have no effect or that cause further problems.

Configuration Issues

IIS 4 has a wide range of configuration options with which you need to be familiar. These options include the installation procedure, default installation directories, default security settings, and locations of most commands and settings (that is, which dialog boxes or menus contain which items). All the relevant items you should be familiar with are detailed in previous chapters. If you're not confident with your knowledge of these basics, be sure to review each chapter and take mental notes. You should also spend time interacting with IIS directly. This will add hands-on experience to the knowledge you've gained from reading.

Web Site Configuration Errors

In the following sections, we review some common configuration errors made with Web sites. These items are grouped by the tabs found on a Web site's Properties dialog box.

Web Site

The following items are configuration errors that are possible on the Web Site tab:

➤ **IP Address** Setting this to a specific IP address enables the site to receive all traffic directed at that IP address. Be sure the DNS entry mapping an IP address to a Fully Qualified Domain Name (FQDN) is correct for the hosted Web site and the selected IP address. IP addresses appear in this pull-down list only if they are defined in the TCP/IP properties via the Protocol tab of the Network applet.

➤ **TCP Port** The default port for HTTP is 80. All Web clients automatically attempt to establish communication with the server over port 80. If you change the TCP port, users must specify this in any URL used to access that site.

Operators

The Operators tab is prone to certain configuration errors. Each user who is specifically added or who is a member of an added group is granted operator privileges to a Web site. A site operator does not need to be a Windows NT system administrator. Site operators have the ability to change logging, set server access permissions, change default documents and footers, and alter content expirations, HTTP headers, and content ratings. Granting operator status to the wrong users can endanger the vitality of your Web site. Not granting operator status to the correct users will prevent them from being able to manage their sites remotely or locally.

Performance

The following items are configuration errors that are possible on the Performance tab:

➤ **Bandwidth Throttling** Setting the bandwidth throttle too low can prevent a Web site from responding quickly if multiple users are accessing the site simultaneously. Also, setting the throttle too high may starve other sites on the same IIS server.

➤ **Keep-Alives** Some Web applications rely on consistent connections with clients to maintain a context stream. If these are disabled, some Web applications may no longer function or may respond to users with improper information.

ISAPI Filters

Be aware that configuration errors are possible on the ISAPI Filters tab. ISAPI filters that are either corrupt or not designed/configured for a Web site can cause the Web site to fail or performance to be degraded.

Home Directory

The following items are sources of possible configuration errors on the Home Directory tab:

➤ **Location** The top three radio buttons on this page are used to define where the resources used by this Web site are stored—locally, network share, or URL. If this is set incorrectly, visitors will not gain access to the correct resources, if anything at all.

➤ **Path** Based on which radio button is selected, this option defines the location (locally, network share, or URL) where resources are pulled. If this is incorrect, visitors will not see the intended resources.

➤ **Access Permissions** The settings of Read and Write determine whether visitors can view documents and upload files. If Read access is not enabled, visitors will receive a 403 HTTP error stating that Read access is forbidden.

➤ **Content Control** If directory browsing is allowed, the list of files in a directory will be displayed in the client browser when a default file is not present in that directory. Otherwise, a user will receive an error that browsing is not allowed.

Documents

The following items are configuration errors that are possible on the Documents tab:

➤ **Default Document** If Default Document is disabled, each URL used to gain access to the site must contain the name of a document; otherwise, a directory listing will be attempted. If the wrong document name is defined, a directory list will be attempted.

 To find broken links quickly and easily, use Content Analyzer to create a report on your site.

➤ **Document Footer** If the content of the footer file is not properly formatted or if it's saved as a file format other than plain text, it may display incorrectly in a client browser.

Directory Security

The following items are configuration errors that are possible on the Directory Security tab:

➤ **Authentication Methods** If Allow Anonymous Access is not defined, only authenticated users (those with valid names and passwords) can gain access to the site. If Anonymous Access is enabled but fails, double-check that Automatic Password Synchronization is enabled.

➤ **Key Manager** If server certificates not issued for a specific server are installed, clients will receive a message stating that the certificate used does not match the server.

➤ **IP Address and Domain Name Restrictions** Because you must set blanket access permission to either Grant or Restrict, and then further refine the setting with exceptions, it's easy to set these backward. Be sure to double-check the restriction methods used.

HTTP Headers

The following items are configuration errors that are possible on the HTTP Headers tab:

➤ **Content Expiration** Setting expiration dates that expire too soon may cause proxy servers to access resources continually in search of current materials. Also, some client browsers can be set to accept only current data, so expired materials may be restricted from being viewed.

➤ **Custom Headers** Defining a header name or its value incorrectly can result in spurious responses by client browsers and proxy servers. Always double-check custom headers to ensure spelling and relevance.

➤ **Ratings** Defining the content's rating level incorrectly prevents users who should not be restricted from gaining access, or it may fail to warn or restrict those users to whom access should be restricted.

➤ **MIME** If a resource accessed via IIS is not being handled properly by a client's browser (such as not calling the proper helper application, failing to automatically play/use the content, or forcing the user to save the content to disk), check the defined MIME types for the Web server.

Custom Errors

The Custom Errors tab is also prone to configuration errors. If you define a custom error, make sure the contents of the defined error properly reflect the information the user needs to handle the error. This is more a user-friendly mistake than an actual error. Always give your visitors enough information so that they can solve the problem themselves or understand that it is out of their control and should be reported to you.

FTP Site Configuration Errors

In the following sections, we review some common configuration errors made on FTP sites. These items are grouped by the tabs found on an FTP site's Properties dialog box.

FTP Site

The following items are configuration errors that are possible on the FTP Site tab:

➤ **IP Address** Setting this to a specific IP address enables a site to receive all traffic directed at that IP address. Be sure that the DNS entry mapping an IP address to an FQDN is correct for the hosted FTP site and the selected IP address. IP addresses appear in this pull-down list only if they are defined in the TCP/IP properties via the Protocol tab of the Network applet.

➤ **TCP Port** The default port for FTP is 21. All FTP clients automatically attempt to establish communication with the server over port 21. If you change the TCP port, users must specify this when attempting to access that site.

Security Accounts

The following items are configuration errors that are possible on the Security Accounts tab:

➤ **Allow anonymous** If Allow Anonymous Access is not defined, only authenticated users (those with valid names and passwords) can gain access to the site. If Anonymous Access is enabled but fails, make sure Automatic Password Synchronization is enabled. If authenticated users are unable to log on, verify that you have not selected to restrict access to anonymous only.

➤ **Adding users** Each user who is specifically added or who is a member of an added group is granted operator privileges to this FTP site. A site operator does not need to be a Windows NT system administrator. Granting operator status to the wrong users can endanger the vitality of your FTP site. Not granting operator status to the correct users will prevent them from being able to manage their sites remotely or locally.

Messages

There really isn't an error on the Messages tab that will prevent proper functioning. You should provide useful information for your visitors, such as contact information and announcement of prosecution for illegal activities, in this section.

Home Directory

The following items are configuration errors that are possible on the Home Directory tab:

➤ **Location** The top radio button on this page defines where the resource used by this FTP site is stored—locally or network share. If this is set incorrectly, visitors will not gain access to the correct resources, if anything at all.

➤ **Path** Based on which radio button is selected, this option defines the location where resources are pulled. If this setting is incorrect, visitors will not see the intended resources.

➤ **Read/Write** If Read access is not granted, users can't download files or view directory contents. If Write access is not granted, users can't upload and delete files. This setting is in addition to the NTFS file and folder object-level settings.

Directory Security

The following item is a configuration error that is possible on the Directory Security tab:

➤ **TCP/IP Access Restrictions** Because you must set blanket access permission to Grant or Restrict for FTP site access, which is then further refined by exceptions, it's easy to set this backward. Be sure to double-check the restriction methods used.

IIS HTTP Errors

The HTTP protocol used to transmit Web pages has a standard set of error codes that are reported to clients in the event of an error. These error codes inform users of problems that have occurred and let them know if there is anything they can do to avoid these errors in subsequent communications.

 To customize a message users receive when an HTTP error occurs, create an HTML file with the custom error message. Then right-click on the Web site, choose Properties, and choose the Custom Error tab. Highlight the error message you'd like to customize, and click Edit Properties. In the resulting Error Mapping Properties dialog box, specify the new HTML file with the new error message.

Here are the seven HTTP errors you should be familiar with:

➤ **400 Bad Request** Due to malformed syntax, the request could not be understood by the server. The client should not repeat the request without modifications.

➤ **401 Unauthorized: Logon Failed** This error indicates that the credentials passed to the server do not match the credentials required to log on to the server. It instructs the user to contact the Web server's administrator to verify that he or she has permission to access the requested resource.

➤ **403 Forbidden: Execute Access Forbidden** This error can be caused if a user tries to execute a CGI, ISAPI, or other executable program from a directory that does not allow programs to be executed. It instructs the user to contact the Web server's administrator if the problem persists.

➤ **404 File Not Found** The Web server cannot find the file or script asked for. The user is instructed to check the URL to ensure that the path is correct and to contact the server's administrator if the problem persists.

➤ **500 Internal Server Error** The Web server is incapable of performing the request. The user is instructed to try the request again later and to contact the Web server's administrator if the problem persists.

➤ **501 Not Implemented** The Web server does not support the functionality required to fulfill the request. The user is instructed to check the URL for errors and to contact the Web server's administrator if the problem persists.

➤ **502 Bad Gateway** The server, while acting as a gateway or proxy, received an invalid response from the upstream server it accessed in attempting to fulfill the request. The user is instructed to contact the Web server's administrator if the problem persists.

 You should take notice that the 400 series HTTP error messages are related to the client, whereas the 500 series HTTP error messages are related to the server.

IIS ODBC Errors

When accessing a Web site that has a connection to a database, the user will be presented with an error message if the ODBC connection is not set up correctly. The following is a list of the most common ODBC errors:

➤ **Data source name not found and no default driver specified** The global.asa file is not firing, possibly because it is not in a directory that has Execute rights. Also, only a File or System (not a User) Data Source Name can be used.

➤ **Logon failed** If you are using standard security, the SQL account name and password are incorrect. If you are using integrated security, check the permissions of the Windows NT user.

➤ **General network error** This error message can be caused by changing the name of a SQL database computer. The DSN may still be referencing the old database computer name.

➤ **General error Unable to open registry key DriverId** The permissions on the DriverId Registry key are not set correctly. Use the Windows NT Registry Editor to modify the permissions appropriately.

➤ **ConnectionOpen (CreateFile())** This error is caused when a user tries to access a database that is on a different computer or that is being called by a UNC. The remote computer may try to validate the user based on the IUSR anonymous account or his Windows NT account, depending on the authenticate method used on the IIS server. Possible solutions are to change the anonymous account to a valid Windows NT account that is accessible from both computers, duplicate the anonymous account on the remote computer, or use Basic Authentication rather than Windows NT Challenge/Response.

Installation Issues

Fortunately, IIS is very simple to install. As discussed in Chapter 2, the installation procedure is often painless, especially if you follow a few simple rules:

1. Install Service Pack 3 (if you're in the U.S. and you want to use 128-bit encryption, use the 128-bit version of Service Pack 3).

2. Install Internet Explorer 4.01.

3. Close all applications, especially those using ODBC or those that offer services similar to IIS (Web, FTP, SMTP, and so on).

If the installation of IIS fails, your only course of action is to attempt to uninstall IIS and then reinstall. In extreme cases, the installation failure causes Windows NT to fail. This may require the reinstallation of Windows NT.

Once IIS is installed, you can test the installation by launching a Web browser and attempting to load the default Web pages from the new installation of IIS (or any document placed in the \InetPub\Wwwroot directory). To do so, use a URL constructed from the IP address, NetBIOS name, or FQDN (if DNS is present) of IIS in the form **http://address/**. If a document fails to load, first check that files actually exist in the Wwwroot directory. Next, verify that the IIS services are started. Finally, check the IIS set and the NTFS-level access control lists (ACLs) for the resources. If none of these actions enables IIS to function, you may need to reinstall IIS and possibly Windows NT as well.

Windows NT Issues

As discussed earlier in this book, IIS is tightly integrated into the Windows NT Server 4 operating system. Therefore, a working knowledge and solid familiarity with Windows NT Server and its management, performance, and administration tools are essential. Due to the integration of IIS and Windows NT Server, it's important to recognize that configuration errors in Windows NT Server can directly affect IIS's ability to operate and function properly.

Knowledge of Windows NT Server is assumed for the IIS certification exam. If you're not already familiar with Windows NT Server or you have not passed the Windows NT Server certification exam, we strongly recommend you take and pass it before moving on to IIS.

The configuration and administration of Windows NT Server can have a direct and profound impact on IIS in four key areas: security, performance, networking, and name resolution. In the following four sections, we look at each of these Windows NT Server-specific issues. However, you should recognize that due to the tight integration of IIS with Windows NT, it can be difficult to distinguish where a problem lies. Several of these topics have been addressed earlier in this book and in this chapter; therefore, some of them overlap.

Windows NT Security

IIS relies on Windows NT security to provide the underlying control mechanism for user access to resources over the information services (Web, FTP, and so on) offered through IIS. If Windows NT security fails to restrict access or grant access correctly, your information services will either be unable to distribute resources or unable to distribute confidential resources.

The ACLs (Access Control Lists) are what control who can use a resource. For most IIS resources (that is, files and folders), ACLs are limited to controlling who can read, write, execute, and delete a specific object. It's important to review the ACLs for all resources hosted by IIS—and even those supposedly outside the reach of IIS—to ensure that all items have properly defined ACLs. Specifically, the IUSR_*servername* user should be granted. Read access to all IIS resources and Execute access on all script resources. The exception is where public access to a resource should be restricted, in which case the IUSR account should have either No Access specifically defined or not be defined at all. Users and groups that control the content of IIS services should be granted Write and/or Delete access to the subsections of those services. All items outside of the IIS roots should either not have the IUSR included in their ACLs or have No Access specified for that account.

You should also keep in mind how multiple group memberships can affect the resultant access for an individual user. The resultant access is the accumulation of all access granted to that user specifically and by all group memberships, except if No Access is specified for that user or for the user's group, in which case that user is denied access.

In a multidomain environment, in addition to ACLs, you also need to monitor trust relationships. Trusts are logical security connections between two domains, where one domain is able to share its resources with the authenticated users from another domain. If either of the domains terminates the trust, access over the trust is canceled. If you suspect user inability to access resources is due to a failed trust, your only course of action is to reestablish the trust.

Another important item to remember is that all user accounts that will be accessing resources over IIS must have the Log On Locally user right. Otherwise, they will not be authenticated on the IIS server and will be prevented from gaining access to retrieve resources. This includes the IUSR_*servername* account and any individual user account that needs direct or special access on the IIS server.

CGI scripts and similar files should be limited, when possible, to Execute only access. This prevents anyone from viewing and modifying them. However, some CGI file types, such as the .IDC and .HTX files for Index Server, require Read access to function properly. In some cases, when a script that only requires Execute access is placed in a directory that offers both Read and Execute access, the client browser will attempt to download the file instead of instructing the server to execute it. In such a case, you should move all Execute-only scripts into one directory and all Execute and Read scripts into another.

Windows NT Performance

As you should know, the ability of a system to process resource requests is only as good as its ability to perform the actions required to fulfill the requests. In other words, a slow or poorly tuned system will offer sluggish or interrupted service. Maintaining a watch over how well your system is supporting its processing load is an important preventive measure. Waiting until a service fails or too much activity causes the system to crash results in increased repair costs, extensive downtime, and disgruntled users.

As discussed in Chapter 8, monitoring and tuning is a key aspect of administering IIS. If you don't maintain the performance of the underlying hardware and operating system, it will be unable to adequately support the heavy activity of a growing IIS user base.

When your IIS server is in danger of overrunning its available resources, you can use several tactics to shackle IIS to limit its resource usage:

➤ **User limits** On the Web Site tab of the Web site's Properties dialog box via MMC, you can restrict the number of simultaneous users. By restricting access to a specified number of users, you gain better control over the performance offered to that limited user base.

➤ **Remove nonessential services** Any service or application that is active on the same Windows NT Server machine that hosts IIS is fighting IIS for access to the limited resources of that system. For larger IIS sites, especially those in which performance is important and/or those with a large user base, no other services or applications should be installed. IIS and only those services and applications essential to the operation of the Web application should be present on the Windows NT Server machine.

➤ **Add more resources** When money is not an issue and upgrading or expanding your current hardware is possible, adding additional RAM, CPUs, faster network/ISP interfaces, and faster/larger storage devices may directly increase the resource availability.

➤ **Optimizing code** If you're using scripts created in-house, CGI, and other custom applications with IIS, take the time to inspect how these utilities allocate, use, and release resources (especially memory and CPU cycles). It's not uncommon for a single server-side application to consume more than its fair share of resources and bring the rest of the system to a standstill. Code that is not optimized is often a direct culprit of declining resources.

➤ **Bandwidth restrictions** You can control, on a global and site basis, the amount of bandwidth used by a Web or FTP site hosted by IIS. By restricting the traffic of one or more sites, you can effectively grant more bandwidth to others.

Windows NT Networking

Windows NT networking is essential to the operation of IIS because it's through the network interface (either to an intranet or to the Internet) that all communication between the server and clients occurs. If this communication pathway is interrupted, terminated, or clogged with traffic, IIS site performance will suffer accordingly.

In relation to Windows NT networking, three problems can occur:

➤ The IIS machine has no network access.

➤ The IIS machine has network access but clients cannot access resources.

➤ Clients receive the wrong resources.

If the IIS machine loses its network connection or that connection becomes unusable for any reason, it should be obvious that access to IIS is not possible. There are several possible causes of network communication loss.

First, the rest of the network or your ISP has somehow failed. This can range from a cable being disconnected to a server crashing. In such cases, check all physical points of failure and test other servers or clients to see if they still have network access.

Second, the network adapter on the IIS system has stopped functioning. This can occur when hardware burns, is disconnected due to movement, or the driver is corrupt. If the NIC fails, check all connections and attempt to restart the machine to see if communication is reestablished. Then, replace/reinstall the driver and/or replace the NIC itself.

Third, the protocol used by IIS is no longer configured correctly or is not the same as that used by the rest of the network. Typically, TCP/IP is the protocol used to transmit IIS-hosted services, but some proxy applications can transport IIS services over IPX. In any case, an incorrectly configured protocol is most often the cause of protocol networking problems. Both making a change to and installing a protocol can result in a system unable to communicate due to incorrect settings. Be sure to double-check the IP address, subnet mask, and default gateway. In some cases, you may need to verify that the routers and gateways in use on your network or between IIS and the ISP are properly configured and functioning.

Windows NT's TCP/IP includes a handful of tools that you can use to determine if you have lost network connectivity. They include PING and TRACERT. Use **PING 127.0.0.1** to determine if the protocol is properly installed. Use **PING** *network server IP address* to determine if the subnet is defined properly (where *network server IP address* is the IP address of another server within the same subnet). Use **PING** *external server IP address* to determine that the gateway is defined properly (where *external server IP address* is the IP address of a server outside of the IIS server's subnet or out on the Internet). If you see a list of replies with times from any of these uses of PING, you know that aspect of IP is probably configured correctly. If you see timeouts, this indicates either that IP is configured incorrectly or the object of the PING is not present.

The second tool, TRACERT, can be used to determine where in the logical order of servers the network communication fails. The command **TRACERT** *external server IP address* lists each server or router encountered between your machine and the external server. If the external server's IP address fails to appear as the last item in the TRACERT list, a breakdown in communication at the last server listed has occurred.

If your IIS server has network access but clients are unable to access resources, this may indicate that the services that normally serve out these resources are not functioning properly. Often, if a service is not functioning, an error message will be displayed on the client stating that a connection with the server could not be established. Make sure that clients have network access by using PING and TRACERT to test the path between the clients and the IIS server. If this test shows the clients to have network access to the IIS server, you can suspect the IIS services.

Use the Services applet or the IIS MMC snap-in to determine whether the IIS-related services are started, paused, or stopped. The relevant services include FTP Publishing, IIS Admin, and World Wide Web Publishing. If they are stopped or paused, restart these services. If this fails, try rebooting the server and testing them again. After a reboot, if the services still fail to function, inspect the Event Viewer logs for dependency failures.

 Remember that a *dependency failure* occurs when a driver, device, or service fails to load, which then causes other drivers, devices, or services to load or function improperly. Take whatever steps are necessary to resolve any dependency failures. As a last course of action, you can reinstall IIS to attempt to repair or replace the services.

If clients are accessing resources from IIS but the resources requested are not the resources returned, a configuration error exists. This configuration error can be in the binding of an IP address with the incorrect Web site or in an IP address improperly defined with an FQDN in DNS.

Windows NT Name Resolution

Name resolution hosted by Windows NT can cause problems with accessing IIS. Because Windows NT uses a wide variety of name resolution schemes (DNS, HOSTS, WINS, and LMHOSTS), it may be difficult to track down the point of failure. DNS is used to manage static mappings of FQDNs (fully qualified domain names) to IP addresses for an entire network. The HOSTS file is used to manage static mappings of FQDNs to IP addresses for a single machine. WINS is used to dynamically manage mappings of NetBIOS names to IP addresses for an entire network. The LMHOSTS file is used to manage static mappings of NetBIOS names to IP addresses for a single machine.

Within an intranet, IIS-hosted sites can be accessed using the NetBIOS name of the server as the domain name in a URL (for example, if the server's NetBIOS name is nts03, a URL could be **http://nts03/staff/default.htm**). However, on larger networks where DNS is present, FQDN is the address method of choice. This is true because most companies with larger networks grant access to their IIS sites (or parts of them) to Internet-based users.

More often than not, DNS name resolution is associated more with IIS than with any of the other methods. You should be aware of and have general troubleshooting knowledge of several issues related to DNS and IIS. These include the following:

➤ **DNS unavailable** If the primary and secondary DNS servers on your local network are unavailable due to system crashes or network communication interruption, clients will be unable to have FQDNs resolved into IP addresses. In other words, they will not be able to reach your site because the address they use will not be directed to IIS.

➤ **Old data** If the IP address has changed but this information has not been altered in DNS, clients will be directed to the old IP address. Therefore, they will not be directed to IIS. If the data has been updated on the primary DNS server, but it is not reflected or synchronized over the other DNS servers on the network, some users will be properly resolved whereas others will not. In this case, you need to investigate the synchronization parameters of your DNS system.

➤ **Incorrect entries** All DNS entries are defined by hand. That means it is easy to introduce errors when alterations or new mappings are performed. An incorrect entry can result in two errors. First, an FQDN can be mapped to an unknown or illegal IP address. Second, an FQDN can be mapped to a wrong IP address that is, however, a valid address within the network.

Practice Questions

Question 1

> When a user opens the URL for an IIS site, he or she is shown a directory listing of the Wwwroot directory instead of being shown the default document. Why? [Check all correct answers]
>
> ❑ a. The directory has Read access set.
>
> ❑ b. Directory browsing is enabled.
>
> ❑ c. A redirection URL is used.
>
> ❑ d. No default is present or the name of the default document does not match the one known by IIS.

Answers b and d are correct. If a user is shown a directory listing, directory browsing is enabled and a default document is not found. The directory must have Read access defined; otherwise, the directory listing won't be displayed. Therefore, answer a is incorrect. A redirection URL does not cause a directory listing to be displayed; it simply takes you to the alternate location. Therefore, answer c is incorrect.

Question 2

> Clients are unable to access the IIS-hosted Web site. In fact, an error message appears stating that a connection with the server could not be established. However, the client is able to access other Internet sites without difficulty. Using PING and TRACERT, it has been determined that IIS is not experiencing any network communication difficulties locally or with the Internet. What could be the problem?
>
> ○ a. Anonymous access is restricted.
>
> ○ b. The router between the IIS server and the Internet is offline.
>
> ○ c. The World Wide Web service is stopped.
>
> ○ d. The client does not have TCP/IP installed.

Answer c is correct. In this situation, it is most likely that the WWW service is stopped. If anonymous access is restricted, an error message stating this restriction would be seen on the client machine instead of the "unable to establish a connection" error. Therefore, answer a is incorrect. If the router is offline, IIS would not be able to use PING and TRACERT on the sites on the Internet. Therefore, answer b is incorrect. If the client does not have TCP/IP installed, other Internet sites are not accessible. Therefore, answer d is incorrect.

Question 3

Clients attempting to access a Web site hosted on IIS receive an HTTP error 403. What could cause this error?

○ a. Write access is enabled.

○ b. Read access is not enabled.

○ c. That client's domain is restricted from the Web site.

○ d. Resources are located on a share.

Answer b is correct. A 403 error occurs if the Web site does not have Read access enabled. Enabling Write access has no effect on Read access. Therefore, answer a is incorrect. If the client was restricted from the Web site, an "access denied" error would be issued instead of a "Read access forbidden" error. Therefore, answer c is incorrect. Pulling resources from a share has no effect on the Read error. Therefore, answer d is incorrect.

Question 4

The password for the IUSR_*servername* account in the User Manager For Domains has been changed, and clients are reporting that they can no longer gain access to the public Web site. Why?

○ a. Automatic password synchronization for the anonymous account has been disabled.

○ b. The new password was less than eight characters long.

○ c. Changing the anonymous account password requires a reinstallation of IIS.

○ d. It takes up to three hours before a new password can be used on Windows NT.

Answer a is correct. The IUSR_*servername* account in the User Manager For Domains must match the Internet Guest account in IIS for anonymous users to gain access to a Web site. If automatic password synchronization were enabled for the anonymous account, any change made to the password in User

Manager For Domains would be reflected in IIS instantly. The length of the password does not matter, unless a Windows NT account policy is in force. Even then, the changed password would be forced to comply with the policy before it would be accepted. Therefore, answer b is incorrect. Changing the anonymous account's password does not require a reinstallation of IIS. Therefore, answer c is incorrect. Windows NT propagates new passwords almost instantly; no waiting period is required. Therefore, answer d is incorrect.

Question 5

Within your company intranet, you have 10 workstations used by temporary employees. You do not want users of these computers to have any access to the Web site hosted on your internal IIS server. Therefore, on the IP Address And Domain Name Restrictions page for the company Web site, you define exceptions for these 10 computers as 10 individual IP addresses. After you make this change, you discover that no clients on the intranet can access the Web site except these 10 computers. What could be the problem?

- ○ a. Individual computers cannot be exceptions. A subnet must be specified.
- ○ b. A reboot of IIS is required before this takes effect.
- ○ c. Anonymous access has been disabled.
- ○ d. The IP Address Access Restrictions option is set to Denied Access.

Answer d is correct. If all but the exception computers can no longer gain access, this means that Denied Access was selected instead of Granted Access. Therefore, answer d is correct. Individual computers and a subnet can be used as exceptions. A reboot of IIS is not required for a change in access restrictions. Therefore, answer b is incorrect. Disabling anonymous access prevents all clients from accessing anonymously, but it does not prevent authenticated users from accessing. This question does not state whether anonymous or authenticated access was affected. Therefore, answer c is incorrect.

Question 6

A client attempting to access a resource on your IIS Web site receives a 404 HTTP error. What does this error mean?

○ a. Due to malformed syntax, the request could not be understood by the server.

○ b. This error indicates that the credentials passed to the server do not match the credentials required to log on to the server.

○ c. The Web server cannot find the file or script requested.

○ d. The server, while acting as a gateway or proxy, received an invalid response from the upstream server it accessed in attempting to fulfill the request.

Answer c is correct. A 404 HTTP error means the Web server cannot find the file or script requested. A 400 HTTP error means, due to malformed syntax, the request could not be understood by the server. Therefore, answer a is incorrect. A 401 HTTP error means the credentials passed to the server do not match the credentials required to log on to the server. Therefore, answer b is incorrect. A 502 HTTP error means the server, while acting as a gateway or proxy, received an invalid response from the upstream server it accessed in attempting to fulfill the request. Therefore, answer d is incorrect.

Question 7

The Index Server files of IDC and HTX require which NTFS permission settings for the IUSR account to function properly? [Check all correct answers]

❑ a. Read

❑ b. Delete

❑ c. Write

❑ d. Execute

Answers a and d are correct. The IDC and HTX files require Read and Execute permissions.

Question 8

In which ways can you improve the performance of an IIS-hosted Web site without spending more money on hardware or network services? [Check all correct answers]

❑ a. Restrict simultaneous users

❑ b. Remove nonessential services

❑ c. Optimize custom code

❑ d. Impose bandwidth restrictions

Answers a, b, c, and d are correct. All of these actions are useful for improving the performance of an IIS-hosted Web site.

Question 9

Which Microsoft TCP/IP tools are used to investigate the network communications of IIS? [Check all correct answers]

❑ a. PING

❑ b. ROUTE

❑ c. TRACERT

❑ d. NBTSTAT

Answers a and c are correct. PING and TRACERT are TCP/IP utilities that are used to test network communications. ROUTE and NBTSTAT are not used to test network communications. Therefore, answers b and d are incorrect.

Question 10

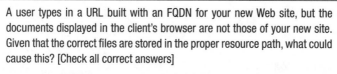

A user types in a URL built with an FQDN for your new Web site, but the documents displayed in the client's browser are not those of your new site. Given that the correct files are stored in the proper resource path, what could cause this? [Check all correct answers]

❑ a. A network share is being used to pull the resources for this new site.

❑ b. DNS mappings associate the FQDN with the wrong IP address.

❑ c. The new Web site is set to the wrong IP address on the Web Site tab.

❑ d. Read access is not enabled in the new site.

Answers b and c are correct. If the wrong Web site appears in a client browser when the correct URL is used, either the DNS mapping is wrong or the site's IP address is wrong. Using a network share for resource storage would not cause this problem. Therefore, answer a is incorrect. If the client was directed to the correct Web site and Read access was disabled, an error message stating such would be displayed. Therefore, answer d is incorrect.

Need To Know More?

 Howell, Nelson, and Ben Forta: *Using Microsoft Internet Information Server 4, Special Edition.* Que Publishing, Indianapolis, IN, 1997. ISBN: 0-7897-1263-6. This book discusses IIS troubleshooting in Chapter 18.

 Some information about troubleshooting IIS can be found on the TechNet CD-ROM or online via the Microsoft IIS Web area at **www.microsoft.com/ntserver/web/**.

 IIS's own online documentation, accessed through Start| Programs|Windows NT 4 Option Pack|Product Documentation, contains information about troubleshooting IIS.

Sample Test #1

In this chapter, we provide pointers to help you develop a successful test-taking strategy, including how to choose proper answers, how to decode ambiguity, how to work within the Microsoft testing framework, how to decide what you need to memorize, and how to prepare for the test. At the end of this chapter, and again in Chapter 15, we include a set of 55 questions on subject matter pertinent to Microsoft Exam 70-087: "Implementing and Supporting Microsoft Internet Information Server 4."

Also, remember that you can take an adaptive practice exam on IIS online at **www.coriolis.com/cip/testcenter/** (the password is ISPTOL51069) to help you prepare even more. Good luck!

Questions, Questions, Questions

There should be no doubt in your mind that you are facing a test full of specific and pointed questions. Currently, the IIS 4 test may be a short-form test or an adaptive test. If it is a short-form test, the exam will consist of 30 questions that you must complete in 60 minutes. If it is an adaptive test (and the software should tell you this as you begin the exam), it will consist of somewhere between 15 and 30 questions (on average) and take somewhere between 30 and 60 minutes.

Whichever type of test you take, for this exam, questions belong to one of five basic types:

➤ Multiple-choice with a single answer

➤ Multiple-choice with one or more answers

➤ Multipart with a single answer

➤ Multipart with one or more answers

➤ Simulations (that is, operating on a GUI screen capture to simulate using IIS 4 tools or utilities with your mouse and/or your keyboard)

Always take the time to read a question at least twice before selecting an answer, and always look for an Exhibit button as you examine each question. Exhibits include graphical information related to a question. An exhibit is usually a screen capture of program output or GUI information that you must examine to analyze the question's contents and formulate an answer. The Exhibit button brings up graphics and charts used to help explain a question, provide additional data, or illustrate page layout or program behavior.

Not every question has only one answer; many questions require multiple answers. Therefore, it's important to read each question carefully, to determine how many answers are necessary or possible, and to look for additional hints or instructions when selecting answers. Such instructions often occur in brackets immediately following the question itself (as they do for all multiple-choice questions in which one or more answers are possible).

Picking Proper Answers

Obviously, the only way to pass any exam is to select enough of the right answers to obtain a passing score. However, Microsoft's exams are not standardized like the SAT and GRE exams; they are far more diabolical and convoluted. In some cases, questions are strangely worded, and deciphering them can be a real challenge. In those cases, you may need to rely on answer-elimination skills.

Almost always, at least one answer out of the possible choices for a question can be eliminated immediately because it matches one of these conditions:

➤ The answer does not apply to the situation.

➤ The answer describes a nonexistent issue, an invalid option, or an imaginary state.

➤ The answer may be eliminated because of the question itself.

After you eliminate all answers that are obviously wrong, you can apply your retained knowledge to eliminate further answers. Look for items that sound correct but refer to actions, commands, or features that are not present or not available in the situation that the question describes.

If you're still faced with a blind guess among two or more potentially correct answers, reread the question. Try to picture how each of the possible remaining answers would alter the situation. Be especially sensitive to terminology; sometimes the choice of words ("remove" instead of "disable") can make the difference between a right answer and a wrong one.

Only when you've exhausted your ability to eliminate answers, but remain unclear about which of the remaining possibilities is correct, should you guess at an answer. An unanswered question offers you no points, but guessing gives you at least some chance of getting a question right; just don't be too hasty when making a blind guess.

 If you're taking a fixed-length or a short-form test, you can wait until the last round of reviewing marked questions (just as you're about to run out of time, or out of unanswered questions) before you start making guesses. If you're taking an adaptive test, you'll have to guess to move on to the next question if you can't figure out an answer some other way. Either way, guessing should be your technique of last resort!

Decoding Ambiguity

Microsoft exams have a reputation for including questions that can be difficult to interpret, confusing, or ambiguous. In our experience with numerous exams, we consider this reputation to be completely justified. The Microsoft exams are tough, and deliberately made that way.

The only way to beat Microsoft at its own game is to be prepared. You'll discover that many exam questions test your knowledge of things that are not directly related to the issue raised by a question. This means that the answers you must choose from, even incorrect ones, are just as much a part of the skill assessment as the question itself. If you don't know something about most aspects of how IIS 4 works and the related tools and utilities found in Windows NT 4, you may not be able to eliminate obviously wrong answers because they relate to a different area of IIS 4 or Windows NT than the one that's addressed by the question at hand. In other words, the more you know about the software, the easier it will be for you to tell right from wrong.

Questions often give away their answers, but you have to be Sherlock Holmes to see the clues. Often, subtle hints appear in the question text in such a way that they seem almost irrelevant to the situation. You must realize that each question is a test unto itself and that you need to inspect and successfully navigate each question to pass the exam. Look for small clues, such as the mention of times, group permissions and names, and configuration settings. Little things like these can point at the right answer if properly understood; if missed, they can leave you facing a blind guess.

Another common difficulty with certification exams is vocabulary. Microsoft has an uncanny knack for naming some utilities and features entirely obviously in some cases, and completely inanely in other instances. Be sure to brush up on the key terms presented at the beginning of each chapter. You may also want to read through the Glossary at the end of this book the day before you take the test.

Working Within The Framework

The test questions appear in random order, and many elements or issues that receive mention in one question may also crop up in other questions. It's not uncommon to find that an incorrect answer to one question is the correct answer to another question, or vice versa. Take the time to read every answer to each question, even if you recognize the correct answer to a question immediately. That extra reading may spark a memory or remind you about an IIS 4 feature or function that helps you on another question elsewhere in the exam.

If you're taking a fixed-length test, you can revisit any question as many times as you like. If you're uncertain of the answer to a question, check the box that's provided to mark it for easy return later on. You should also mark questions you think may offer information that you can use to answer other questions. On fixed-length or short-form tests, we usually mark somewhere between 25 and 50 percent of the questions on exams we've taken. The testing software is designed to let you mark every question if you choose; use this framework to your advantage. Everything you will want to see again should be marked; the testing software can then help you return to marked questions quickly and easily.

For fixed-length or short-form tests, we strongly recommend that you first read through the entire test quickly, before getting caught up in answering individual questions. This will help to jog your memory as you review the potential answers and can help identify questions that you want to mark for easy access to their contents. It will also let you identify and mark the really tricky questions for easy return as well. The key is to make a quick pass over the territory to begin with, so that you know what you're up against, and then to survey that territory more thoroughly on a second pass, when you can begin to answer all questions systematically and consistently.

If you're taking an adaptive test, and you see something in a question or one of the answers that jogs your memory on a topic, or that you feel you should record if the topic appears in another question, write it down on your piece of paper. Just because you can't go back to a question in an adaptive test doesn't mean you can't take notes on what you see early in the test, in hopes that it might help you later in the test.

 For adaptive tests, be sure to take notes on what you see in various questions. Sometimes, what you record from one question, especially if it's not as familiar as it should be or reminds you of the name or use of some utility or interface details, can help you on other questions later on.

Finally, some Microsoft tests combine 15 to 25 adaptive questions with 10 fixed-length questions. In that case, use our recommended adaptive strategy for the adaptive part, and the recommended fixed-length or short-form strategy for the fixed-length part.

Deciding What To Memorize

The amount of memorization you must undertake for an exam depends on how well you remember what you've read, and how well you know the software by heart. If you are a visual thinker, and you can see the drop-down menus and dialog boxes in your head, you won't need to memorize as much as someone who's less visually oriented. The tests will stretch your recollection of commands, tools, utilities, and functions related to how IIS 4 works in the Windows NT environment.

At a minimum, you'll want to memorize the following kinds of information:

➤ Details about the IIS components: WWW service, FTP service, SMTP service, NNTP service, Index Server, and Certificate Server

➤ How to configure IIS 4 on a Windows NT 4 machine, including basic and advanced configuration elements

➤ Configuration of HTTP including HTTP keep-alives and host headers

➤ How to determine proper Web and NTFS permissions

If you work your way through this book while sitting at a machine with IIS 4 installed, and you try to manipulate the features and functions of the various IIS 4 commands, tools, and utilities as they're discussed throughout, you should have little or no difficulty mastering this material. Also, don't forget that The Cram Sheet at the front of the book is designed to capture the material that is most important to memorize; use this to guide your studies as well.

Preparing For The Test

The best way to prepare for the test—after you've studied—is to take at least one practice exam. We've included one here in this chapter (and another in Chapter 15) for that reason; the test questions are located in the pages that follow (and unlike the preceding chapters in this book, the answers don't follow the questions immediately; you'll have to flip to Chapter 14 to review the answers separately for this practice test, and to Chapter 16 to review the answers for the second practice test).

Give yourself 90 minutes to take the exam, keep yourself on the honor system, and don't look at earlier text in the book or jump ahead to the answer key. When your time is up, or you've finished the questions, you can check your work in Chapter 14 or Chapter 16. Pay special attention to the explanations for the incorrect answers; these can also help to reinforce your knowledge of the material. Knowing how to recognize correct answers is good, but understanding why incorrect answers are wrong can be equally valuable.

Taking The Test

Relax. Once you're sitting in front of the testing computer, there's nothing more you can do to increase your knowledge or preparation. Take a deep breath, stretch, and start reading that first question.

There's no need to rush; you have plenty of time to complete each question and to return to those questions that you skip or mark for return (if you are taking a fixed-length or short-form test). If you read a question twice and remain clueless, you can mark it if you're taking a fixed-length or short-form test; if you're taking an adaptive test, you'll have to guess and move on. Both easy and difficult questions are intermixed throughout the test in random order. If you're taking a fixed-length or short-form test, don't cheat yourself by spending too much time on a hard question early in the test, thereby depriving yourself of the time you need to answer the questions at the end of the test. If you're taking an adaptive test, don't spend more than five minutes on any single question—if it takes you that long to get nowhere, it's time to guess and move on.

On a fixed-length or short-form test, you can read through the entire test, and before returning to marked questions for a second visit, figure out how much time you've got per question. As you answer each question, remove its mark. Continue to review the remaining marked questions until you run out of time or you complete the test.

On an adaptive test, set a maximum time limit for questions (we recommend no more than five minutes if you're completely clueless), and watch your time on long or complex questions. If you hit your limit, it's time to guess and move on. Don't deprive yourself of the opportunity to see more questions by taking too long to puzzle over questions, unless you think you can figure out the answer. Otherwise, you're limiting your opportunities to pass.

That's it for pointers. Here are some questions for you to practice on.

Sample Test #1

Question 1

A digital signature performs two functions—it indicates the identity of the sender, and encrypts the signed message.

○ a. True

○ b. False

Question 2

A user performs a query using an Index Server query form on the office intranet. The results from the user's query fail to list the SALES1997.DOC file, which the user knows contains the words "April" and "1997". What could be the reason for this? [Check all correct answers]

❑ a. The user was not authenticated.

❑ b. The user does not have Read access to the file.

❑ c. Another user was accessing the document at the time the query was performed.

❑ d. The file is not included in the corpus.

Question 3

As a busy Webmaster, you would like to automate the process of creating regular reports on the popularity of your Web site. However, you're concerned about the performance of your under-powered server. You've already set up the W3C extended log to take the data you need. Which of the following actions can you add to the Scheduler that won't compromise performance on your server?

○ a. Look up HTML titles.

○ b. Resolve IP addresses.

○ c. Perform Whois organization queries.

○ d. All of the above; this is all good information for reports to management.

○ e. None of the above; each of these actions is performance-intensive on the server.

Question 4

As the Webmaster of the growing company Web site, you're getting a number of complaints from users: Pages are too slow to load, text browsers just can't search through your site, and a number of links just end up in space.

You've already used the Verify Links tool. Which types of data can you get on these issues without having to go through the time and trouble of using a Usage Import of a log file? [Check all correct answers]

❑ a. Perform a quick search for all images without HTML **<ALT>** tags.

❑ b. Do a quick search for all pages above 32K.

❑ c. Create a Site Summary report.

❑ d. Check the links and HTML tags on each page one by one. There's no other way to be sure what is and isn't working.

Question 5

In what ways can you maximize performance of your IIS server when using SSL encryption? [Check all correct answers]

❑ a. Only encrypt the directories that require SSL encryption.

❑ b. Use SSL encryption on the entire site rather than on individual directories.

❑ c. Increase the processor speed of the server.

❑ d. Add more RAM to the server.

Question 6

Clients attempting to access a Web site hosted on IIS receive HTTP error 403. What could cause this error?

○ a. Write access is enabled.

○ b. Read access is not enabled.

○ c. That client's domain is restricted from the Web site.

○ d. Resources are located on a share.

Question 7

Creating a key certificate request is an integral step of what process?

○ a. Installing IIS 4

○ b. Configuring a Web server to offer SSL-based secure communications

○ c. As a client, purchasing a product with a credit card over a secure link

○ d. Applying Service Pack 3 to Windows NT Server

Question 8

For an intranet, if the server name is "marketing", you can reach the Web site's home directory by typing which one of the following URLs within the browser's URL text box?

○ a. **http://localhost/marketing**

○ b. **http://marketing**

○ c. **http://www.iis.com/marketing**

○ d. None of the above

Question 9

You are the Webmaster for your company's Internet Web site. You would like to administer your Web site, but you are behind a firewall. What port do you need to open on the firewall to administer your Web site remotely?

○ a. 80

○ b. 8080

○ c. The randomly assigned port for your default Web site

○ d. The randomly assigned port for your administration Web site

Question 10

If you do not have Read access to a file on the FTP server, you cannot perform which of the following operations? [Check all correct answers]

❑ a. Download the file

❑ b. Read the file

❑ c. Write to the file

Question 11

If you need to make modifications to the certificate key mappings for a Web site, which administration utility can you use?

○ a. Internet Service Manager snap-in

○ b. Server Manager

○ c. Internet Service Manager HTML

○ d. Certificate Server

Question 12

IIS can be administered through which interfaces or utilities? [Check all correct answers]

❑ a. Internet Service Manager MMC snap-in

❑ b. A command prompt

❑ c. Internet Service Manager Administrative wizard

❑ d. Internet Service Manager HTMLA via a Web browser

Question 13

IIS is used to host four Web sites, named SITE1, SITE2, SITE3, and SITE4. You enable bandwidth throttling for the server/computer and set it to 4,096K. SITE3 and SITE4 are the most popular sites hosted by your installation of IIS. You want to grant each of them twice the bandwidth of the other sites. Which modification should you perform?

○ a. Set server/computer-level bandwidth throttling to 8,192KB.

○ b. Set service/site-level bandwidth throttling to 2,046KB for SITE1 and SITE2.

○ c. Set service/site-level bandwidth throttling to 8,192KB for SITE3 and SITE4.

○ d. This cannot be done with IIS 4.

Question 14

In addition to IIS 4 and Windows NT Server, what is another component required to enable 128-bit data encryption?

○ a. An InterNIC-assigned domain name

○ b. Microsoft Transaction Server

○ c. Service Pack 3

○ d. Microsoft Certificate Server

Question 15

You need to enable W3C logging on each of your company's 1,200 Web servers. What is the most efficient method of performing this task?

○ a. Use host headers

○ b. Use Windows Scripting Host

○ c. Through the Web Site tab of each server

○ d. Through the Home Directory tab of each server

Question 16

One of your users cannot connect to IIS. You have checked everything on the user's machine, including the TCP/IP configuration and IP address. Everything looks fine. How do you verify that IIS is installed and up and running on the server properly? [Check all correct answers]

❑ a. Open Internet Explorer 4.01 on the server and verify that the connection to the localhost is okay.

❑ b. Make sure both the network and IIS are running.

❑ c. Make sure the WWW service is configured properly.

❑ d. Make sure the TCP/IP protocol stack is installed.

Question 17

You are the Webmaster for a company called LANW. A user performs a query using an Index Server query form on the company's intranet. The results from the user's query are not relevant to the information they are seeking. The user is searching on the words "LANW", "COPYRIGHT", and "plastic". What should you do to make the user's queries more accurate?

○ a. Add the words "LANW" and "copyright" to the noise word list.

○ b. Increase the size of the word list.

○ c. Delete the user's Internet Explorer cache.

○ d. Delete the server's cache.

Question 18

The IIS SMTP and NNTP services can be administered and managed through which utilities or interfaces? [Check all correct answers]

❑ a. Server Manager

❑ b. IIS's MMC snap-in

❑ c. Network Monitor

❑ d. An HTML interface

Question 19

The Index Server files of IDC and HTX require which permission settings for the IUSR account to function properly? [Check all correct answers]

❑ a. Read

❑ b. Delete

❑ c. Write

❑ d. Execute

Question 20

The NNTP service of IIS supports which of the following functions or features? [Check all correct answers]

❑ a. Hosting of multiple discussion groups

❑ b. Access to standard Usenet newsfeeds

❑ c. Moderated groups

❑ d. SSL-secured transmissions

Question 21

What is a certificate authority (CA)?

○ a. The single worldwide distribution point for client identities

○ b. An Internet standards organization, similar to IETF and IEEE, that sets the requirements for certificates

○ c. A division of the National Security Council (NSC) with the sole purpose of cracking down on computer fraud

○ d. A third-party organization that is trusted to verify the identity of servers and individuals

Question 22

What is the default port for the WWW service?

○ a. 80

○ b. 81

○ c. 82

○ d. 83

Question 23

What tool is included with IIS 4 to simplify the troubleshooting process of Active Server Pages?

○ a. Java Virtual Machine

○ b. Script Debugger

○ c. W3C logging

○ d. ODBC drivers

Question 24

When a user opens the URL for an IIS site, the user is shown a directory listing of the wwwroot directory instead of being shown the default document. Why? [Check all correct answers]

❑ a. The directory has Read access set.

❑ b. Directory browsing is enabled.

❑ c. A redirection URL is used.

❑ d. No default is present or the name of the default document does not match the one known by IIS.

Question 25

While you are trying to install IIS, the installation fails due to insufficient privileges. How do you resolve this problem?

○ a. Reboot the machine.

○ b. Log on the machine as Administrator and reinstall IIS.

○ c. Reinstall IIS with all the components of Windows NT Option Pack.

○ d. Share your root directory.

Question 26

Where are the files that comprise the Administrative HTML tools for remotely managing IIS stored by default?

○ a. \Inetpub\Iisadmin

○ b. \Winnt\System32\Inetsrv\Iisadmin

○ c. \Program Files\Inetput\Admin

○ d. \Inetpub\Adminroot

Question 27

Which of the following tools can you use to monitor the performance of Index Server? [Check all correct answers]

❑ a. Index Server MMC snap-in

❑ b. Performance Monitor

❑ c. HTML Administration

❑ d. An IDA script

Question 28

Which IIS component offers programmers the ability to create three-tiered applications for Internet deployment?

○ a. The NNTP service

○ b. Transaction Server

○ c. Certificate Server

○ d. Index Server

Question 29

Which Microsoft TCP/IP tools are used to investigate the network communications of IIS? [Check all correct answers]

❏ a. PING

❏ b. ROUTE

❏ c. TRACERT

❏ d. NBTSTAT

Question 30

Which Windows NT Server 4 update installs the password-filtering security component?

○ a. Windows NT Service Pack 3

○ b. Windows NT Option Pack

○ c. Internet Explorer 4.01

○ d. Windows NT Server 4

Question 31

Which of the following are needed to install Internet Information Server 4? [Check all correct answers]

❏ a. A local network connection

❏ b. An NTFS partition

❏ c. A computer with at least the minimum hardware required to support Windows NT Server 4

❏ d. The TCP/IP protocol installed

❏ e. Access to the Option Pack distribution files

Question 32

Which of the following software components are requirements for the installation of IIS 4? [Check all correct answers]

❑ a. Service Pack 3 for Windows NT Server 4

❑ b. Index Server

❑ c. Internet Explorer 4.01

❑ d. Windows NT 4 Workstation

Question 33

Which of the following are true statements about IIS 4 and the other services that are included in the Windows NT Option Pack? [Check all correct answers]

❑ a. HTML, text, Microsoft Office, and Adobe PDF documents can be searched.

❑ b. Client identities can be tracked and verified.

❑ c. A single Web server can be copied to three or more other servers simultaneously.

❑ d. Applications can communicate even if network connections are broken.

Question 34

Which of the following do you need before creating a virtual directory?

○ a. A physical path

○ b. Read and Write permissions

○ c. Gopher

○ d. An IP address

Question 35

Which of the following Index Server indexes is stored only in memory?

O a. Word lists

O b. Persistent index

O c. Shadow index

O d. Master index

Question 36

Which of the following measures are used to secure the SMTP service of IIS?
[Check all correct answers]

❑ a. SSL identity verification

❑ b. Windows NT Challenge/Response authentication

❑ c. Reverse DNS lookup

❑ d. IP address and domain name restrictions

Question 37

One of your users is attempting to access a SQL database through your Web
site and receives a "general network error." Which of the following problems
could be causing this error?

O a. The user doesn't have sufficient rights to access the database.

O b. The user doesn't have sufficient rights to access resources within
the database.

O c. The Web service is no longer running.

O d. The name of the SQL database computer has been changed.

Question 38

Which technology is used most often to establish secure communications over networks where data interception is possible?

○ a. CRC

○ b. Encryption

○ c. TCP/IP

○ d. DHCP

Question 39

Which views are available in the Site Server Express Content Analyzer? [Check all correct answers]

❏ a. Orthogonal

❏ b. Tree

❏ c. Cyberbolic

❏ d. Visual

❏ e. Web

Question 40

Why must you install Internet Explorer 4.01 before installing IIS 4?

○ a. To browse the Web.

○ b. Because Internet Explorer 4.01 installs various system DLLs on the server that provide functionality for the Microsoft Management Console, the Microsoft Java VM, and so on.

○ c. Because HTMLA works only with Internet Explorer 4.01.

○ d. Because the script debugger works only with Internet Explorer 4.01.

Question 41

Windows NT Challenge/Response is a built-in Windows NT security feature. What technology can you use to implement similar functionality independent of the operating system? [Check all correct answers]

❑ a. CGI scripts

❑ b. Active Server Pages with ActiveX controls

❑ c. Visual Basic

❑ d. Visual C++

❑ e. Perl

Question 42

One of your users is attempting to access a SQL database through your Web site and receives the following error: "Data source name not found and no default driver specified." Which of the following problems could be causing this error? [Check all correct answers]

❑ a. A "User" type DSN is being used.

❑ b. A "System" type DSN is being used.

❑ c. The server does not have the most current drivers.

❑ d. The DSN is not configured correctly.

Question 43

With MMC, you have the ability to add or remove an individual snap-in; however, once it's added, you cannot save the configuration for future sessions.

○ a. True

○ b. False

Question 44

Within your company intranet, you have 10 workstations used by temporary employees. You do not want users of these computers to have any access to the Web site hosted on your internal IIS. Therefore, on the IP Address And Domain Name Restrictions page for the company Web site, you define exceptions for these 10 computers as 10 individual IP addresses. After you make this change, you discover that no clients on the intranet can access the Web site except these 10 computers. What could be the problem?

○ a. Individual computers cannot be exceptions. A subnet must be specified.

○ b. A reboot of IIS is required before this takes effect.

○ c. Anonymous access has been disabled.

○ d. The IP Address Access Restrictions option is set to Denied Access.

Question 45

You're running a Web site for a winery in the state of Washington. There's a steady stream of users from all over the country who go to your Web site to purchase wines and to get advice on wine making. You're looking to customize the site to provide the best possible experience for your users. You're even considering the use of a mirror site in Delaware if you can show sufficient demand from the East Coast. Which of the following preformatted Report Writer reports could help you meet this need? [Check all correct answers]

❑ a. IP Server

❑ b. Geography

❑ c. Browser And Operating System

❑ d. Referrer

❑ e. Path

Question 46

One of your users is attempting to access a SQL database through your Web site and receives the "login failed" error. Which of the following problems could be causing this error?

○ a. The user does not have sufficient rights to access the database.

○ b. The user does not have sufficient rights to access resources within the database.

○ c. The Web service is no longer running.

○ d. The SQL database has been changed from 16-bit named pipes to a 32-bit TCP connection.

Question 47

You can configure IIS to block specific IP addresses from accessing and using which of the following services? [Check all correct answers]

❑ a. Web

❑ b. FTP

❑ c. Gopher

❑ d. Telnet

Question 48

If you secure your Web site, **www.domain.com**, using SSL encryption, how must your users change the URL to access your site?

○ a. **http://www.domain.com**

○ b. **https://www.domain.com**

○ c. **httpssl://www.domain.com**

○ d. **shttp://www.domain.com**

Question 49

You have been the IIS administrator for your company for more than a year. The Internet content for your company's Web site has grown, and you are asked to create a proprietary authentication program for the site. As the Web site administrator, you are asked to choose the design technique. What technique would you choose? [Check all correct answers]

❑ a. Create an ISAPI filter to authenticate all the users.

❑ b. Create a CGI script to authenticate all the users.

❑ c. Create a user account on Windows NT for all the users.

Question 50

You must manually start a virtual Web or FTP server.

○ a. True

○ b. False

Question 51

You want to create a new Index Server catalog for a Web site. The corpus of the Web site is 500MB. How much space will be required by the catalog?

○ a. 100MB

○ b. 200MB

○ c. 500MB

○ d. 800MB

Question 52

You would like to design an HTML form that accepts data from the user, processes the data on IIS, and returns results to the browser. Choose the IIS extensions for this type of implementation. [Check all correct answers]

❑ a. JScript

❑ b. VBScript

❑ c. CGI

❑ d. ASP

Question 53

Your public Web server also hosts a private data area. You have configured Index Server to index every document stored on the server in both the Web root and the data directory. All the files in the data directory are set so that only internal users have Read access. If an external user performs a search using a word that exists in one or more files from both the Web root and the data directory, how will items from the data directory appear in the results lists?

- ○ a. They will appear without hyperlinks.
- ○ b. They will appear with authentication fields to gain access.
- ○ c. They will appear just as any item from the Web root.
- ○ d. They will not appear, and the external user will be unaware of their presence.

Question 54

Your supervisor has just read an article that mentioned the power of inference algorithms. She asks you to explain to her what an inference algorithm is and what it has to do with measuring the performance of the Web server. Which of the following would be an accurate description?

- ○ a. An inference algorithm is a program that uses fuzzy logic to perform tasks such as HTML title lookups and IP address resolution. Because it simplifies the lookup of items such as DNS files, it improves performance of these otherwise high-intensity tasks.

- ○ b. An inference algorithm is a set of calculations that improves logging speed in IIS. Without it, ODBC logging would be a process that would overcome all but the fastest processors with at least 64MB of memory.

- ○ c. An inference algorithm works like a statistical correction factor for things such as requesting data in an ODBC-compliant log file. Without it, Web pages with 100 thumbnail images would appear to be many times more popular than they really are.

- ○ d. An inference algorithm works like a set of statistical correction factors for things such as IP address resolution and database caching. Without it, database references to cached data would not be possible.

- ○ e. An inference algorithm is a set of calculations that improves the speed of Site Server Express Report Writer.

Question 55

Which of the following settings can be found in the Metabase?

○ a. MIME type settings for the server

○ b. MIME type settings for the Web service

○ c. The location of the SMTP log files

○ d. The size of the corpus used by Index Server

Answer Key #1

1. b	15. b	29. a, c	43. b
2. a, b, d	16. a, b, c, d	30. a	44. d
3. e	17. a	31. c, d, e	45. b, c, e
4. a, b, c	18. b, d	32. a, c	46. a
5. a, c	19. a, d	33. a, b, d	47. a, b
6. b	20. a, c, d	34. a	48. b
7. b	21. d	35. a	49. a, b
8. b	22. a	36. a, b, c, d	50. a
9. d	23. b	37. d	51. b
10. a, b	24. b, d	38. b	52. a, b, c, d
11. a	25. b	39. b, c	53. d
12. a, b, d	26. b	40. b	54. c
13. c	27. a, c, d	41. a, c, d, e	55. b
14. c	28. b	42. b, c, d	

Question 1

Answer b is correct. False; a digital signature is used only to indicate the identity of the sender; it's not used to encrypt data.

Question 2

Answers a, b, and d are correct. The nonappearance of a known file in a results list can be due to a user not being authenticated, a user not having at least Read access, or the file not being part of the corpus. Because a query is performed against an index and not the original file, it's not affected by the status of the document. Therefore, answer c is incorrect.

Question 3

Answer e is correct. HTML title lookup, IP address resolution, and Whois organization queries are all resource-intensive operations and should be avoided whenever possible when performance is an issue. However, if you can find a time of day when demand on this server is low, it's certainly possible to schedule these operations for specific times. It would be helpful to find out when these times are through the appropriate report; however, you don't know what these times are right now. Therefore, answers a, b, c, and d are incorrect.

Question 4

Answers a, b, and c are correct. Not everyone has a browser that shows images. When a text-based browser gets to an image without HTML <ALT> tags, the browser stops. In general, pages with more than 32KB are too slow to load for all modem users. A Site Summary report is a useful overview of the status of key quick search items on the Web site. Because you've already used the Verify Links tool, broken links will be reported. It isn't necessary to go into a Web page to check all the links. Therefore, answer d is incorrect.

Question 5

Answers a and c are correct. To minimize processor utilization, you should encrypt only the directories that require SSL encryption rather than encrypting the entire Web server. Also, SSL is CPU-intensive rather than memory-intensive, so increasing the processor will help minimize performance degradation.

Question 6

Answer b is correct. A 403 error occurs if the Web site does not have Read access enabled. Enabling Write access has no effect on Read access. Therefore, answer a is incorrect. If the client was restricted from the Web site, an "Access denied" error would be issued instead of a "Read access forbidden" error. Therefore, answer c is incorrect. Pulling resources from a share has no effect on the read error. Therefore, answer d is incorrect.

Question 7

Answer b is correct. Creating a key certificate request is an integral part of configuring a Web server to offer SSL-based secure communications. Installing IIS and applying Service Pack 3 do not require a key request. Therefore, answers a and d are incorrect. As a client, purchasing a product with a credit card over a secure link does not require a key request to be generated, but it does rely on the Web server to have installed a certificate already. Therefore, answer c is incorrect.

Question 8

Answer b is correct. For an intranet, the Web site's home directory is mapped to the server name; "http://marketing" represents a direct mapping between the Web site's home directory and the server name. None of the other options represents this direct mapping. Therefore, answers a, c, and d are incorrect.

Question 9

Answer d is correct. As long as authentication is set up correctly, the URL to administer a Web site remotely includes the randomly assigned port for the administration Web site. Therefore, answers a, b, and c are incorrect.

Question 10

Answers a and b are correct. Downloading a file is equivalent to a Read operation. Because there's no Read access on the file, you can neither read nor download the file. To be able to write to the file, you must have Write access to the file, which is a separate permission from Read and does not rely on Read access. Therefore, answer c is incorrect.

Question 11

Answer a is correct. Only the locally accessible ISM snap-in can be used to manage certificate mappings. The Server Manager is not involved with certificate management. Therefore, answer b is incorrect. ISM HTML does not have the ability to manage certificate mappings. Therefore, answer c is incorrect. The Certificate Server is only used to issue certificates if you want to be a certificate authority—but it's also not used to map certificates to Web sites. Therefore, answer d is incorrect.

Question 12

Answers a, b, and d are correct. IIS is administered through an MMC snap-in and HTMLA. Some administration features can also be accomplished through a command prompt with the help of the Windows Scripting Host. IIS does not have an Administrative wizard. Therefore, answer c is incorrect.

Question 13

Answer c is correct. The correct modification is to set service/site-level bandwidth throttling to 8,192KB for SITE3 and SITE4. This will grant twice the bandwidth granted to SITE1 and SITE2 for both SITE3 and SITE4. Setting server/computer-level bandwidth throttling to 8,192KB will not specifically grant twice the bandwidth to SITE3 and SITE4; instead, it will just double the total bandwidth shared by all four sites. Therefore, answer a is incorrect. Setting service/site-level bandwidth throttling to 2,046KB for SITE1 and SITE2 will not double the available bandwidth to SITE3 and SITE4 but will only force SITE3 and SITE4 to compete for the 4,096KB server/computer throttle limit. Therefore, answer b is incorrect. Throttling by site and by computer is possible with IIS. Therefore, answer d is incorrect.

Question 14

Answer c is correct. Service Pack 3 is the component required for 128-bit data encryption. IIS does not need a true Internet domain name assigned by the InterNIC, Microsoft Transaction Server, or Microsoft Certificate Server to use 128-bit encryption. Therefore, answers a, b, and d are incorrect.

Question 15

Answer b is correct. The most efficient method of accomplishing such a task on a large number of servers is by using the Windows Scripting Host to create commands that will run on each of the servers. Using a host header enables a Web server to use multiple IP addresses. Therefore, answer a is incorrect. Manually making the change to each of the servers would be incredibly slow and inefficient. Also, there is no such thing as a Web Site tab. Therefore, answers c and d are incorrect.

Question 16

Answers a, b, c, and d are correct. First, you want to check whether both the network and IIS are running. Next, you want to check whether the TCP/IP protocol stack is installed. Then, check whether the WWW service is configured properly. Finally, to test if everything is working right, open Internet Explorer on the server and verify the connection to the localhost.

Question 17

Answer a is correct. It's generally a good idea to add your Web site's most popular words to the noise word list so queries have more accurate results. Increasing the size of the word list will not provide more accurate results. Therefore, answer b is incorrect. Deleting the user's cache or the server's cache will not generate more accurate results. Therefore, answers c and d are incorrect.

Question 18

Answers b and d are correct. The IIS SMTP and NNTP services can be administered through the IIS MMC snap-in or through separate HTML interfaces. Server Manager and Network Monitor are not used to administer these services. Therefore, answers a and c are incorrect.

Question 19

Answers a and d are correct. The IDC and HTX files require Read and Execute permissions.

Question 20

Answers a, c, and d are correct. The IIS NNTP service supports multiple discussion groups, moderated groups, and SSL. IIS's NNTP service is unable to access Usenet newsfeeds. It's restricted to host discussion groups within a single server. Therefore, answer b is incorrect.

Question 21

Answer d is correct. A certificate authority (CA) is a third-party organization that is trusted to verify the identity of servers and individuals. A CA is not a single worldwide distribution point for client identities. This type of entity does not currently exist. Therefore, answer a is incorrect. A CA is not an Internet standards organization similar to IETF and IEEE that sets the requirements for certificates. Therefore, answer b is incorrect. A CA is not part of the NSC. Therefore, answer c is incorrect.

Question 22

Answer a is correct. The default port for the WWW service is 80. Therefore, answers b, c, and d are incorrect.

Question 23

Answer b is correct. The Script Debugger is the tool included with IIS 4 that simplifies the troubleshooting process of Active Server Pages. The Java Virtual Machine is not a troubleshooting tool for ASP files. Therefore, answer a is incorrect. W3C logging is a troubleshooting tool for the Web server as a whole. Therefore, answer c is incorrect. ODBC drivers are not troubleshooting tools; they enable database application communications. Therefore, answer d is incorrect.

Question 24

Answers b and d are correct. If a user is shown a directory listing, directory browsing is enabled and a default document is not found. The directory must have Read access defined; otherwise, the directory listing won't be displayed. Therefore, answer a is incorrect. A redirection URL does not cause a directory listing to be displayed; it simply takes you to the alternate location. Therefore, answer c is incorrect.

Question 25

Answer b is correct. While you're installing IIS, Setup needs to create some directories, as well as give share access to others. Only a Windows NT administrator can do this. None of the other options will resolve this problem. Therefore, answers a, c, and d are incorrect.

Question 26

Answer b is correct. The IIS Administration HTML tool files are stored in \Winnt\System32\Inetsrv\Iisadmin, by default. The other listed folders are incorrect. Therefore, answers a, c, and d are incorrect.

Question 27

Answers a, c, and d are correct. Index Server can be administered through its MMC snap-in, through HTML Administration, or through an IDA script. Index Server can be monitored, but not administered, through Performance Monitor. Therefore, answer b is incorrect.

Question 28

Answer b is correct. Transaction Server offers programmers the ability to create three-tiered applications for Internet deployment. The NNTP service is used to host discussion groups; Certificate Server allows your site to be a certificate authority; and Index Server offers content indexing and searching. Therefore, answers a, c, and d are incorrect.

Question 29

Answers a and c are correct. PING and TRACERT are TCP/IP utilities that are used to test network communications. ROUTE and NBTSTAT are not used to test network communications. Therefore, answers b and d are incorrect.

Question 30

Answer a is correct. Windows NT Service Pack 3 installs a number of new security components and application programming interfaces, including the password-filtering security component. The Windows NT Option Pack installs IIS 4. Therefore, answer b is incorrect. Internet Explorer 4.01 installs various system DLLs, thus providing functionality for the Microsoft Management Console, the Microsoft Java VM, and so on. Therefore, answer c is incorrect. Windows NT Server 4 installs Windows NT. Therefore, answer d is incorrect.

Question 31

Answers c, d, and e are correct. You need a machine that supports the minimum hardware requirements to install Windows NT Server 4. The TCP/IP protocol is also required for IIS. Access to the Option Pack distribution files can be via an Internet connection to the Microsoft Web site or on a CD-ROM. You don't need a local network connection (because IIS can be an isolated or standalone machine) or an NTFS partition for installing Windows NT or IIS. Therefore, answers a and b are incorrect.

Question 32

Answers a and c are correct. Service Pack 3 and Internet Explorer 4.01 are installation requirements for IIS 4. Index Server is not a requirement of IIS 4. Therefore, answer b is incorrect. Windows NT 4 Workstation is not a requirement of IIS 4. In fact, IIS is not supported on Windows NT Workstation. Therefore, answer d is incorrect.

Question 33

Answers a, b, and d are correct. Answer a refers to Index Server, answer b refers to Certificate Server, and answer d refers to Message Queue Server. The statement in answer c is incorrect. Site Server Express can replicate only one server to one server. Only the full Enterprise version of Site Server can replicate one server to multiple servers.

Question 34

Answer a is correct. When creating the virtual directory, you need to provide the directory's physical path. If you do not grant the Read and Write permissions for the directory, the client browser may not be able to browse the virtual directory; however, you can grant these permissions at a later stage. IIS 4 does not support Gopher. Also, you need an IP address for a virtual server, not a virtual directory. Therefore, answers b, c, and d are incorrect.

Question 35

Answer a is correct. Only word lists are stored in memory. Persistent, shadow, and master indexes are stored on a hard drive. Therefore, answers b, c, and d are incorrect.

Question 36

Answers a, b, c, and d are correct. The SMTP service can be secured using any of these methods.

Question 37

Answer d is correct. An ODBC general network error may be caused by the DSN not being able to access the server because the DSN may still be referencing the old database computer name. Insufficient rights would invoke an error indicating so, not a general network error. Therefore, answers a and b are incorrect. If the Web service were no longer running, an ODBC error would not have occurred; a Web server error would have occurred. Therefore, answer c is incorrect.

Question 38

Answer b is correct. Encryption is the technology used to establish secure communications over insecure networks. CRC is a technology used to verify the integrity of transmitted data; it's not associated with security. Therefore, answer a is incorrect. TCP/IP is a network protocol. Secure communications can occur over it, but TCP/IP does not directly provide for security. Therefore, answer c is incorrect. DHCP is a technology used to dynamically configure clients. Therefore, answer d is incorrect.

Question 39

Answers b and c are correct. The tree and cyberbolic views are the two views available in Site Server Express Content Analyzer. The other answers are not options in Content Analyzer. Therefore, answers a, d, and e are incorrect.

Question 40

Answer b is correct. IIS 4 uses the system DLLs that Internet Explorer 4.01 installs. You don't need to use Internet Explorer to browse the Web—you can use any other browser. Therefore, answer a is incorrect. The HTMLA works with many other browsers, not just IE 4.01. Therefore, answer c is incorrect. Although it is true that the script debugger only works with IE 4.01, the script debugger is merely an optional component. Therefore, answer d is incorrect.

Question 41

Answers a, c, d, and e are correct. You can use Visual Basic, Visual C++, and Perl to create CGI programs. A CGI program runs independent of the operating system, as long as the program does not use or call any functions specific to the operating system. Active Server Pages with ActiveX controls is Windows-platform-specific. Therefore, answer b is incorrect.

Question 42

Answers b, c, and d are correct. An ODBC DSN not found error may be caused by an incorrectly configured data source name, and a DSN requires a File or System DSN. Also, this error could be caused by the server not having the most current ODBC drivers. A User DSN can't be used. Therefore, answer a is incorrect.

Question 43

Answer b is correct. This statement is false, MMC has the ability to save the configuration of each console as an MSC file for use in subsequent sessions.

Question 44

Answer d is correct. If all but the exception computers can no longer gain access, this means that Denied Access was selected instead of Granted Access. Individual computers and a subnet can be used as exceptions. Therefore, answer a is incorrect. A reboot of IIS is not required for a change in access restrictions. Therefore, answer b is incorrect. Disabling anonymous access prevents all clients from accessing anonymously, but it does not restrict authenticated user access. This question does not state if anonymous or authenticated access was affected. Therefore, answer c is incorrect.

Question 45

Answers b, c, and e are correct. A Geography report will help you determine the distribution of where your users are coming from. Knowing the browser of most of your users will help determine the type of add-ons that are more important for your site (for example, ActiveX for MSIE or Java for Netscape). The Path report shows how your users are navigating through the site and therefore helps determine whether you need to change the locations and sizes of some pages, images, and other objects to make navigation easier. There is no IP Server report. Therefore, answer a is incorrect. The Referrer report provides data on where users are coming from (which ISPs they use). Although this can provide useful data on where your advertising is working best on the Web, this does not address the user experience once he or she has reached your site. Therefore, answer d is incorrect.

Question 46

Answer a is correct. An ODBC logon failed error is usually caused by the user not having sufficient rights to the SQL server database. A user would receive an Access Is Denied error message if he or she could not access a resource within the SQL Server database. Therefore, answer b is incorrect. If the Web service was no longer running, an ODBC error would not have occurred; a Web server error would have occurred. Therefore, answer c is incorrect. An inability to access the DSN would cause a general network error. Therefore, answer d is incorrect.

Question 47

Answers a and b are correct. You can configure both Web and FTP services to block specific IP addresses. IIS 4 does not support Gopher or Telnet. Therefore, answers c and d are incorrect.

Question 48

Answer b is correct. To access a Web site that uses SSL encryption, the URL must begin with http://. Answers a, c, and d are incorrect.

Question 49

Answers a and b are correct. Answer a is the most efficient technique because the approach uses an ISAPI filter. ISAPI implementation consumes fewer server resources compared to a CGI implementation. Answer b is less efficient (but still correct) because an ISAPI solution is faster than a CGI solution. Answer c is not an option because you do not want to create a Windows NT user account for each user. Therefore, answer c is incorrect.

Question 50

Answer a is correct. This is a true statement. When you first create a virtual Web or FTP server, the server's default state is Stopped. Therefore, answer b is incorrect.

Question 51

Answer b is correct. The index catalog is typically 40 percent of the corpus, so 200MB is required in this scenario.

Question 52

Answers a, b, c, and d are correct. Both JScript and VBScript are scripting languages you can use with ASP. ASP is an alternative to CGI, and CGI is the standard Web mechanism for transmitting data between the client and server.

Question 53

Answer d is correct. Items from an ACL-restricted directory will not appear in the results list for a user without proper access privileges. That user will be unaware of the existence of those documents because Index Server will not even show the file name of restricted items to unauthorized users. Because Index Server will not display restricted items to unauthorized users in any way, answers a, b, and c are incorrect. Even when items are included in the index files used by a search to which the current user does not have valid access, these items are not displayed in the results list.

Question 54

Answer c is correct. Without inference algorithms, a Web page with 100 thumbnail images would get 101 hits each time a user links to it, which would make the page seem much more popular than a text-only page that gets only one hit for each time a user links to it. Inference algorithms correct for this discrepancy. However, they only address the data related to hits, requests, visits, users, and organizations. Although IP address resolution is loosely related to organizations, database caching is not an inference algorithm function. Therefore, answer d is incorrect. None of the other answers is related to the function of inference algorithms. Therefore, answers a, b, and e are incorrect.

Question 55

Answer b is correct. Only IIS-specific settings are stored in the Metabase. MIME settings for the server, the location of the SMTP log files, and the size of the corpus used by Index Server are not IIS-specific and thus would not be kept in the Metabase. Therefore, answers a, c, and d are incorrect.

Sample Test #2

See Chapter 13 for Sample Test #1 and pointers to help you develop a successful test-taking strategy, including how to choose proper answers, how to decode ambiguity, how to work within the Microsoft testing framework, how to decide what you need to memorize, and how to prepare for the test. In this chapter, we include another sample test on subject matter pertinent to Microsoft Exam 70-087: "Implementing and Supporting Microsoft Internet Information Server 4." After this chapter, you will find the answer key to this test.

Also, remember that you can take an adaptive practice exam on IIS online at **www.coriolis.com/cip/testcenter/** (the password is ISPTOL51069) to help you prepare even more. Good luck!

Question 1

If you want to view a representation of your Web site and its links, which IIS component would you use?

○ a. Microsoft Transaction Server

○ b. Microsoft Message Queue Server

○ c. Site Server Express

○ d. Microsoft Management Console

Question 2

Your domain name is currently set to one of your subsidiaries, but you want all of your email messages coming from your IIS server to seem as if they are coming from your corporate domain name. Which SMTP service setting should you use to define this parameter?

○ a. Masquerade Domain

○ b. Smart Host

○ c. Virtual Host

○ d. Badmail

Question 3

Which of the following lines of code should you add to the first line in the following script so that the script runs on the server?

```
<SCRIPT LANGUAGE=VBScript>
<!--
Option Explicit

Dim validCreditCardNumber
Sub Submit_OnClick
     validCreditCardNumber = True
     Call CheckCreditCardNumber(CreditCardNumber
       Field.Value,
       "Please enter your credit card number.")
     If validCreditCardNumber then
          MsgBox "Thank you for your order"
     End if
End Sub
</SCRIPT>
```

○ a. **EXECUTEAT=SERVER**

○ b. **RUNAT=SERVER**

○ c. **PARSEAT=SERVER**

○ d. None of the above

Question 4

You have configured a virtual directory on your IIS server called "Chris Mizrany" but some users cannot access this new directory. What is the most likely cause of this problem?

○ a. You have not started the virtual directory.

○ b. You have not started the Web site.

○ c. The virtual directory name has a space in it.

○ d. The virtual directory name has capitalized letters in it.

Question 5

You are the administrator of an IIS Web server that hosts an NNTP service. The newsgroups on the NNTP site have grown so large that your users would like to search their contents. How can you enable this functionality?

○ a. Implement Microsoft Index Server. Use an .IDQ file to search the newsgroups.

○ b. Implement ODBC connections to a SQL Server. Use SQL queries to search the newsgroups.

○ c. Instruct users to use their newsgroup readers to search the newsgroups.

○ d. Do nothing. It is not possible to search the contents of newsgroups.

Question 6

You are the administrator for a company's Internet presence, and their Web site is continually being attacked. By checking your IIS logs, you've determined the attacking user has an IP address assigned to a local ISP. What is the most practical way to protect the Web site from future attacks by this user?

○ a. Disable anonymous access.

○ b. Install a certificate on the server.

○ c. Configure the Web site to deny access to the attacker's IP address.

○ d. Configure the Web site to deny access to the IP address range of the attacker's ISP.

Question 7

The maximum number of FTP connections supported by your IIS Server is 1,000, and the server has reached its limit. When the next user connects to the server, what message does IIS display?

○ a. A warning message

○ b. No message

○ c. A welcome message

○ d. An exit message

Question 8

You are the administrator of a Web server on your company's intranet. Your boss has made it clear that users should be able to access your Web site using a friendly name rather than by its IP address. The entire user base uses Windows NT 4 Workstation. Which of the following technologies allows you to accomplish this request? [Check all correct answers]

❑ a. HOSTS

❑ b. LMHOSTS

❑ c. WINS

❑ d. DNS

Question 9

Log files in IIS 4 are set up by Web site. To use the IIS 4 log files, a number of parameters have to be set in Usage Import to match what has been set in the properties of each Web site. Which of the following do these settings include? [Check all correct answers]

❑ a. Default home page URL

❑ b. Time zone

❑ c. Spider list

❑ d. HTML **<ALT>** tags

❑ e. Domain

Question 10

In which ways can you improve the performance of an IIS-hosted Web site without spending more money on hardware or network services? [Check all correct answers]

❑ a. Add RAM.

❑ b. Remove nonessential services.

❑ c. Run applications in their own memory space.

❑ d. Increase the maximum number of connections.

Question 11

Shannon would like to download a Web site to her computer so that she can make test modifications to the site without affecting the production server. Which of the following is a component of IIS that provides a convenient way of accomplishing this task?

○ a. Microsoft Index Server

○ b. Internet Service Manager

○ c. Microsoft Content Deployment

○ d. Microsoft Content Analyzer

Question 12

The path to your Web site is E:\Inetpub\wwwroot. To which of the following paths can you make a virtual directory? [Check all correct answers]

❏ a. E:\Inetpub

❏ b. E:\Inetpub\wwwroot\bowling

❏ c. C:\bowling

❏ d. D:\Sports\bowling

Question 13

You have created a virtual Web site with its own IP address. You try to access the site by typing the new IP address into the address bar of IE. You receive a message saying "Connection cannot be established." What is the most likely cause of this problem?

○ a. You have not started the virtual Web site.

○ b. IE is trying to use WINS rather than DNS.

○ c. You do not have the correct permissions.

○ d. You need to add the port number to the URL.

Question 14

You need to change the domain name of 300 Web sites to end with .com rather than .edu. Which of the following tools provides the most efficient way to accomplish this task?

○ a. Content Analyzer

○ b. Windows Scripting Host

○ c. HTMLA

○ d. MMC

Question 15

Which technology is used most often to establish secure communications over networks where data interception is possible?

○ a. CRC

○ b. Basic authentication

○ c. SSL

○ d. TCP/IP

Question 16

Which feature of HTTP 1.1 helps increase the loading speed and the processing rate of ASP files?

○ a. Chunked transfers

○ b. Host headers

○ c. Pipelining

○ d. Persistent connections

Question 17

Which of the following are requirements for the installation of IIS 4? [Check all correct answers]

❑ a. Service Pack 3

❑ b. Internet Explorer 4.01+

❑ c. Windows NT Option Pack

❑ d. Windows NT 4 Server

Question 18

You set up a Web site on your intranet. When a user tries to access the site, he receives an error message that says, "Error 401.2, Browser does not support required encryption method." What is most likely the cause of this error?

○ a. The user does not have the appropriate permissions.

○ b. The site uses Windows NT Challenge/Response.

○ c. The browser does not support SSL.

○ d. The site has an invalid certificate.

Question 19

You have created a virtual directory on your Web site that points to a directory on a NetWare server by using a UNC path. You configure script access in IIS for the Scripts directory. You have found that you are unable to read the files on the NetWare server by using the virtual directory. What should you do?

○ a. Add the IUSR_*computername* account access to the file permissions on the NetWare server.

○ b. Move the data from the NetWare server to the Windows NT Server. Create a virtual directory to point to the Windows NT Server.

○ c. Add Execute permissions to the virtual directory.

○ d. Change the path to the NetWare server by using the IP address rather than the UNC path.

Question 20

You are using Internet Service Manager to administer a Web site, and you would like to change the administrator port to 3359. How can you accomplish this task?

○ a. Change the SSL port number for the Administrator site to 3389.

○ b. Change the TCP/IP port number for the Administrator Web site to 3389.

○ c. Change the TCP/IP port number for the Default Web site to 3389.

○ d. Do nothing. By default, 3389 is the port for the Administrator Web site.

Question 21

You install the SMTP service on your IIS server. Users report that it takes up to 48 hours to receive undeliverable message notification. Which of the following configuration changes could you make to decrease the time it takes for users to receive these notifications? [Check all correct answers]

❑ a. Decrease the retry interval to 30 minutes.

❑ b. Increase the maximum retries to 60.

❑ c. Decrease the maximum retries to 30.

❑ d. Limit the number of connections to 1,000.

Question 22

Which of the following are the characteristics of the Windows NT Challenge/Response authentication scheme? [Check all correct answers]

❑ a. Encrypts the password

❑ b. Authenticates a user

❑ c. Is a component of SSL

❑ d. Prompts a user for his or her name and password

Question 23

You can configure IIS to block specific IP addresses from accessing and using which of the following services? [Check all correct answers]

- ❑ a. Web
- ❑ b. SMTP
- ❑ c. FTP
- ❑ d. Gopher

Question 24

If you only have Read access to a directory on an FTP server, which of the following operations can you perform? [Check all correct answers]

- ❑ a. Download a file from the directory
- ❑ b. Upload a file to the directory
- ❑ c. Read a file in the directory
- ❑ d. Modify a file in the directory

Question 25

A digital signature performs two functions: It indicates the identity of the sender, and it encrypts an email message.

- ○ a. True
- ○ b. False

Question 26

What is a certificate authority (CA)?

- ○ a. The single worldwide distribution point for client identities
- ○ b. An Internet standards organization, similar to IETF and IEEE, that sets the requirements for certificates
- ○ c. A division of the National Security Council (NSC) with the sole purpose of cracking down on computer fraud
- ○ d. A third-party organization that is trusted to verify the identity of servers and individuals

Question 27

If you secure a Web site called **www.domain.com** using SSL encryption, how must you change the URL to access the secured pages?

○ a. **http://www.domain.com/ssl/**

○ b. **httpssl://www.domain.com**

○ c. **https://www.domain.com**

○ d. **shttp://www.domain.com**

Question 28

The IIS MMC snap-in alters the rebar menu to grant you one-button access to which standard Windows NT Server utilities? [Check all correct answers]

❑ a. Performance Monitor

❑ b. Server Manager

❑ c. Registry Editor

❑ d. Event Viewer

❑ e. User Manager For Domains

❑ f. Network Monitor

Question 29

To administer your IIS server using MMC through a firewall, which port needs to be open on the firewall?

○ a. 80

○ b. 21

○ c. The randomly generated port for HTMLA

○ d. The NBT port

Question 30

Creating a key certificate request is an integral step of what process?

○ a. Installing IIS 4

○ b. Configuring a Web server to offer SSL-based secure communications

○ c. As a client, purchasing a product with a credit card over a secure link

○ d. Applying Service Pack 3 to Windows NT Server

Question 31

Which of the following measures are used to secure the SMTP service of IIS? [Check all correct answers]

❑ a. SSL identity verification

❑ b. Windows NT Challenge/Response authentication

❑ c. Reverse DNS lookup

❑ d. IP address and domain name restrictions

Question 32

If you change the default SSL port from 443 to 993, what is the syntax of the URL used to access the site?

○ a. **http://www.*domain*.com:993/**

○ b. **https:/www.*domain*.com/**

○ c. **https://www.*domain*.com:993/**

○ d. None. The SSL port can only be 443.

Question 33

For a Windows NT-based intranet, if the server name is "johnh", you can reach the Web site's home directory by typing which one of the following URLs within the browser's URL textbox?

○ a. **http://johnh**

○ b. **http://johnh.domain.com**

○ c. **http://www.iis.com/johnh**

○ d. **http://www.johnh.com**

Question 34

Your Perl script currently works on your original IIS server, but you've moved your application to a different server, and the Perl script is no longer functioning. What is the most likely cause of this problem?

○ a. The script must be recompiled.

○ b. You must first convert the script to a batch file.

○ c. You must install a Perl interpreter on the new server.

○ d. You must assign Write permissions to the script's directory.

Question 35

Which of the following methods is the best way to minimize CPU utilization on an IIS server?

○ a. Use 128-bit encryption.

○ b. Use 40-bit encryption.

○ c. Enable SSL on the entire Web site.

○ d. Enable SSL only where required.

Question 36

Under the SMTP service of IIS, what happens to email messages that cannot be delivered to their intended recipient? [Check all correct answers]

- ❑ a. They are sent to a default remote SMTP server.
- ❑ b. They are returned to the sender.
- ❑ c. They are stored in the local queue.
- ❑ d. They are deposited in the Badmail directory.

Question 37

The Action and View pull-down command lists that are customized by each snap-in are found on which standard MMC component or area?

- ○ a. Scope pane
- ○ b. Status bar
- ○ c. Rebar
- ○ d. Results pane

Question 38

An FTP server can be administered through which interfaces or utilities? [Check all correct answers]

- ❑ a. MMC
- ❑ b. Internet Explorer
- ❑ c. Internet Service Manager Administrative Wizard
- ❑ d. A command prompt

Question 39

A client attempting to access a resource on your IIS Web site receives a 404 HTTP error. What does this error mean?

○ a. Due to malformed syntax, the request could not be understood by the server.

○ b. This error indicates that the credentials passed to the server do not match the credentials required to log on to the server.

○ c. The Web server cannot find the file or script requested.

○ d. The server, while acting as a gateway or proxy, received an invalid response from the upstream server it accessed in attempting to fulfill the request.

Question 40

If you need to monitor the throughput of a specific FTP site, which Performance Monitor object added by IIS should you select counters from?

○ a. FTP Service

○ b. Internet Information Services Global

○ c. Web Service

○ d. Active Server Pages

Question 41

What is the default port for the FTP service?

○ a. 20

○ b. 21

○ c. 25

○ d. 80

Question 42

Which of the following setting changes will improve the performance of a high-volume Web site?

○ a. Disable HTTP keep-alives

○ b. Set Web timeouts to 1,800 seconds

○ c. Set Performance Tuning to fewer than 10,000

○ d. Connect a T3 to IIS

Question 43

Which of the following file types usually contains the query form for Microsoft Index Server?

○ a. HTML

○ b. HTX

○ c. IDQ

○ d. IDC

Question 44

The password for the IUSR_*servername* account in the User Manager For Domains has been changed, and clients are reporting that they can no longer gain access to the public Web site. Why?

○ a. Automatic password synchronization for the anonymous account has been disabled.

○ b. The new password was less than eight characters long.

○ c. Changing the anonymous account password requires a reinstallation of IIS.

○ d. It takes up to three hours before a new password can be used on Windows NT.

Question 45

You have been asked to publish a Web map on your company Web site. For security reasons, you have been asked to exclude information from the internal sales servers. The password-protected entry page to the sales server is several levels below the Web site home page. The Honor Robot Protocol box in the General tab of the Mapping Options dialog box is not checked. In your Content Analyzer Web map, you see a robot icon at the firewall to the sales server. What do you do to protect the sales server from searches?

○ a. Get rid of this robot; otherwise, the rest of the world will have easy access to your company's confidential sales information.

○ b. When you explore the site, limit the levels explored so that the Content Analyzer spider can't get to the secured area of the sales server.

○ c. Create a separate secure Web site for the sales server. Delete all links from your Web site to the secure area.

○ d. The Robot protocol icon is okay, but you need to make sure that the Honor Robot Protocol checkbox in the General tab of the Mapping Options dialog box is checked.

○ e. If you see the Robot protocol icon, it's too late. The secure part of your site has already been penetrated by someone else's spider.

Question 46

The IIS SMTP service can host multiple user mailboxes, so clients with POP3-compliant user agents (email client software) can retrieve messages.

○ a. True

○ b. False

Question 47

Your boss has asked you for a quick "big picture" review of the company's Web site's layout. Which type of report should you create?

○ a. Report Writer Big Picture Report

○ b. Report Writer Executive Summary

○ c. Quick search for broken links and unavailable objects

○ d. Content Analyzer Executive Summary

Question 48

Which of the following is a Microsoft TCP/IP troubleshooting tool that is used to view the hops from a source to a destination computer?

○ a. PING

○ b. FQDN

○ c. TRACERT

○ d. TRACE

Question 49

You are the administrator of a Web site whose home directory is C:\Web. You have files that you would like to make available from this Web site, but they reside in the C:\other directory on the same server. Which of the following actions provides the best method to add these files to your Web site?

○ a. Add a virtual directory for the files, and assign it the path of C:\other.

○ b. Move all of the files from the C:\other directory to the C:\Web directory.

○ c. Add a virtual directory to the new directory, and assign it the path of \\servername\other.

○ d. Change the home directory for the default Web site to C:\other.

Question 50

Site Server Express creates a template database named MSUSAGE during its installation. Which database file extension does it carry?

○ a. SQL

○ b. JET

○ c. MDB

○ d. SSE

Question 51

What is the maximum strength of data encryption that can be used by an IIS server in the United States when communicating with other clients in the United States?

○ a. 40

○ b. 128

○ c. 512

○ d. 1,024

Question 52

The SMTP service automatically processes email placed or copied into a specific directory. What is the directory named?

○ a. Drop

○ b. SortTemp

○ c. Queue

○ d. Pickup

Question 53

An NTFS partition is required to install IIS 4.

○ a. True

○ b. False

Question 54

Your company has developed a software product and would like potential customers to download a free evaluation copy from its Web site. Which of the following is the least complicated, most efficient way to accomplish this?

○ a. Create a Web form where users register themselves and you mail them a disk with the free software.

○ b. Use Microsoft Merchant Server to configure the download facility.

○ c. Place the software on the FTP site and set the FTP directory to Read Only. Point the interested users to this site.

○ d. Install a proxy server and then use IIS's FTP service to facilitate the download.

Question 55

You have created a Web page that includes only information you'd like to have as a standard footer on all of your Web pages. Of the following, choose the most efficient methods of including the footer in each page. [Check all correct answers]

❑ a. Use SSI to include the page in all Web pages.

❑ b. Use the Default Directory tab of the Web Site Properties sheet.

❑ c. Use the Documents tab of the Web Site Properties sheet.

❑ d. Use the Microsoft Script Debugger.

Answer Key #2

1. c	15. c	29. d	43. a
2. a	16. a	30. b	44. a
3. b	17. a, b, c, d	31. a, b, c, d	45. d
4. c	18. b	32. c	46. b
5. a	19. a	33. a	47. b
6. d	20. b	34. c	48. c
7. a	21. a, c	35. d	49. a
8. a, b, c, d	22. a, b	36. b, d	50. c
9. a, e	23. a, b, c	37. c	51. b
10. b	24. a, c	38. a, b, d	52. d
11. d	25. b	39. c	53. b
12. a, b, c, d	26. d	40. a	54. c
13. a	27. c	41. b	55. a, c
14. b	28. a, b, d, e	42. d	

Question 1

Answer c is correct. Site Server Express contains Content Analyzer, which can provide a representation of a Web site and its links. Microsoft Transaction Server is the IIS component that enables you to track communications based on the client. Therefore, answer a is incorrect. MMQS is a distributed application communications system and would not supply a representation of a Web site. Therefore, answer b is incorrect. MMC is the control interface for all the IIS components. Therefore, answer d is incorrect.

Question 2

Answer a is correct. The Masquerade Domain setting is used to define an alias domain for the SMTP server. A smart host is a designated SMTP server to route outgoing messages through. Changing this parameter would not affect the origin's domain name. Therefore, answer b is incorrect. There is no setting called Virtual Host for the SMTP service. Therefore, answer c is incorrect. Badmail is the term used for undeliverable messages that cannot be returned to the sender. Therefore, answer d is incorrect.

Question 3

Answer b is correct. **RUNAT=SERVER** is the keyword. The others are not. Therefore, answers a, c, and d are incorrect.

Question 4

Answer c is correct. Some older browsers do not support URLs with spaces. Only virtual sites, not virtual directories, need to be started. Therefore, answer a is incorrect. Because some users can access the Web site, obviously the Web site is already started. Therefore, answer b is incorrect. Directories in IIS are not case-sensitive. Therefore, answer d is incorrect.

Question 5

Answer a is correct. On the Home Directory tab of the NNTP Site Properties sheet, an administrator can enable the option to index the news content. An .IDQ (Internet Data Query) file can then be created to access that NNTP index. This is the method of choice. Therefore, answers b and d are incorrect. Newsgroup readers can usually search by the title of the newsgroup, but not by the content of the messages themselves. Therefore, answer c is incorrect.

Question 6

Answer d is correct. On the Directory Security tab for the Web Site Properties sheet, you can set IP address restrictions for who can access your Web site. Because the attacker most likely was assigned an IP address dynamically from a pool of addresses the ISP has, you should deny the entire range of addresses the user could have. Therefore, answer c is incorrect. Disabling anonymous access would deny everyone else access as well. Therefore, answer a is not the most practical solution. Installing a certificate on the server would not restrict the attacker's access. Therefore, answer b is incorrect.

Question 7

Answer a is correct. Because the maximum connections limit is reached, IIS displays a maximum connections warning message (that is, the message you specify within the Messages tab of the FTP Site Properties sheet). Therefore, answer b is incorrect. The server displays a welcome message only if the server lets the user access the site. Therefore, answer c is incorrect. The server displays an exit message if a user has already connected to the site and then disconnects from the site. Therefore, answer d is incorrect.

Question 8

Answers a, b, c, and d are correct. Because the Web site is on an intranet rather than on the Internet, users can use DNS, as well as WINS to access the server. LMHOSTS and HOSTS files can also serve as methods to access the server's names because they can resolve IP addresses to a NetBIOS or domain name, respectively.

Question 9

Answers a and e are correct. Without the default home page URL and server domain, Usage Import cannot identify the right database for the site. The time zone is set in Usage Import to make sure that log data from different servers of a Web site, such as a mirror site in a different part of the world, is synchronized. By definition, you want times in a site to match their local time zones. Therefore, answer b is incorrect. Spider lists and images without HTML <ALT> tags are not part of the setup for IIS logging. Therefore, answers c and d are incorrect.

Question 10

Answer b is correct. Removing nonessential services may directly increase the resource availability for IIS. Adding RAM may also increase resource availability, but RAM is hardware and must be paid for. Therefore, answer a is incorrect. Running applications in their own memory space is good for debugging, but decreases the performance of the Web site. Therefore, answer c is incorrect. Increasing the maximum number of connections may actually decrease performance if the Web site is very busy. Therefore, answer d is incorrect.

Question 11

Answer d is correct. Shannon can use Content Analyzer, which is a component of Site Server Express, to map from a URL and download the entire Web site to a local computer. Neither Microsoft Index Server nor the Internet Service Manager provide ways to download an entire site. Therefore, answers a and b are incorrect. Microsoft Content Deployment is a part of the full-featured Site Server suite, not Site Server Express. Therefore, answer c is incorrect.

Question 12

Answers a, b, c, and d are correct. Any directory, whether it exists on the same server or on a different server, can be referenced as a virtual directory in IIS. A directory that physically exists on a different server is referenced by a UNC name.

Question 13

Answer a is correct. When you first create a virtual Web site, the default state is Stopped, so you must manually start the site in order to access it. Because you are trying to access the site by its IP address, DNS and WINS are not used. Therefore, answer b is incorrect. Not having the correct permissions would produce an "Access is denied" error message. Therefore, answer c is incorrect. Because a unique IP address is being used, a unique port number is not necessary; the site most likely uses the default port of 80. Therefore, answer d is incorrect.

Question 14

Answer b is correct. Windows Scripting Host provides an easy way to make multiple changes to multiple Web sites easily. Content Analyzer provides an easy way to make multiple changes, but only on one Web site at a time. Therefore, answer a is incorrect. Although these changes can be made with the HTLMA and MMC, the tasks would be long, tedious, and inefficient. Therefore, answers c and d are incorrect.

Question 15

Answer c is correct. SSL is a type of encryption used to establish secure communications over insecure networks. CRC is a technology used to verify the integrity of transmitted data; it's not associated with security. Therefore, answer a is incorrect. Basic authentication is a method used to gather a name and password from users; however, its data is not secured, and data interception on the network could gather these names and passwords. Therefore, answer b is incorrect. TCP/IP is a network protocol. Secure communications can occur over it, but TCP/IP does not directly provide for security. Therefore, answer d is incorrect.

Question 16

Answer a is correct. Chunked transfer is a delivery method that improves ASP performance. Host headers are the primary means by which IIS 4 hosts multiple Web sites over a single IP address. Therefore, answer b is incorrect. Pipelining is the process of handling multiple client requests without requiring the client to wait for a server response. Therefore, answer c is incorrect. A persistent connection is a communication feature in which a single connection between the server and client is maintained to transfer multiple resources. Therefore, answer d is incorrect.

Question 17

Answers a, b, c, and d are correct. Service Pack 3, Internet Explorer 4.01, and the Windows NT Option Pack are minimum software requirements for installing IIS 4. Also, IIS is supported only on Windows NT 4 Server.

Question 18

Answer b is correct. Many older browsers do not support the Windows NT Challenge/Response authentication method. Different error messages will occur when the user has insufficient permissions, does not support SSL, or views an invalid certificate. Therefore, answers a, c, and d are incorrect.

Question 19

Answer a is correct. The anonymous account must be added to the NetWare server for a user to access it. Moving the files would defeat the purpose of adding the virtual directory to the Web server. Therefore, answer b is incorrect. Changing the IIS permissions to Execute would not solve the problem. Therefore, answer c is incorrect. Using a UNC is the only way to add a virtual directory whose content lives on a different server. Therefore, answer d is incorrect.

Question 20

Answer b is correct. Within the Web site tab of the Administrator Web site, the TCP Port can be modified to reflect the port at which a user can access the site. Changing the SSL port or the port to the Default Web site would not affect the port of the Administrator Web site. Therefore, answers a and c are incorrect. For the Administrator Web site, the port is dynamically created when you install IIS, so there is no set default. Therefore, answer d is incorrect.

Question 21

Answers a and c are correct. In the Delivery tab of the SMTP Site Properties sheet, the maximum retries is set at 48 and the retry interval is set to 60 minutes by default. This means that once an hour (every 60 minutes), the undeliverable email message will try to be sent, and this will happen 48 times, so 48 hours later, the user will receive the notification. If the Retry Interval were changed to 30 minutes, the user would receive a notification after only 24 hours, and if the Maximum Retries setting was changed to 30, the user would receive a notification after only 30 hours. However, increasing the maximum retries would actually increase the time it takes for users to receive the notification. Therefore, answer b is incorrect. Limiting the number of connections would not solve the problem; it would only keep users from accessing the SMTP server. Therefore, answer d is incorrect.

Question 22

Answers a and b are correct. Windows NT Challenge/Response encrypts user names and passwords and authenticates users. SSL (Secure Socket Layer) is a method of securing a Web site, but Windows NT Challenge/Response is not one of its components. Therefore, answer c is incorrect. Unlike basic authentication, Windows NT Challenge/Response does not prompt the user for his or her name and password; instead, the name and password are passed in seamlessly in the background. Therefore, answer d is incorrect.

Question 23

Answers a, b, and c are correct. Through the Directory Security tab, you can configure Web, FTP, and SMTP services to block specific IP addresses. IIS 4 does not support Gopher. Therefore, answer d is incorrect.

Question 24

Answers a and c are correct. Read access allows you to download and read files. Write access would be required to upload new files or to modify existing files to the directory. Therefore, answers b and d are incorrect.

Question 25

Answer b is correct. A digital signature is used only to indicate the identity of the sender; it is not used to encrypt data. Therefore, answer a is incorrect.

Question 26

Answer d is correct. A certificate authority (CA) is a third-party organization that is trusted to verify the identity of servers and individuals. A CA is not a single worldwide distribution point for client identities. This type of entity does not currently exist. Therefore, answer a is incorrect. A CA is not an Internet standards organization. Therefore, answer b is incorrect. A CA is not part of the NSC. Therefore, answer c is incorrect.

Question 27

Answer c is correct. The correct syntax of a URL for a Web site that uses SSL encryption is **https://www.domain.com**. Therefore, answers a, b, and d are incorrect.

Question 28

Answers a, b, d, and e are correct. The IIS snap-in modifies the MMC rebar to give single-button access to Performance Monitor, Server Manager, Event Viewer, and User Manager For Domains. The Registry Editor and Network Monitor are not accessed via the MMC IIS snap-in rebar. Therefore, answers c and f are incorrect.

Question 29

Answer d is correct. You must configure your firewall to allow traffic on the NBT (NetBIOS over TCP/IP) port used by IIS. Port 80 is the port used by the Web server itself and port 21 is the port used by the FTP server, both of which are not actually necessary when administering IIS using the MMC. Therefore, answers a and b are incorrect. The randomly generated port for the Administration Web site would have to be opened if you were going to administer your site using HTMLA. However, because you will be administering the IIS server using MMC instead, this port number is not necessary.

Question 30

Answer b is correct. Creating a key certificate request is an integral part of configuring a Web server to offer SSL-based secure communications. Installing IIS and applying Service Pack 3 do not require a key request. Therefore, answers a and d are incorrect. As a client, purchasing a product with a credit card over a secure link does not require a key request to be generated, but it does rely on the Web server to have already installed a certificate. Therefore, answer c is incorrect.

Question 31

Answers a, b, c, and d are correct. The SMTP service can be secured using any of these methods.

Question 32

Answer c is correct. The only correct URL for accessing an SSL-secured site with a nonstandard port is **https://www.*domain*.com:993/**. The protocol must be changed to **https**. Therefore, answer a is incorrect. Because the SSL protocol expects to be transmitted through port 443, the different port must be defined in the URL. Therefore, answer b is incorrect. Port 443 is the default port for SSL, but it can be changed. Therefore, answer d is incorrect.

Question 33

Answer a is correct. **Http://johnh** should be used because an intranet generally uses WINS to map the IP address with the NetBIOS name of the computer. The other options would require DNS. Therefore, answers b, c, and d are incorrect.

Question 34

Answer c is correct. For a Perl script to execute on an IIS server, a Perl interpreter must be installed. Unlike binary applications, a Perl script does not need to be compiled. Therefore, answer a is incorrect. Converting a Perl script to a batch file is unnecessary. Therefore, answer b is incorrect. A CGI program does not need Write permissions. Therefore, answer d is incorrect.

Question 35

Answer d is correct. SSL is CPU-intensive so it should only be used on directories that require it. The encryption strength has no impact on the server's CPU utilization. Therefore, answers a and b are incorrect. Because SSL is CPU-intensive, enabling SSL on the entire Web site would increase CPU usage. Therefore, answer c is incorrect.

Question 36

Answers b and d are correct. First, undeliverable email is returned to the sender. If it can't be returned, it's placed in the Badmail directory. Undeliverable email is not sent to a remote SMTP server, nor is it stored in the local queue. Therefore, answers a and c are incorrect.

Question 37

Answer c is correct. MMC's rebar hosts the Action and View command lists. The scope pane, status bar, and results pane are components of MMC but do not host these lists. Therefore, answers a, b, and d are incorrect.

Question 38

Answers a, b, and d are correct. With the use of the Internet Service Manager MMC snap-in, HTMLA, and the Windows Scripting Host, an FTP server can be administered with MMC, Internet Explorer, or a command prompt.

An Internet Service Manager Administrative Wizard does not exist. Therefore, answer c is incorrect.

Question 39

Answer c is correct. A 404 HTTP error means the Web server cannot find the file or script requested. Malformed syntax would produce a 400 HTTP error. Therefore, answer a is incorrect. Non-matching credentials would produce a 401 HTTP error. Therefore, answer b is incorrect. An invalid upstream response would produce a 502 HTTP error. Therefore, answer d is incorrect.

Question 40

Answer a is correct. You should use the FTP Service object because it enables you to select the instance of a single site. The IIS Global object does not have granular focus on sites. Therefore, answer b is incorrect. The Web service object is not for FTP sites. Therefore, answer c is incorrect. The ASP object is not related to a specific site's throughput but rather the overall performance of scripting. Therefore, answer d is incorrect.

Question 41

Answer b is correct. The default port for the FTP service is 21. Therefore, answers a, c, and d are incorrect.

Question 42

Answer d is correct. Using a T3 line will improve the site's performance by allowing more hits per day, more simultaneous users, and more objects transmitted per second. Disabling HTTP keep-alives, increasing Web timeouts, and setting Performance Tuning to fewer than 10,000 will only degrade the performance of IIS. Therefore, answers a, b, and c are incorrect.

Question 43

Answer a is correct. An HTML document usually contains the Microsoft Index Server query form. An HTX file is an HTML extension file that is used to format a query's results. Therefore, answer b is incorrect. An IDQ file is a file with parameters that are used to define the scope and restrictions of a query. Therefore, answer c is incorrect. An IDC file is used to connect to a database. Therefore, answer d is incorrect.

Question 44

Answer a is correct. The IUSR_*servername* account in the User Manager For Domains must match the Internet Guest account in IIS for anonymous users to gain access to a Web site. If automatic password synchronization was enabled for the anonymous account, any change made to the password in User Manager For Domains would instantly be reflected in IIS. Therefore, answer a is correct. The length of the password does not matter, unless a Windows NT account policy is in force. Even then, the changed password would be forced to comply with the policy before it would be accepted. Therefore, answer b is incorrect. Changing the anonymous account's password does not require a re-installation of IIS. Therefore, answer c is incorrect. Windows NT propagates new passwords almost instantly; no waiting period is required. Therefore, answer d is incorrect.

Question 45

Answer d is correct. The Robot protocol, when honored, actually acts as a firewall to the automated Content Analyzer and search engine spiders. This can be confusing, because spiders are actually sometimes known as robots, and the Robot protocol stops robots. Therefore, answers a and e are incorrect. Although limiting the levels searched may prevent getting to the secured area entry page, it would also prevent searching through other areas of the site that could also be important. Therefore, answer b is incorrect. Even though it's technically possible to create a separate Web site for the secure sales area, anyone creating a Web page on the main site can create links to the secure area. Without the Robot protocol, the sales area is not as secure as it could be. Therefore, answer c is incorrect.

Question 46

Answer b is correct. This statement is false. The IIS SMTP service does not include POP3 support or the ability to host multiple mailboxes. All mail sent to the SMTP service for the domains hosted by this service is deposited in the Drop folder and must be read with a text editor or a UA that can import text email messages. Therefore, answer a is incorrect.

Question 47

Answer b is correct. The Report Writer Executive Summary report provides a "big picture" view on the status of your Web site. There is no Report Writer

Big Picture Report, nor is there a Content Analyzer Executive Summary. Therefore, answers a and d are incorrect. A quick search for broken links and unavailable objects will give you quick, detailed information on links that are no longer working and pages and other objects that are no longer available. Because these searches provide heavy detail on each problem link and object, they are not appropriate for an overview of the site. Therefore, answer c is incorrect.

Question 48

Answer c is correct. Windows NT 4 users can use the TRACERT command to view the hops from a source to a destination computer. PING is used to test network connectivity between the source and the destination computers. Therefore, answer a is incorrect. FQDN and TRACE are not Microsoft TCP/IP troubleshooting tools. Therefore, answers b and d are incorrect.

Question 49

Answer a is correct. Adding a virtual directory with the path of C:\other is the best solution because users can simply access the existing home directory as usual, and within the URL, the new directory will seem as if it is simply a subdirectory within that home directory. Moving the files from the C:\other directory to a subdirectory in the Web directory would work, but is an unnecessary step. Therefore, answer b is incorrect. Because the directory resides on the same server as the default directory, it should be referenced as a local path rather than a UNC. Therefore, answer c is incorrect. Changing the home directory to C:\other would defeat the purpose because the files in C:\Web would no longer be accessible. Therefore, answer d is incorrect.

Question 50

Answer c is correct. The correct file extension for MSUSAGE is .MDB. Answer a is incorrect because .SQL is the extension for a .SQL database. Jet is a technology, not a file extension. Therefore, answer b is incorrect. The .SSE extension is fictitious. Therefore, answer d is correct.

Question 51

Answer b is correct. The strongest encryption that can be used within the United States is 128-bit encryption. In most cases, 40-bit encryption is the strongest encryption that can be used across U.S. borders. Therefore, answer a is incorrect. 512 and 1,024 bits are encryption strengths for certificates that are used for identity verification, not data encryption. Therefore, answers c and d are incorrect.

Question 52

Answer d is correct. The Pickup directory serves as an inbox for email messages to be copied. All files in this directory are automatically processed by the SMTP service. The Drop directory is where all messages directed at the domains hosted by this SMTP service are stored. Therefore, answer a is incorrect. SortTemp is just a storage folder for temporary files. Therefore, answer b is incorrect. Queue is the folder used by the SMTP service that holds all active messages in the process of being delivered. Therefore, answer c is incorrect.

Question 53

The correct answer is b. This statement is false. An NTFS partition is recommended, but not required, to install IIS. Therefore, answer a is incorrect.

Question 54

Answer c is correct. The FTP service's primary function is to allow users to download and upload files easily. Creating a Web form for users to register themselves and then mailing them a disk is not a state-of-the-art solution. Therefore, answer a is incorrect. You can use the Microsoft Merchant Server to design and build Web storefronts that may include a file download facility, but this is not really necessary because IIS's FTP service suffices. Therefore, answer b is incorrect. The proxy server has no role as far as implementing a download facility is concerned. Therefore, answer d is incorrect.

Question 55

The correct answers are a and c. By using a SSI (Server Side Include), you can easily make a change to the footer information, and the changes will automatically appear in each of the Web pages. Likewise, you can enable a document footer using the Documents tab of the Web Site Properties sheet, and every page will automatically have the standard footer included. The Default Directory tab does not include any options that allow you to include footers on Web pages. Therefore, answer b is incorrect. The Script Debugger is used to debug Web applications. Therefore, answer d is incorrect.

Glossary

. . . .

.ASP (Active Server Page file)—The extension applied to an ASP script. ASP scripts usually include both HTML code and server-side scripting.

.HTM (HTML file)—An extension applied to all standard HTML (Hypertext Markup Language) documents.

.HTX (HTML Extension file)—The extension used with one of the files involved in the resolution of a query. The HTX file is used to format the query results for presentation back to the user.

.IDA (Internet Data Administration file)—The extension for a file that contains queries that allow a user to administer and monitor Index Server.

.IDQ (Internet Data Query file)—The extension used for one of the files involved in the resolution of a query. The IDQ file specifies how the query from the form is to be processed.

AATP (Authorized Academic Training Program)—A program that authorizes accredited academic institutions of higher learning to offer Microsoft Certified Professional testing and training to their students. The institutions also are allowed to use the Microsoft Education course materials and Microsoft Certified Trainers.

ACL (access control list)—A list of users and computers that defines who can use a resource and who cannot.

Active client—An application that includes built-in support for ActiveX technology and supports client-side scripting (for example, Internet Explorer).

Active platform—The foundation of designing and developing Internet and intranet business solutions using Microsoft tools and technologies. A three-tier client/server model, the Active platform is an extensible component-based architecture.

Active Server—A Web server or similar application that supports server-side scripting (also known as *Active Server Pages*).

Active Server components—A collection of IIS prepackaged components that allow you to build your ASP applications quickly and efficiently.

Active Server objects—Five core server objects that constitute the core functionality of ASP. These server objects contain methods and properties that you can configure to meet your application requirements.

ActiveX—A suite of technologies you can use to deliver business solutions over the Internet and intranets.

ActiveX controls—A stripped-down version of OLE controls with their size and speed optimized for use over the Internet.

ADO (Active Data Object)—Probably the most important and popular ASP component, ADO is used to build data-driven dynamic Web applications.

alias—A short name for a directory that is easy to use and remember.

anonymous account—The IUSR_*servername* account created by IIS for Web and FTP services that can access only the files and applications for which the system administrator grants permission.

ARP (Address Resolution Protocol)—A Network layer protocol that associates logical (IP) addresses to physical (MAC) addresses.

ASPs (Active Server Pages)—A Web programming technique that enriches commerce and business communications by improving script management. ASP files can execute with a transaction. Therefore, if the script fails, the transaction is aborted.

assessment exam—Similar to the certification exam, this type of exam gives you the opportunity to practice answering test questions at your own pace.

ATEC (Authorized Technical Education Center)—The location where you can take a Microsoft Official Curriculum course taught by Microsoft Certified Trainers.

automatic password synchronization—When the server automatically synchronizes the FTP or Web site password with the Windows NT password for anonymous users.

bandwidth—The range of frequencies that a communications medium can carry. For baseband networking media, the bandwidth also indicates the theoretical maximum amount of data that the medium can transfer. For broadband networking media, the bandwidth is measured by the variations that any single carrier frequency can carry.

bandwidth throttling—Limits the total bandwidth used by all IIS sites to the kilobytes per second defined in the associated field.

Boolean—A form of algebraic logic that consists of only two opposite states, such as on or off, yes or no, or true or false.

bottleneck—The component of a computer or network that is preventing at least one other component from operating at its maximum efficiency.

CA (certificate authority)—A third party that issues certificates and claims to have verified the identity of a server or an individual.

cache—A temporary storage area that holds current information and is able to provide that information faster than other methods.

catalog—The highest level of content organization within Index Server. The catalog is also known as the Master Index.

CATALOG.WCI—The default catalog file created by Index Server.

certificate—A digital signature issued by a third party (called a certificate authority or CA) that claims to have verified the identity of a server or an individual.

Certificate Server—A component installed with IIS's Web and FTP services that gives individual Web servers the ability to issue, revoke, and renew X.509 digital certificates to clients.

chunked transfers—A method of data transmission that greatly increases the efficiency of delivering Active Server Pages.

chunking—The process of breaking a transmission into multiple pieces of different sizes, each with its own header and size indicator.

client software—See *UA (user agent)*.

COM (Component Object Model)—Microsoft's groundwork of the ActiveX platform. Used to support interprocess communications and designed to promote software interoperability.

computer name—The name of a computer on a LAN that is specific to an individual workstation or server.

configuration error—An error that occurs in the installation procedure, default installation directories, default security settings, or locations of most commands and settings.

connection timeout—The maximum time a client connection can exist without any activity.

Content Analyzer—A Site Server Express tool that is used to visualize what is and is not working on a Web site.

content filters—The file format-specific add-ons that enable Index Server to index the contents of non-Microsoft documents.

cookie—A marker downloaded to a PC that identifies a specific user to a Web site.

corpus—The collection of all documents that Index Server is configured to monitor and index.

CRL (certificate revocation list)—Maintained by the CA, the list of all invalid certificates.

CryptoAPI—This application programming interface (API) allows programmers to create applications that can use or even rely upon cryptography without requiring knowledge of the encryption system. The CryptoAPI separates applications from encryption, thus enabling an application without modification to use different types or new technologies of encryption.

custom error—A customized error message.

cut score—On a Microsoft Certified Professional exam, the lowest score a person can receive and still pass.

database—A collection of information arranged and stored so that data can be accessed quickly and accurately.

decryption—The necessary flip side of encryption. Decryption is the process of unscrambling data.

decryption key—The mathematical inverse of the encryption key. The decryption key unscrambles encrypted data to extract the original.

dependency error—When a driver, device, or service fails to load, which then causes other drivers, devices, or services to load or function improperly.

DHCP (Dynamic Host Configuration Protocol) server—A service used in a TCP/IP environment to dynamically assign IP addresses and other IP settings to clients upon bootup.

digital certificate—An electronic identification and verification tool used to secure online commerce and other transactions.

digital signatures—The private key of the sender.

directory browsing—An IIS content control that allows users to navigate through the directory structure on the IIS server. To prevent this, uncheck Directory Browsing Allowed. By default, IIS lets the users browse through the directory structure.

directory security—An IIS setting used to secure the directories on your FTP or Web server. You can choose to grant or deny access to all or specific directories on your FTP server. For a Web server, you can configure authentication methods, secure communications, and IP and domain name restrictions.

DNA (Distributed interNet Applications)—A Windows platform architectural framework that enables the deployment of scalable, multitier, distributed computing solutions over any type of network.

DNS (Domain Name Service)—A service that resolves host names (such as microsoft.com) into IP addresses (such as 207.68.145.42).

drop directory—Where all messages directed at the domains hosted by an SMTP service are stored.

encryption—The process of scrambling data (message, streaming multimedia, data files, and so on) into a form that is unusable and unreadable by anyone except the intended recipient.

encryption key—An electronic mathematical formula used to scramble data.

ERD (emergency repair disk)—The disk that contains files and other resources that can be used to repair the system partition of a Windows NT computer.

event auditing—The security activity of recording a log of events or occurrences on a computer system.

Exam Preparation Guides—Guides that provide information specific to the material covered on Microsoft Certified Professional exams to help students prepare for the exams.

Exam Study Guide—Short for Microsoft Certified Professional Program Exam Study Guide. Contains information about the topics covered on more than one of the Microsoft Certified Professional exams.

firewall—A piece of equipment or software that is used to secure an Internet connection.

FTP (File Transfer Protocol)—An application protocol that is used for file transfer, file manipulation, and directory manipulation.

Gopher—A large database that provides search capabilities. Gopher is no longer supported in version 4 of IIS.

host headers—A delivery and communication mechanism used by IIS to distribute multiple sites using transferred session information.

HTMLA—The HTML administration tool.

HTTP (Hypertext Transfer Protocol)—The World Wide Web protocol that allows for the transfer of HTML documents over the Internet or intranets.

HTTP 1.1—A version of the HTTP protocol that supports several improvements to the Web communication process.

HTTP errors—A standard set of error codes that are reported to clients in the event of an error.

HTTP headers—An IIS setting that lets you configure information such as content expiration, content rating, custom headers, and MIME maps.

HTTP keep-alives—A request that the Web server keeps a communication connection open across multiple requests.

IDC (Internet Database Connector)—A tool that lets you connect IIS to 32-bit relational databases, including Microsoft SQL Server, Microsoft Access, Microsoft FoxPro, Sybase SQL Server, dBASE, and so on. The IDC is an ISAPI DLL (HTTPODBC.DLL) server extension.

IIS (Internet Information Server)—Web server software by Microsoft; included and implemented with Windows NT Server.

IIS directory—The location on IIS in which you store files, including ASP scripts and other programs.

index—The database of all remaining words extracted from the corpus after it has been handled by the content filters, word breakers, normalizers, and noise word filters.

Index Server—A component of IIS that brings site content indexing and searching to IIS-hosted Web sites.

inference algorithm—A statistical correction factor for situations, such as hits, that are not recorded due to proxy server caching.

Internet—The collection of TCP/IP-based networks around the world. Information on nearly every subject is available in some form somewhere on the Internet.

intranet—An internal, private network that uses the same protocols and standards as the Internet.

IP (Internet Protocol)—A Network layer protocol that provides source and destination addressing and routing.

IP address—Four sets of numbers, separated by decimal points, that represent the numeric address of a computer attached to a TCP/IP network, such as the Internet.

IPX/SPX (Internetwork Packet Exchange/Sequenced Packet Exchange)— Novell's NetWare protocol, reinvented by Microsoft and implemented in Windows NT under the name NWLink. It's fully compatible with Novell's version and, in many cases, is a better implementation than the original.

ISAPI filter—A program, typically a DLL file, that responds to the events during an HTTP request's processing.

ISDN (Integrated Services Digital Network)—A form of digital communication that has a bandwidth of 128Kbps.

ISM (Internet Service Manager)—In older versions, this was the tool used to manage IIS. Internet Service Manager is now a component of MMC and the Web-based administration tool.

ISP (Internet Service Provider)—A service company that sells network access to the Internet. An ISP purchases bandwidth in bulk and, in turn, resells it in smaller packages.

job function expert—A person with extensive knowledge about a particular job function and the software products/technologies related to that job. Typically, a job function expert is currently performing the job, has recently performed the job, or is training people to do the job.

LAN (local area network)—A network that is confined to a single building or geographic area and comprised of servers, workstations, peripheral devices, a network operating system, and a communications link.

mailroot directory—The directory in which all the messages handled by the SMTP service are stored.

master index—Created when all current shadow indexes and the current master index are integrated into a new master index. There is always only one master index (also called a *catalog*).

masquerade domain—A setting used to define an alias domain for the SMTP Server, used to provide an alias that an email message can use to make it seem as though the email is coming from a Web server other than the one it is being sent from.

maximum connections message—The warning message users see when they connect to the FTP site and it has already reached the maximum number of connections.

MCP (Microsoft Certified Professional)—An individual who has taken and passed at least one certification exam.

MCSD (Microsoft Certified Solution Developer)—An individual who is qualified to create and develop solutions for businesses using the Microsoft development tools, technologies, and platforms.

MCSE (Microsoft Certified Systems Engineer)—An individual who is an expert on Windows NT and the Microsoft BackOffice integrated family of server software. This individual also can plan, implement, maintain, and support information systems associated with these products.

MCSE+I (Microsoft Certified Systems Engineer + Internet)—An individual who is an expert on Windows NT and the Microsoft BackOffice integrated family of server software, plus Internet-related technology.

MCT (Microsoft Certified Trainer)—An individual who is qualified by Microsoft to teach Microsoft Education courses at sites authorized by Microsoft.

Message Queue Server—A component of the Windows NT Server 4 Option Pack that enables applications to communicate via a message queue system, even when remote systems are offline.

Metabase—A high-speed, memory-resident, hierarchical system used as a storage device for most of the configuration parameters used by IIS.

Microsoft Certificate Server—This application is used to organize, issue, renew, and revoke private certificates without relying on a third-party external CA.

Microsoft Certification Exam—A test created by Microsoft to verify a test-taker's mastery of a software product, technology, or computing topic.

Microsoft Certified Professional Certification Update—A newsletter for Microsoft Certified Professional candidates and Microsoft Certified Professionals.

Microsoft official curriculum—Microsoft education courses that support the certification exam process and are created by the Microsoft product groups.

Microsoft Proxy Server 2—Acts as an IPX-to-IP gateway for LAN clients, as a firewall to protect the internal network from the external network, and as a cache area for Internet objects that allows faster response time when a client requests an Internet object, such as a URL.

Microsoft Roadmap To Education And Certification—An application, based on Microsoft Windows, that takes you through the process of deciding what your certification goals are and informs you of the best way to achieve them.

Microsoft Sales Fax Service—A service through which you can obtain Exam Preparation Guides, fact sheets, and additional information about the Microsoft Certified Professional Program.

Microsoft Script Debugger—A utility used to debug application scripts. It can be invoked from only within Internet Explorer.

Microsoft Solution Provider—An organization, not directly related to Microsoft, that provides integration, consulting, technical support, and other services related to Microsoft products.

Microsoft TechNet—A service provided by Microsoft that gives helpful information via a monthly CD-ROM. TechNet is the primary source of technical information for people who support and/or educate end users, create automated solutions, or administer networks and/or databases.

MMC (Microsoft Management Console)—A Windows-based tool that provides users with total management of all services and applications within a single utility.

MMC snap-in—The primary means by which IIS is configured locally.

MOLI (Microsoft Online Institute)—An organization that makes training materials, online forums and user groups, and online classes available.

MRI (multiple-rating item)—An item that gives you a task and a proposed solution. Every time the task is set, an alternate solution is given, and the candidate must choose the answer that gives the best results produced by one solution.

MSDN (Microsoft Developer Network)—The official source for Software Development Kits (SDKs), Device Driver Kits (DDKs), operating systems, and programming information associated with creating applications for Microsoft Windows and Windows NT.

MTS (Microsoft Transaction Server)—An IIS component that allows distributed transaction applications to be developed for IIS.

NDA (nondisclosure agreement)—A legal agreement signed both by Microsoft and by a vendor, rendering certain rights and limitations.

NetBEUI (NetBIOS Extended User Interface)—A simple Network layer transport protocol developed to support NetBIOS networks.

NetBIOS (Network Basic Input/Output System) interface—The networking service used by Windows NT to communicate NetBIOS-level (typically name space) information to other network members.

network—A collection of server and client computers that communicates to share wire-based resources.

network adapter card—A synonym for "network interface card (NIC)." Refers to the hardware device that mediates communication between a computer and one or more types of networking media.

NNTP (Network News Transfer Protocol)—The protocol used to distribute, retrieve, inquire about, and post Network News articles.

NNTP service—A service designed to host private discussion forums. Does not support news feeds or message replication from the global USENET NNTP news services.

node—An object that can be managed through MMC by means of an installed snap-in.

noise word—A language-specific word that offers no useful content and is not stored in the index.

NOISE.ENU—The filename of the noise word list.

normalizer—A software tool that standardizes words emitted by a word breaker. Standardization includes removing capitalization, plurality, and punctuation. Plus, the normalizer identifies and removes noise words from the index.

NTFS (New Technology File System)—A file system used in Windows NT that supports file-level security, fault tolerance, and file-level compression.

NTLM (NT LAN Manager) authentication—An authentication technique the browser uses to encrypt and send a password across the network.

ODBC (Open Database Connectivity)—A standard API (application programming interface) used to construct platform/application-independent databases.

Option Pack—The Microsoft Windows NT Server 4 product distribution that contains IIS 4 (and its subcomponents), Transaction Server 2, Message Queue Server Standard Edition, Site Server Express, and Connection Services for Microsoft RAS.

OS (operating system)—A software program that controls the operations on a computer system.

packet filter—An Internet Service Manager (ISM) option that controls inbound access to a network on a packet level. By utilizing this option, users can accept or deny traffic based on packet types, datagrams, or packet fragments.

PCT (Private Communication Technology)—An encryption technology similar to SSL.

performance tuning—The process or task of improving the performance of a computer by locating and eliminating bottlenecks.

permissions—A level of access assigned to files or folders. Permissions determine who has access rights to those files or folders.

persistent connections—A communication mechanism used to send multiple objects over fewer connections. This reduces communication overhead and improves performance.

persistent index—The combination of one or more word lists into a file stored on hard drive. Also called a *shadow index*.

pickup directory—An inbox for email messages to be copied. All files in this directory are automatically processed by the SMTP service.

PICS (Platform for Internet Content Selection) rating—A rating given to a Web site that provides control over what content can be accessed by which audiences.

pipelining—Used by HTTP 1.1 to allow clients to send multiple requests without waiting for a server's response. Pipelining improves response time and Web display performance.

policies—The evaluation of requests and assignment of new certificates is governed through the use of policies. Policies are installed by an administrator and instruct the Certificate Server to accept, deny, or delay a request based on the contents of the request. Policies are written in Java, Visual Basic, or C/C++.

proxy server—A software product that acts as a moderator or go-between for a client and a remote host. Most proxy servers also offer content caching and firewall capabilities.

public key encryption—The form of cryptology used by IIS. In this system, both the server and the client use two keys—a private key and a public key.

PWS (Personal Web Server or Peer Web Services)—A scaled-down version of IIS that works only on Intel-based Windows 95, Windows 98, or Windows NT Workstation systems.

query—Another word for *search*. More specifically, the term used to describe the data sent from an Index Server Web page to the server-side script that attempts to locate matches within the corpus.

queue—The folder used by the SMTP service for storage of messages actively being delivered.

RDS (Remote Data Service)—A database connection tool that enables client-side data caching in Web applications to reduce server traffic and overhead.

rebar—The MMC command bar that lists node- and object-specific commands.

Registry—A database that stores all the configuration information for Windows NT.

Report Writer—A Site Server Express tool that is used to mine information from the Usage Import Database.

Resource Kit—The additional documentation and software utilities distributed by Microsoft to provide information and instruction on the proper operation and modification of its software products.

resultant access—The accumulation of all types of access granted to a user specifically and by all group memberships, except if No Access is specified for that user or for a group to which that user is a member, in which case the user is denied access.

Results pane—The right pane of the MMC console. It displays the contents of the selected node.

robot—Also called a *spider*. An automated tool used to explore links.

Robot protocol—A protocol or behavioral control language used to define how a robot (crawler, spider, and so on) interacts with a specific Web site.

RPC (Remote Procedure Call)—A programming interface that allows software applications running on separate computers on different networks to use each other's services.

Scope pane—The left pane of the MMC console. It displays the namespace tree where all items to be managed, called *nodes*, are listed.

secure communication—An IIS security feature that directs the client browser to establish an encrypted link to a directory or file on the system, which enables a secure communication link between the browser and the server.

secure envelopes—The public key encryption of the sender.

security—The protection of data by restricting access to authorized users.

server-centric—A term that implies that most of the actual execution or work of the application occurs on the server instead of on the client.

server-side scripting—Another name for Active Server Pages.

Service Pack—A suite of updates and hot fixes for a particular application or operating system. Service Pack 3 for Windows NT is a requirement for IIS 4 and its related components.

SGC (Server Gated Crypto)—An extension to SSL that grants IIS the ability to use 128-bit encryption.

shadow index—The combination of one or more word lists into a file stored on a hard drive. Also called a *persistent index*.

Site Server Express—An express version of Microsoft Site Server that is included with the IIS 4 Option Pack. This application gives you a wide variety of analysis tools to keep tabs on your Web sites, as well as several publishing utilities to ease content issuance.

smart host—A designated SMTP server through which to route all outgoing email messages. Smart hosts are usually used to ensure that the most efficient or the most secure route is being use to route the messages.

SMTP (Simple Mail Transfer Protocol)—The protocol used to exchange mail between a mail client and server.

SMTP service—A client service that allows Web applications to send and receive email messages.

snap-in—A product or service specific to COM or DCOM object management utilities.

SortTemp—A storage folder for temporary files.

spamming—The act of sending a lot of unsolicited, anonymous, untraceable email.

spider—See *robot*.

SQL Server—A Microsoft product that supports a network-enabled relational database system.

SSL (Secure Sockets Layer)—An industry-standard protocol used to establish secure communications between a Web server (or other information service server) and a client.

SSL Client Authentication (SSLCA)—Another and more secure authentication scheme (added to the existing set of three—anonymous, basic/clear text, and Microsoft Challenge/Response).

SSL Handshake protocol—The higher layer of the SSL protocol that is used to coordinate between a client and server on an encryption algorithm to use for further secured communications.

SSL Record protocol—The lower-layer SSL protocol that operates just above the Transmission Layer Protocol (TCP). It encapsulates higher-level protocols; therefore, it's a security scheme that is flexible and application protocol-independent.

subnet—A portion or segment of a network.

subnet mask—A 32-bit address that indicates how many bits in an address are being used for the network ID.

TCP (Transmission Control Protocol)—A connection-oriented Transport layer protocol that accepts messages of any length from the upper layers and provides transportation to another computer. TCP is responsible for packet fragmentation, as well as reassembly and sequencing.

TCP/IP (Transmission Control Protocol/Internet Protocol)—The most commonly used network protocol and the central protocol of the Internet.

TCP port—A representation of a data stream.

three-tiered programming architecture—A system in which the components of an application are positioned in three distinct locations.

trusts—Logical security connections between two domains in which one domain is able to share its resources with the authenticated users from another domain.

UA (user agent)—A standard email client utility. Also called *client software*.

Unicode—A 16-bit system used to encode characters and letters from many different languages.

Unix—An interactive time-sharing operating system developed in 1969 by a hacker to play games. This system developed into the most widely used industrial-strength computer operating system in the world, and ultimately supported the birth of the Internet.

URL (Universal Resource Locator)—The addressing scheme used to identify resources on the Internet.

Usage Import—A Site Server Express tool that brings Web site logs into a database, which then can be refined by Report Writer into any number of formats.

user authentication and authorization—An IIS security feature that simplifies the logon process because the user provides the logon information only once rather than logging on to both IIS and Windows NT.

virtual directory—A local or remote directory in which a user uses an alias to access its path in the URL.

virtual server—Additional Web and FTP sites hosted on the same IIS server.

W3C extended log file format—A standardized log file format created by the W3C.

WAN (wide area network)—A network that spans geographically distant segments. Often, the distance of two miles or more is used to define a WAN; however, Microsoft equates any RAS connection as establishing a WAN.

word breaker—A software tool that takes the stream of characters emitted by a content filter and breaks it into words based on known language-dependent syntax and structure rules.

word list—The list of non-noise words and relevant properties extracted from a document. This list only exists in memory.

WSH (Windows Scripting Host)—A language-independent scripting host for 32-bit Windows platforms.

Index

CORIOLIS HELP CENTER

Here at The Coriolis Group, we strive to provide the finest customer service in the technical education industry. We're committed to helping you reach your certification goals by assisting you in the following areas.

Talk to the Authors

We'd like to hear from you! Please refer to the "How to Use This Book" section in the "Introduction" of every Exam Cram guide for our authors' individual email addresses.

Web Page Information

The Certification Insider Press Web page provides a host of valuable information that's only a click away. For information in the following areas, please visit us at:

www.coriolis.com/cip/default.cfm

- Titles and other products
- Book content updates
- Roadmap to Certification Success guide
- New Adaptive Testing changes
- New Exam Cram Live! seminars
- New Certified Crammer Society details
- Sample chapters and tables of contents
- Manuscript solicitation
- Special programs and events

Contact Us by Email

Important addresses you may use to reach us at The Coriolis Group.

eci@coriolis.com

To subscribe to our FREE, bi-monthly on-line newsletter, *Exam Cram Insider*. Keep up to date with the certification scene. Included in each *Insider* are certification articles, program updates, new exam information, hints and tips, sample chapters, and more.

techsupport@coriolis.com

For technical questions and problems with CD-ROMs. Products broken, battered, or blown-up? Just need some installation advice? Contact us here.

ccs@coriolis.com

To obtain membership information for the *Certified Crammer Society*, **an exclusive club for the certified professional.** Get in on members-only discounts, special information, expert advice, contests, cool prizes, and free stuff for the certified professional. Membership is FREE. Contact us and get enrolled today!

cipq@coriolis.com

For book content questions and feedback about our titles, drop us a line. This is the good, the bad, and the questions address. Our customers are the best judges of our products. Let us know what you like, what we could do better, or what question you may have about any content. Testimonials are always welcome here, and if you send us a story about how an Exam Cram guide has helped you ace a test, we'll give you an official Certification Insider Press T-shirt.

custserv@coriolis.com

For solutions to problems concerning an order for any of our products. Our staff will promptly and courteously address the problem. Taking the exams is difficult enough. We want to make acquiring our study guides as easy as possible.

Book Orders & Shipping Information

orders@coriolis.com

To place an order by email or to check on the status of an order already placed.

coriolis.com/bookstore/default.cfm

To place an order through our online bookstore.

1.800.410.0192

To place an order by phone or to check on an order already placed.

CERTIFIED CRAMMER SOCIETY

PHI SLAMMA CRAMMA

breed apart, a cut above the rest—a true professional. Highly skilled and superbly trained, certified IT professionals are unquestionably the world's most elite computer experts. In an effort to appropriately recognize this privileged crowd, The Coriolis Group is proud to introduce the Certified Crammer Society. If you are a certified IT professional, it is our pleasure to invite you to become a Certified Crammer Society member.

Membership is free to all certified professionals and benefits include a membership kit that contains your official membership card and official Certified Crammer Society blue denim ball cap emblazoned with the Certified Crammer Society crest—proudly displaying the Crammer motto "Phi Slamma Cramma"—and featuring a genuine leather bill. The kit also includes your password to the Certified Crammers-Only Web site containing monthly discreet messages designed to provide you with advance notification about certification testing information, special book excerpts, and inside industry news not found anywhere else; monthly Crammers-Only discounts on selected Coriolis titles; *Ask the Series Editor* Q and A column; cool contests with great prizes; and more.

GUIDELINES FOR MEMBERSHIP

Registration is free to professionals certified in Microsoft, A+, or Oracle DBA. Coming soon: Sun Java, Novell, and Cisco. Send or email your contact information and proof of your certification (test scores, membership card, or official letter) to:

Certified Crammer Society Membership Chairperson
THE CORIOLIS GROUP, LLC
14455 North Hayden Road, Suite 220, Scottsdale, Arizona 85260-6949
Fax: 480.483.0193 • Email: ccs@coriolis.com

APPLICATION

Name:

Address:

Society Alias:

Choose a secret code name to correspond with us and other Crammer Society members.
Please use no more than eight characters.

Email: